THE CULTURE OF THE COLD WAR

THE AMERICAN MOMENT
Stanley I. Kutler, Editor

THE
CULTURE
OF THE
COLD
WAR

BY

STEPHEN J.
WHITFIELD

THE JOHNS HOPKINS
UNIVERSITY PRESS
BALTIMORE • LONDON

This book is dedicated, with love, to
RON AND DEENA

© 1991 The Johns Hopkins University Press
All rights reserved
Printed in the United States of America

The Johns Hopkins University Press
701 West 40th Street
Baltimore, Maryland 21211
The Johns Hopkins Press Ltd., London

The paper used in this book meets the minimum requirements of American
National Standard for Information Sciences—
Permanence of Paper for
Printed Library Materials, ANSI Z39.48-1984.

Library of Congress Cataloging-in-Publication Data

Whitfield, Stephen J., 1942–
The culture of the cold war / Stephen J. Whitfield.
p.   cm. — (The American moment)
Includes bibliographical references (p.   ) and index.
ISBN 0-8018-4081-3 (hardcover). — ISBN 0-8018-4082-1 (pbk.)
1. United States—Popular culture—History—20th century.   2. Cold
war—Social aspects—United States.   I. Title.   II. Series.
E169.12.W47   1990   306'.0973—dc20   90-4599 CIP

CONTENTS

FOREWORD

Anti-Communism has been a recurring theme in American political life for more than a century. But because the perceived threat from international Communism receded by the beginning of the 1990s, we run the risk of remembering the nation's crusade against Communism as an isolated historical happening, one that affected only diplomatic and military policies of the Cold War. On the contrary, that struggle deeply scarred the nation's social order as well.

Vigilance against Communism was a national priority during the darkest days of the Cold War, from the late 1940s until the mid-1950s. Abroad, the government mobilized alliances and vast military resources to combat Soviet expansionism, both real and imagined. At home, politicians vied with one another to demonstrate their devotion to the cause of the "Free World." "McCarthyism" is the convenient historical shorthand to describe the political behavior of the period, but it was far more than a phenomenon associated with a relatively obscure junior senator from Wisconsin. The national fetish with anti-Communism pervaded American society, and nowhere is this more apparent than in the popular culture of the era. Few could escape or miss the message.

Literature, movies, art, and the media—particularly the then-new form, television—consistently hammered the theme of an enemy within, working to subvert the American Way of Life. Movies justified informing on the behavior of one's family or friends; popular novels glorified trampling on constitutional and democratic values in pursuit of the necessary end of destroying the Communist menace; and organized religion sanctified the crusade against Godless Communism. Stephen J. Whitfield has skillfully recalled that cultural milieu. His engaging summaries and vignettes of events are linked to an analysis informed with criticism, empathy, and wit—and one that deftly combines a civil libertarian and an anti-Communist perspective.

The domestic war against Communism had profound consequences beyond political results. The cultural assault on Communism unleashed a fear and loathing that weakened and even subdued traditional commitments to an open society and the Rule of Law. The hypocrisy and self-righteousness that animated so much of anti-Communism had a corrosive effect that proved more real than the spies or subversives. Whitfield's work is timely, for it reminds us that intolerance and demands for conformity assault and strain the fragile bonds of our pluralist society.

Stanley I. Kutler

THE UNIVERSITY OF WISCONSIN
MADISON, WISCONSIN

ACKNOWLEDGMENTS

In thinking about the 1950s, and then writing this book, I have incurred many debts. A fellow graduate student, David Axeen, taught me the phrase "Cold War liberalism," which he meant somewhat pejoratively. Readers should nevertheless be advised of my belief that this orientation remains the soundest guide to a historical consideration of the period, which did not confine the political choices to Cardinal Spellman or Lillian Hellman. But I have benefited over the years from pungent conversations with Phillip M. Weitzman and Henie Lustgarten, who disagree. Nor can the debts that I very much owe to two particular historians, Richard S. Tedlow and Raymond O. Arsenault, be easily repaid. By assuming that a manuscript is guilty unless proven innocent, Richard H. King has continued to demonstrate the compatibility of skepticism and friendship. Edward S. Shapiro, David M. Oshinsky, James B. Gilbert, David Starr, and Thomas Doherty also read—in whole or in part— an earlier draft of *The Culture of the Cold War*. I am grateful for their criticism, their learning, their instruction, and their encouragement; but they are not to blame for my stubbornness or for the errors that persist. As consulting editor of this series and as an authority on this period, Stanley I. Kutler was both noodge and Nestor; he made this book happen. This is also the right moment to thank Michael Rothschild, another child of the fifties, whose reactions to the cinema of that era shaped my own and whose memories remain much sharper. Because of a paid leave of absence from Brandeis University, the completion of this book was possible. But because my wife, Lee, wanted to live in southern France, the completion of this book was also fun. That is only one reason why my deepest gratitude is reserved for her.

1

POLITICIZING CULTURE:
SUSPICIOUS MINDS

In 1951, one of the prisoners in a New York jail awaiting sentencing under the Smith Act for conspiring to advocate the violent overthrow of the American government was George Charney. The chairman of the state's Communist party and a member of the national committee, he became acquainted with an Italian-American hoodlum named Bob Raymondi, who since his teens in Brooklyn had associated with Murder, Inc., and was a veteran of seventeen years as an inmate of Dannemora. While dominating the prison population, Raymondi also sought to compensate for his poor formal education by chatting with the Marxist-Leninists who had been inserted among the other prisoners. One Saturday, Raymondi's sister visited him and was startled to learn how close he had gotten with Charney and others convicted under the Smith Act. "My God, Bob," she warned. "You'll get into trouble."

In this era, a specter was haunting America—the specter of Communism. Trying to exorcise it were legislators and judges, union officials and movie studio bosses, policemen and generals, university presidents and corporation executives, clergymen and journalists, Republicans and Democrats, conservatives and liberals. The specter that, a century earlier, Marx and Engels had described as stalking the continent of Europe was extending itself to the United States, looming over a nation that had prided itself on its historical immunity to the apocalyptic tragedies of the either/or. What *The Communist Manifesto* had traced as the fault lines of politics seemed to be cracking open the American landscape as well. By introducing ideological politics, Communism became more loathed than organized crime, exacerbating fears that were to distort and enfeeble American culture throughout the late 1940s and the 1950s.

The animus against Communism was not concocted of phantasms; it was rooted in reality. If judged in the light of liberal democratic ideals, of the promise inherent in personal autonomy and of the conventions of ordinary decency, Communism *was* evil. Indeed, the system that the Bolsheviks had created in the Soviet Union and had imposed beyond their borders was even more hideous in its devastation of humane values than many of its most vocal opponents in the 1950s realized. The monstrous scope of the slave labor camps known as the Gulag Archipelago was then sketchily known and its misery scarcely imagined. Few Americans knew of the deliberate famine in the Ukraine in the early 1930s, which may have cost almost as many lives as the Nazi murder of European Jewry a decade later. Founded upon subjugation and terror, the Soviet system was devoted to the violation of the humanitarian ideals of the Enlightenment, crushing hope of both resistance and reform. Stretching across eleven time zones, this totalitarian empire was so vast that Vladivostok was closer to Honolulu than to Leningrad; but its dynamism reeked of random death.

The British Sovietologist Robert Conquest once asked Tibor Szamuely about the rationale of the military purges of the 1930s. In a grisly way, Conquest found it understandable that Stalin had executed Marshal Tukhachevsky, but why was Marshal Yegorov shot? Szamuely, himself a survivor of the Gulag Archipelago, replied, "Why not?" Immediately after the dictator himself died in 1953, the *Washington Post's* Herblock drew a cartoon—for which he won a Pulitzer Prize—that had the grim reaper telling Stalin, "You were always a great friend of mine, Joseph." The largest killing fields of the twentieth century were among his legacies. But Stalinism was also an international political organization, centered in Moscow, which sought to apply the Soviet model elsewhere. In the late 1940s and the 1950s, this *was* the Communist system; and the Sino-Soviet split that erupted by the end of the decade produced no deviation from the pattern of the closed society. (The Chinese regime duplicated it instead.)

In the West, including the United States, Stalinism inspired adherents and sympathizers to an extent that Nazism never did. For it appealed to feelings of human solidarity, to the brotherhood of the dispossessed and the excluded, especially when the Great Depression had dramatized the twin failures of free enterprise and the ethos of individualism. Before the incredible scale of Stalin's purges had become credible, Communism could present itself as the activated legacy of the Enlightenment. The aura of idealism that emanated from its militant apparatus required novel responses to the character of the Soviet Union and its satellites. Because this form of totalitarianism generated champions and collaborators in the West, a relatively open society confronted a unique threat to its operations; and those who wished to reform as well as defend democratic institutions had to puzzle through for the first time appropriate means of resistance to such a movement. The secrecy and authoritarianism of Communist cadres flung down an unprecedented challenge, for they sought to enjoy the rights and benefits of a largely free society in order to demolish it. These clandestine and cohesive parties took their signals from a foreign power hostile to Western political values, and they could offer no principled objections to violent revolution under the right circumstances. The Cold War was therefore more than a geopolitical contest between the two major states which filled the power vacuum after World War II. When the British Communists tried to affiliate with the Labour party in 1946, its chairman explained his opposition in a pamphlet. "Organized as a conspiracy," Harold Laski wrote in *The Secret Battalion*, "their major desire is not to select the best possible leadership in ability and character for the end Socialism desires; it is to get those on whom they can count for uncritical and devoted obedience to their orders into the key positions of a movement or party they enter to use for their own purposes."

Though the Communists generally called themselves "progressives," this book also refers to them as Stalinists—not because I am oblivious to the harshness of the term, but because that is precisely what they were. They habitually offered alibis for mass murder and denounced as "slander" the effort to expose Soviet crimes. To call them Stalinists is also a reminder to readers that American Communists were enemies of civil liberties, which they disdained as "bourgeois" but which they invoked in their own behalf when opportune. They themselves remained mini-totalitarians, even when incurring penalties in the United States for beliefs that were voluntarily chosen. Because their commitment to civil liberties was so fraudulent, American Communists earned little sympathy when their rights were unfairly withdrawn—and thus bore some responsibility for the suppression that they endured.

That the organization was so unappealing helps explain why the American political system had such a phobic overreaction in the late 1940s and the 1950s. Communism was a threat *to* the United

States, as the literary critic Philip Rahv phrased it in 1952; but it was not a threat *in* the United States, where the danger was often wildly overestimated. The battalion of Stalinists may have been secret, but it was too negligible to divert the course of American history. Though evidence of infiltration could be detected from Hollywood to Harvard, Party membership hovered around forty-three thousand by 1950, around thirty-two thousand a year later. A nation of about one hundred fifty million people included as many members of, say, the Finnish Evangelical Lutheran church (Suomi Synod) as there were Stalinists. The Party and its outriders could inflict mischief in a few trade unions or in some advanced social movements, but the cost that American society paid to crush domestic Communism was disproportionate. For the repression weakened the legacy of civil liberties, impugned standards of tolerance and fair play, and tarnished the very image of a democracy. This Red Scare was not a collective tragedy, but it was a disgrace.

In Italy, which had so recently emerged from the ordeals of Fascist dictatorship, Nazi occupation, and military destruction, a fifth of the population could be counted on to vote the Communist ticket—without stirring the fears that racked so many Americans. The proportion of Communist voters was comparable in France, which was geographically close enough to Russia to have evoked the dread—early in the nineteenth century—of Cossacks watering their horses at the Place de la Concorde. But no widespread attacks on civil liberties, no cultural distortions, occurred in the name of anti-Communism in France. In April 1954, Prime Minister Winston Churchill refused to establish a royal commission to investigate domestic Communism in Great Britain, where no parliamentary inquisitions of any "un-British activities committee" could run amuck and inhibit political expression. In thus diverging from its Western allies, the United States repudiated two of the Four Freedoms for which World War II had so recently been fought; for freedom of speech and freedom from fear were among the entitlements that the late President Roosevelt had enunciated. Within a decade after the ghastly slaughter that the Four Freedoms were supposed to redeem, the United States had transparently violated such ideals.

1

To the novelty of the secret battalions as a cause of the Red Scare must be added the impossibility of getting at their ultimate source. It is tempting to interpret the excessive reaction to domestic Communism as a product of frustration, especially after September 1949, when President Harry S Truman announced that the Soviets had detonated an atomic bomb. The sudden end of the American nuclear monopoly meant that Communism could be extirpated only at the price of catastrophic violence. Oddly enough, not everyone shrank from the prospect of World War III, perhaps because the United States had already unleashed nuclear weapons to end World War II. Frustration with the receding advantages of the Allied victory in 1945 helps to account for popular willingness to accept the further use of atomic weapons during the Cold War. Toying with the initiation of such devastation was, in any event, an index of how dreaded the Soviet specter had become.

In the summer of 1949, before Truman's announcement, Gallup pollsters learned that 70 percent of Americans were *against* their government's pledge of no first use of such bombs. The loss of the nuclear monopoly did not immediately cause the majority of those polled to reconsider the acceptability of using atomic weapons. Instead, the announcement of a Soviet blast, according to historian Paul Boyer, "accelerated the shift toward viewing the atomic bomb not as a terrible scourge to be eliminated as quickly as possible, but as a winning weapon to be stockpiled with utmost urgency." Senator Brien McMahon (D-Conn.), chairman of the Joint Congressional Committee on Atomic Energy, was prepared to think the unthinkable. He told David Lilienthal, who headed the Atomic Energy Commission, that a preventive nuclear attack on the Soviet Union was the only way to avoid an ultimate, planetary holocaust.

McMahon's views were shared by the once-influential journalist H. L. Mencken, who was not joking when he proposed war upon "the Russian barbarians," so that, "in the end, if we are lucky, there will be something resembling a civilized peace in Christendom." In a few postwar statements, the British philosopher Bertrand Russell also recommended that the United States threaten the Soviet Union with nuclear destruction, if Moscow did not cooperate in the quest for world peace and order. Philosopher James Burnham announced in 1950 that World War III had already begun. The American decision to retaliate with atomic weapons against Soviet targets was therefore a question not of ethics but of expediency, in a war that could no longer be categorized as *preventive but as current*. Another Gallup poll, released in August 1950, found that 28 percent of those queried were in favor of dropping the atomic bomb in Korea, where war had erupted two months earlier when Communist forces crossed the 38th parallel. By November 1951, the figure had jumped to 51 percent supporting use of the bomb on "military targets." After truce negotiations in Korea had begun in the summer of 1951, Senator Margaret Chase Smith (R-Me.) expressed hopes for the success of the talks. If not, she suggested that her country "drop the atomic bomb on these barbarians." A weapon so powerful that the flash from its testing was reflected on the moon thus cast a long shadow on national strategy as well.

How far anti-Communism might be pressed within the executive branch was revealed in the last week of August 1950, when President Truman's secretary of the navy recommended a "preventive war." He was Francis P. Matthews, an Omaha millionaire who, from 1941 till 1950, had chaired the Chamber of Commerce's Committee on Socialism and Communism. In a Boston speech, Matthews declared that he "would be willing to pay any price to achieve a world at peace, even the price of instituting a war." Opposing forces, he conceded, "would brand our program as imperialist aggression. We could accept that slander with complacency, for in the implementation of a strong affirmative, peace-seeking policy, though it cast us in a character new to a true democracy—an initiator of a war of aggression—it would win for us a proud and popular title—we would be the first aggressors for peace." This version of pacifism was so peculiar, in fact, that a few days later Truman was compelled to repudiate it. Within two weeks, the president also fired the secretary of defense, who was Matthews's immediate superior, and brought General George C. Marshall back to the Pentagon. Matthews, a papal chamberlain who had headed the Knights of Columbus, was hustled off to Ireland as the new ambassador there. (Blessed are the peacemakers.) General Orville Anderson, the commandant of the Air War College, was also retired after boasting that the air force was poised and ready for orders to drop nuclear bombs on Moscow.

The Republican administration that succeeded Truman's in 1953 was more willing to brandish nuclear weaponry. In taking office, Dwight D. Eisenhower invoked the threat of nuclear retaliation to end the stalemate of the Korean War and told army general Lawton Collins in May, "It might be cheaper, dollar-wise, to use atomic weapons in Korea than to continue to use conventional weapons." For reasons other than thrift, the administration again tried nuclear blackmail during the crisis over the offshore Chinese islands in 1954–55, even though the president knew that Quemoy and Matsu were not essential to the defense of Formosa in the event of a Communist attack from the mainland. Though considerably more powerful than the bombs dropped on Japan a decade earlier, "tactical atomic explosives are now conventional," Vice-President Richard M. Nixon asserted.

Perhaps the closest call came when American forces were not even near the scene, however—during the final phase of an ally's colonial war in Vietnam. In March 1954, three key figures advocated an air strike, involving three atomic bombs, to aid the French garrison that the Communist Viet Minh was besieging at Dien Bien Phu: Nixon, Secretary of State John Foster Dulles, and Admiral Arthur W. Radford, who served as chairman of the Joint Chiefs of Staff. But army general Matthew B. Ridgway, a tough paratrooper whose trademark live grenades dangled from his chest, opposed the recommendation. With the British government balking at intervention and Congress unwilling to authorize U.S. troops in Vietnam, Eisenhower refused to accept the Joint Chiefs' split recommendation. Had Congress and the Western allies agreed, the president apparently would have accepted the proposal of the Joint Chiefs of Staff in May 1954 to retaliate with atomic bombs in case of Chinese intervention.

General Nathan Twining later second-guessed the refusal of his commander in chief to contemplate nuclear war in Vietnam: "I still think it would have been a good idea [to have taken] three small tactical A-bombs—it's a fairly isolated area, Dien Bien Phu—no great town around there, only Communists and their supplies. You could take all day to drop a bomb, make sure you put it in the right place. No opposition." The result, the air force chief added, would have been to "clean those Commies out of there[,] and the band could play the *Marseillaise* and the French could march out of Dien Bien Phu in fine shape."

A facility for entertaining the possibility of nuclear war—and indeed for considering its instigation—stemmed almost inevitably from the doctrine of "massive retaliation" that the Republicans introduced into statecraft and salesmanship during the Cold War. Its chief theoretician was a secretary of state who was himself the nephew and grandson of earlier secretaries of state. John Foster Dulles had managed to condemn the "materialistic emphasis" of American society while spending his adult life as a Wall Street lawyer. And though his corporate clients must have been puzzled by his insistence on the need to "regain confidence in our spiritual heritage" and to "reject totally the Marxian thesis that material things are primary and spiritual things only secondary," no one could doubt his animosity to Marxism as a creed. A Presbyterian minister's son, Dulles had chaired the Commission for a Just and Durable Peace of the Federal Council of Churches, which asserted in 1946 that "differences" with the USSR "will never be removed by compromise or surrender."

The prospect of terror might work, however, and Dulles did not seem to flinch from accelerating Armageddon. In March 1953 he told the National Security Council that, while "in the present state of world opinion we could not use an A-bomb, we should make every effort now to dissipate this feeling." The minutes of this meeting record that "the President and Secretary Dulles were in complete agreement that somehow or other the tabu which surrounds the use of atomic weapons would have to be destroyed." Two years later Dulles went public with a threat to drop atomic bombs. After all, as he remarked on the phone to General Twining, "there [is] no use of having stuff, and never being able to use it." Mere deterrence would, presumably, be wasteful. Dulles had also promised in a 1952 campaign speech in Buffalo that a Republican administration would use "all [sic] means to secure the liberation of Eastern Europe," and in a radio address the following January he had assured the peoples behind the Iron Curtain that his nation would back their efforts to emancipate themselves.

But the doctrine of massive retaliation soon collided with the dictates of sanity. After the secretary of state informed the Council on Foreign Relations in January 1954 that "instant retaliation" would be the American reaction to Communist aggression, members of Congress wondered how the response could be immediate without a declaration of war by the Senate and House of Representatives, as the Constitution provided. London also told Washington that no American bombers would be permitted to take off for Russian targets from British bases without the consent of the British government. (In George Orwell's dystopian novel 1984, published five years earlier, the political importance of his country was reduced to its strategic location: Airstrip One.) In Canada, Secretary of State for External Affairs Lester B. Pearson also wondered how Dulles could be so casual about Soviet retaliation that might culminate in inconceivable devastation. The secretary of state may well have scared his allies more than he intimidated the enemy.

For despite such pugnacious promises, the administration offered nothing tangible to the East Berlin workers who threw rocks at Soviet tanks in June 1953, or to the Hungarians who tried to withdraw from the Warsaw Pact and ended up defending themselves against a Soviet invasion in November 1956. When Poles seemed about to resist the Russians in October 1956, the secretary of state got on the radio to warn that, in case of a Soviet intervention, the United States would not interpose itself. The Warsaw Pact became the only alliance in history whose military campaigns were conducted entirely against its own members; and when Dulles's bluff was called, he folded. "Liberation" had been a sham all along. Even he realized that the rattling of nuclear weapons would not erase the evil and that, if force were used in the attempt to beat the devil, not only the Captive Nations would be decimated in the process. From that prospect even the exorcist shrank, which made Republican foreign policy largely continuous with the postwar strategy of containment that it was supposed to repudiate. During the 1952 campaign, Nixon had scorned the Democrats' diplomacy as Secretary of State "Dean Acheson's College of Cowardly Communist Containment," and Dulles had used the GOP campaign platform to denounce containment as "negative, futile and immoral." But his own policies proved to be no more militant or vigorous than his predecessor's, though his phrasemaking was certainly more provocative. His flair for creating major crises was so irrepressible that, according to Prime Minister Churchill, Dulles was "a bull . . . who carries his china closet with him." This disproportion between rhetoric and action generated a paradox. Dean Acheson had not vowed to defend South Korea, but then his administration did so—at a cost of 54,246 American lives. Dulles promised to emancipate the Captive Nations, and then did *not* do so—with tragic consequences for the embattled East Germans, Poles, and Hungarians. In fact, the only governments that the Republican administration contrived to overthrow were in Iran and Guatemala, where non-Communist nationalist regimes tried to acquire Western properties.

2

Since a preventive nuclear war to roll back the Soviets was excluded as a policy option, anti-Communism seemed to redouble its energies at home. The invulnerability of so resolute an enemy as the Soviet Union was novel to American statecraft, and this fact helps render intelligible the punitive and malicious excesses of the Red Scare. Forbearance was too ambiguous. Unable to strike directly at the Russians, the most vigilant patriots went after the scalps of their countrymen instead. Since Stalin and his successors were out of reach, making life difficult for Americans who admired them was more practicable. Since NATO would not come to the rescue of Eastern Europe, at least some politically suspect writers could be kept from traveling to Western Europe. Since breath could not be restored to all the victims whom the N.K.V.D. murdered, at least some Hollywood screenwriters could be sent to prison. Since the Korean War was a stalemate, perhaps the Cold War could be won at home. And also because few citizens could sustain a lively interest in foreign policy, anti-Communism was intensified on American soil.

With the source of the evil so elusive and so immune to risk-free retaliation, American culture was politicized. The values and perceptions, the forms of expression, the symbolic patterns, the beliefs and myths that enabled Americans to make sense of reality—these constituents of culture were contaminated by an unseemly political interest in their roots and consequences. The struggle against domestic Communism encouraged an interpenetration of the two enterprises of politics and culture, resulting in a philistine inspection of artistic works not for their content but for the *politique des auteurs*. Censors endorsed the boycott of films that they had not seen; vigilantes favored the removal from library shelves of books that they had not read.

The confusion of the public and private realms was also characteristic of the era. Thus, the Federal Bureau of Investigation compiled dossiers on novelists who seemed unduly critical of their native land, and the bureau got into the movie business by secretly filming the patrons of a left-wing bookstore, Four Continents, in New York. At the same time, some representatives of Hollywood presented themselves to Congress as authorities on the theory and tactics of Marxism-Leninism. An awed member of the House Committee on Un-American Activities (HUAC) hailed even the mother of musical star Ginger Rogers as "one of the outstanding experts on communism in the United States," for example. While legislators were interrogating musicians and actors about their beliefs, university administrators were using political instead of academic criteria to evaluate the fitness of teachers. Even as some clergymen were advocating ferocious military measures to defeat an enemy that was constantly described as "atheistic," government officials were themselves asserting that the fundamental problem presented by Communism was not political but spiritual.

Citizens were expected to enlist in the Cold War. Neutrality was suspect, and so was a lack of enthusiasm for defining American society as beleaguered. Near the end of playwright Arthur Miller's testimony before HUAC, a congressman asked him to help make literature *engagé*. "Why do you not direct some of that magnificent ability you have to fighting against well-known Communist subversive conspiracies in our country and in the world?" Representative Clyde Doyle (D-Cal.) asked. "Why do you not direct your magnificent talents to that, in part? I mean more positively?" The right of officialdom to interfere in cultural affairs was so taken for granted that occasional skepticism stood out. On one occasion a senator, his young aides, and a right-wing newspaper columnist were discussing with Martin Merson, the assistant director of the International Information Agency, whether to blacklist the music of Aaron Copland, the nation's most distinguished composer. Sitting in on "the Copland colloquy," Merson "was suddenly struck by the ludicrousness of the whole evening's performance. [Roy M.] Cohn, [G. David] Schine, [Senator Joseph R.] McCarthy, [George] Sokolsky, and for that matter the rest of us, meeting to discuss the manners and morals of our times. By whose appointment? By what right? What qualification did any of us have?" No more, certainly, than did Congressman Donald L. Jackson (R-Cal.), who objected to the participation of the Soviet Union's most honored composer at the "Cultural and Scientific Conference for World Peace," held in New York in 1949: "[Dmitri] Shostakovich has the same right to attend a cultural conference as a rattlesnake has to be at the altar of a church."

To record the obtuse folly of such unearned opinions, to be troubled by such interventions so far from the normal field of legislative jurisdiction, does not mean that the politics of an artist should never be noticed—or criticized. Nor is it true that political arguments against a work of art are inherently illegitimate, for they can uncover the intentions behind an object as well as its implications. But when such a standard becomes pervasive and intensive, and so potent in its effects that countless careers are ruined and the public cannot make its own choices in the marketplace of ideas, then the United States has come to resemble, rather uncomfortably, the sort of society to which it wishes to be contrasted. A society that imposes political standards upon its art, or demands of its artists certain sorts of citizenship tests (uncritical loyalty, abject repentance), is too much like totalitarianism. Congressman Jackson could not have realized how abjectly Shostakovich himself lived in terror of Stalin, a dictator who knew what he liked in music. Creativity is unlikely to flourish where the tastes of officials matter.

In the United States the application of political tests was not systematic, though it was not entirely haphazard either. Sometimes the tests were imposed by agencies of the federal government and were designed to intimidate other branches or the private sector. Sometimes the demands of hyperpatriotism reflected the efforts of private employers, sometimes of self-appointed monitors of political morality who acted with official complicity. Sometimes the private sphere was ahead of the government in such efforts at regulation and purification. But the effect was the same: the suffocation of liberty and the debasement of culture itself. Even by the narrowest chauvinistic criteria of the Cold War, the United States thus diminished its ability in the global struggle to be seen as an attractive and just society. The politicization of culture might win the allegiance of those who cherished authority, but not of those who valued autonomy. The politicization of culture might appeal to reactionaries abroad, but not to foreigners who appreciated creativity or critical thought.

And though the state was intimately involved in restricting liberty, it acted with popular approval and acquiescence; the will of the majority was not thwarted. In effect, Americans imposed a starchy repression upon themselves, and without denying rights to minorities—certain political factions on the right, for example. Indeed, American Legionnaires and the Catholic War Veterans were exercising their First Amendment rights in seeking to prevent other Americans from attending particular films and plays. The opportunity to dissuade other citizens from patronizing an institution or an individual has long been included in the definition of a democracy, and the marketplace—including the marketplace of ideas—has accepted the notion that unpopularity is decisive. No company, including a movie studio or a television network, is obligated to keep on its payroll those from whom the public has explicitly withdrawn its favor. Nor did principled foes of the right to boycott condemn such tactics; differences arose only over the choice of targets.

Government agencies acted improperly because they barged into areas where they did not belong and thus corrupted the sphere of expression that the First Amendment was designed to protect. In denying to the assorted talents who contributed to the nation's culture a level playing field, the House Committee on Un-American Activities, the Subcommittee on Investigations of the Senate Committee on Government Operations, the Senate Internal Security Subcommittee, and the Federal Bureau of Investigation were the most conspicuous offenders. To acknowledge that their efforts were often clumsy, spasmodic, and feckless, or that some citizens were plucky enough to defend themselves, is proof that a genuinely totalitarian impulse could gain little traction on American soil. But to minimize the danger that such interference posed is like saying that fear of rape is unfounded because its attempt was bungled or resisted.

The historian can nevertheless draw the happy conclusion that the culture of the Cold War was by no means synonymous with the culture of the 1950s, and in that asymmetry one can distinguish a relatively free society from a political system with totalitarian tendencies. The drive to inhibit art and thought left much untouched, and what was exempt from the scorched-earth policy of the patriots remains among the adornments of American culture. Three novels of the era, for example, belong on any reasonably short list of the canon of American fiction: J. D. Salinger's *The Catcher in the Rye* (1951), Ralph Ellison's *Invisible Man* (1952), and Vladimir Nabokov's *Lolita* (1955). Except for the final—and least satisfactory—section of Ellison's classic, none of these novels was political. At least one work of social thought is also destined to endure: David Riesman's *The Lonely Crowd* (1950). Major interpretations of the implications of the Freudian legacy were produced by Herbert Marcuse, Norman O. Brown, and Philip Rieff.

Perhaps the most famous book that a disciple of Freud ever wrote was Erik H. Erikson's *Childhood and Society* (1950). Its publication coincided with the author's resignation on principle from the University of California at Berkeley, because—although Erikson was willing to state that he was not a Communist—he refused to accept such a stipulation in his contract; and he protested the dismissals of his colleagues. "My field includes the study of 'hysteria,' private and public, in 'personality' and 'culture,'" Erikson explained. "I would find it difficult to ask my subject of investigation (people) and my students to work with me, if I were to participate without protest in a vague, fearful, and somewhat vindictive gesture devised to ban an evil in some magic way—an evil which must be met with much more searching and concerted effort." Erikson's career did not suffer because of his courageous act, for he was soon appointed to the Austen Riggs Center in Massachusetts. Long after *Childhood and Society* had been translated into a dozen languages, Berkeley gave him an honorary degree. At its best, thought and expression in the 1950s was subtle and radiant, and some of that work was apolitical.

Poetry followed its own direction, resisting virtually all the pressures of politics. One oddly reassuring sign was the choice of Ezra Pound to receive the Bollingen Prize in 1949, because the judges concluded that—despite his pro-Fascist beliefs—the verse that he had written the previous year was better than anyone else's. His politics had apparently not befouled his poetry. Confined to a lunatic ward in a Washington, D.C., hospital since late 1945, Pound was declared mentally incompetent so that he would not have to stand trial for broadcasts from Radio Rome during World War II. *The Pisan Cantos* extended—possibly into a cul-de-sac—the aesthetic achievements of modernism. But they were the work of a traitor. The 1949 award was so controversial because to honor poetry is also to reward a poet, and Pound's crankiness was so obnoxious that it inspired no apologists. The American Legion did not protest the award, despite his recent broadcasts to G.I.'s from the enemy side.

The responsibility of giving subsequent Bollingen prizes was nevertheless entrusted to Yale University rather than the Library of Congress. But when Communists were involved, apolitical judgments were more difficult to exercise.

The culture of the 1950s was therefore not monochromatic, and it would be unfair to encapsulate the era in the title of the series of paintings that Josef Albers executed in the 1950s: "Homage to the Square." Both Faulkner and Hemingway won Nobel Prizes within five years of each other for their earlier fiction; and the greatness of Eugene O'Neill was posthumously recognized in 1956, when *The Iceman Cometh* (1939) was revived and *A Long Day's Journey into Night* (1941) was first produced on Broadway. The trajectory of the work of writers like Saul Bellow, Flannery O'Connor, John Updike, Bernard Malamud, and James Baldwin was unaffected by the demands of the Cold War. The capital of Western painting shifted from Paris to New York. But even after underscoring such fertility, diversity, and vigor, and even after insisting upon the sunny-side-up ease that permeated much of society and that can evoke such nostalgia, it must be acknowledged that the Cold War also narrowed and altered American culture. This form of politicization arose because super-patriots themselves adopted the methods of their Communist enemies, and because the axis of partisan politics shifted so dramatically to the right.

3

Central to totalitarianism, for example, was the denial of what the political philosopher Hannah Arendt had called "the right to have rights." For both the Third Reich and the Soviet Union had turned certain groups into pariahs, whose exclusion from the political community was so complete that they could make no claims upon it. Nothing so absolute happened in the 1950s to American Communists, or those believed to be Communists, or those who might be sympathetic to Communists. But their "right to have rights" was imperiled. Their opportunities for political association and utterance, their freedom of movement, their chances of employment (even when the risk to national security was irrelevant), were all withdrawn or seriously curtailed. Eisenhower's 1954 State of the Union address had even proposed depriving Communists of their citizenship. According to a national poll that Harvard's Samuel A. Stouffer administered, 80 percent of the populace agreed with the president's suggestion; 52 percent wanted all Communists jailed; 77 percent wanted them banned from the radio. For good measure, 42 percent of those polled thought that *no* member of the press should be permitted to criticize the "American form of government."

For Stalinism was considered so dangerous and so sinister that democratic procedures could be suspended in the effort to combat it, and so urgent and pervasive was this crisis that anti-Communism assumed some of the same guises as its target. The most ardent variety of anti-Communism became, in the phrase of the political scientist Michael Paul Rogin, a species of "political demonology," in which the threat was exaggerated, intensified, and finally dehumanized. "The counter-subversive needs monsters to give shape to his anxieties and to permit him to indulge his forbidden desires," Rogin argued. "Demonization allows the counter-subversive, in the name of battling the subversive, to imitate his enemy."

Consider that the Committee on Socialism and Communism of the Chamber of Commerce proposed in 1946 and 1948 to remove liberals, socialists, and Communists from opinion-forming agencies. Communists, fellow-travelers, and "dupes" would not be permitted to teach in schools, or work in libraries, or write for newspapers, or participate in the entertainment industries. By 1952, this advocacy of thought control had become the official position of the Chamber of Commerce. Those of dubious political reliability would also be prohibited from employment in "any plant large enough to have a labor union"—thus foreclosing for radical workers as well as left intellectuals opportunities to earn a living. The implementation of such purges could not be entrusted to authorities but was to be a civic responsibility. Local members of the Chamber of Commerce were advised to "be on the alert for Communist sympathizers in your community," to "find out from reputable sources such as *Counterattack, Alert* or the American Legion about Communist sympathizers in the entertainment field," to be on the lookout for Communists "promoting appeasement in the name of peace," to "support patriotic ex-Communists who cooperate with the FBI," and to "identify public officials . . . displaying softness toward Communism." The systematic scope of the political mobilization that the Chamber of Commerce recommended was a facsimile of totalitarianism.

Another example of this mimetic effect was the attitude toward historical knowledge. About three months after Stalin's death, his successors on the Presidium of the Soviet Central Committee decided to shoot Lavrentii P. Beria, the secret police chief. Soon thereafter the owners of the *Great Soviet Encyclopedia* received so important an article on the Bering Straits that readers were instructed to cut out with a razor blade the published biography and photo of

Beria and insert the new geographic information instead. The late head of the M.V.D. thus sank into a black hole of oblivion. The next year the American poet Langston Hughes published a set of biographical essays, *Famous American Negroes,* and acceded to the wishes of his publisher (Dodd, Mead) by dropping the entry on W.E.B. Du Bois, who was the most distinguished Afro-American intellectual who ever lived. But by 1954 Du Bois had also become a reliable fellow traveler, and thus he risked transformation into a nonperson. He was not even mentioned in Hughes's chapter on Booker T. Washington, who had been Du Bois's chief antagonist in the black community at the turn of the century. Such Orwellian airbrushing of history was more arbitrary, ephemeral, and inefficient than in the Soviet Union, and in the United States such efforts at inducing amnesia could also backfire. Less than a decade later, several publishers yielded to right-wing intimidation and dropped from their own history textbooks the name of—among others—Langston Hughes.

The difference between Stalinist Russia and America—even when the superpatriots could play out their most vindictive fantasies— was still extreme, however. In the Soviet Union, the penalties for dissidence were lethal; countless innocent citizens were tortured, suffering ostracism and penury even if they managed to survive. For other Soviet citizens, the right to privacy, as well as the option to be nonpolitical, was also denied. During a 1934 writers' conference in Moscow, Isaac Babel had puckishly championed a right to silence. Three years later the self-proclaimed "master of the genre of silence" was arrested; he died—perhaps shot to death—in the Gulag Archipelago in 1939 or 1940. A phrase like "the great fear," coined just before the French Revolution and applied by historian David Caute to American society during the Cold War, fits Stalinist Russia best of all.

In the United States, the penalties for political dissidence were capricious. The sanctions were generally economic and social rather than legal. The victims of this Red Scare were usually deprived of their livelihood, not of their lives. For the "natural" tendency of Bolshevism was domination and subjugation, the denial of legitimacy to any political opposition. "We are all Chekists," Lenin had once asserted to Party comrades, affirming their complicity with the secret police. The "natural" tendency of the American political system, however, has been the give-and-take of partisan bargaining, the compromises negotiated according to the accepted rules of a rambunctious democracy. Jefferson's first inaugural address had proclaimed that "every difference of opinion is not a difference of principle. . . . We are all Republicans, we are all Federalists." And the few Americans who were not might well have meditated on the virtues of such comity.

4

If the third president of the United States was perhaps the first to articulate the ideal of consensus, the thirty-fourth seemed to embody it. Virtually everyone liked Ike. The Americans for Democratic Action (ADA), chock full of implacably liberal Democrats, pleaded with him to run for the presidency in 1948, though he was neither a liberal nor even a Democrat. Four years later, the Democratic party's candidate, Governor Adlai E. Stevenson of Illinois, complained that major daily newspapers favored Eisenhower "before they knew what that candidate stood for, or what his party platform would be, or who his opponent was, or what would be the issues of the campaign." After the election, Stevenson therefore had trouble sympathizing with newspaper editors who feared for the two-party system had Eisenhower lost. Even though the Republicans had till 1952 been excluded from the White House longer than either party since the Civil War, a GOP that controlled 90 percent of the press, Stevenson conjectured, would somehow have survived "one of the longest and loudest deathbed scenes in history."

Stevenson garnered more votes than Truman had in 1948—more votes than Franklin D. Roosevelt had won in 1940 and 1944, more votes, in fact, than any previous *victorious* candidate had attracted, except Roosevelt in his first two campaigns. But Ike's popularity stretched far. "Eisenhower has the simplicity, the closeness and contactfulness [*sic*] of genital characters," the refugee psychotherapist Wilhelm Reich remarked on the night of the 1952 election. "I do not know him, really, personally; but that is what I feel about him." Henry Wallace, the presidential candidate of the Communist-backed Progressive party in 1948, came out publicly for the Republican incumbent in 1956, claiming that Ike was sincere about peace and had indeed adopted Wallace's own ideas. The Beat novelist Jack Kerouac, who propounded a feral vision of life as "kicks," did not fit the profile of the typical Republican, but he supported Ike that year too. The Reverend Martin Luther King, Jr., who had spearheaded the resistance to racial segregation in Alabama, voted for the GOP in 1956. The ship of state had become a love boat. Only the Twenty-second Amendment, itself a Republican device to inflict a posthumous defeat on Roosevelt, blocked Eisenhower from a third term in 1960.

This consensus was pitched to the right of center. Otherwise it would not have won the allegiance of the most famous of the repentant ex-Communists, Whittaker Chambers, who seemed to infer from the GOP victory in 1952 that the Antichrist had been defeated (at least momentarily). Chambers had suffered a heart attack soon after leaving the polling booth, and when he recovered consciousness recalled that "the little nurse, who had been sitting in a corner, hurried over to see what I wanted. I asked: 'Who has won the election?' She left for a few minutes and returned to say: 'General Eisenhower.' I could not believe it and made her go over the key states. They were all for Eisenhower. Then I fell asleep. But our beginnings never know our ends." As the ultimate witness against the sins of Communism, Chambers exuded more authority than any other private citizen in explaining the stakes of the Cold War. "At issue," he wrote in his 1952 autobiography, "was the question whether this sick society, which we call Western civilization, could in its extremity still cast up a man whose faith in it was so great that he would voluntarily abandon those things which men hold dear, including life, to defend it." The author presented himself as such a man, but so gaunt a martyrdom was not to be his destiny. The *Saturday Evening Post* paid $75,000 for the serial rights to *Witness* and excerpted the autobiography for eight weeks. NBC invited him to read the foreword, his "Letter to My Children," on both radio and television. *Witness* was a Book-of-the-Month Club selection as well as the number nine bestseller of 1952.

The author especially treasured the note that another ex-Communist, the French novelist and critic André Malraux, had sent him after reading *Witness:* "You are one of those who did not return from Hell with empty hands." Though Chambers fancied himself a "revolutionist" in the ravaged company of Malraux, novelist Arthur Koestler, and Margarete Buber-Neumann (a survivor of both the Nazi and Soviet camps), he had served as an espionage courier in America, where his descent into the inferno of totalitarianism was vicarious. If Chambers had gone to hell and back at all, he had traveled tourist class. But the self-dramatizing force of his book, its wrenching psychological plunges, its riveting disclosures, its urgent political message, and its soaring rhetorical energy touched many readers—especially conservatives. Nixon, who owed his own meteoric rise to Chambers's credibility, listed *Witness* as one of his three favorite books (along with *War and Peace* and Senator Robert La Follette's autobiography). John Wayne, the most popular actor of the 1950s, claimed to have reread *Witness* often and to have memorized long sections of it. He gave one of his daughters *Witness* on her sixteenth birthday. Chambers was the only conservative quoted by another film star, Ronald Reagan, in his own autobiography, *Where's the Rest of Me?* (1965).

Such readers undoubtedly gave credence to Chambers's claim that "when I took up my little sling and aimed at Communism, I also hit something else. What I hit was the forces of that great socialist revolution, which, in the name of liberalism . . . has been inching its ice cap over the nation for two decades." *Witness* reinforced the effort to discredit liberalism itself. For the Cold War consensus put the heirs of the Jeffersonian Republicans on the defensive, and the balance of American politics shifted to the mid-twentieth century counterparts of the Federalists. It was not accidental that the strongest proponents of the regimentation of the mind had been the foremost critics of the regulation of property, nor that the most energetic advocates of thought control often resented government efforts to control the economy. The Cold War put the reformist strategies of the New Deal and the Fair Deal on ice, as though those experiments were part of the continuum that stretched all the way to Moscow. From the perspective of a resurgent right, the regulation of capitalist abuses that Roosevelt had begun easily shaded into something more sinister.

Thus, the 1946 congressional elections, according to the chairman of the GOP National Committee, offered voters a graphic choice between "Communism and Republicanism." Six years later, Nixon told the *Kansas City Star* that "there's one difference between Reds and Pinks. The Pinks want to socialize America. The Reds want to socialize the world and make Moscow the world capital. Their paths are similar; they have the same bible—the teachings of Karl Marx." The Pinks, Nixon argued, included the New Deal or progressive wing of the Democratic party. Among them had been his opponent in his rock 'em-sock 'em senatorial campaign of 1950, Helen G. Douglas, who was "pink right down to her underwear." Claiming that she "follows the Communist Party line," Nixon received the largest plurality of any politician elected to the Senate that year.

During the 1954 congressional campaign, the vice-president charged the ADA with "selling socialism under the guise of liberalism. It is practicing the greatest deception of the century." Though Eleanor Roosevelt and Ronald Reagan had been among the liberal anti-Communists who founded the organization, the Republican National Committee asserted that the ADA "has its roots deeply embedded in the Communist inspired 'Popular Front' movement that united both factions of Marxism, i.e., Communists and Socialists." A House Republican newsletter also labeled the ADA "a leading front organization for Marxist Socialism in the United

States," as though oblivious to the group's consistent *opposition* to Marxist socialism as well as its 1948 appeal to Eisenhower to seek the presidency. In 1956, Stevenson expressed his appreciation that the GOP attacks had mellowed, for in that campaign Nixon associated the Democrats only with socialism rather than Communism. These tactics were not ineffective; by the end of the 1940s, the age of reform was over.

The temptation to note a historical irony cannot be resisted, for the denunciations of socialism coincided with its decomposition. Never in the twentieth century had the democratic left been so paralyzed. Norman Thomas, who had led the Socialist Party of America for a generation, urged his colleagues not to bother running a presidential candidate in 1952, since he had attracted only 139,521 votes four years earlier. The Socialists nevertheless put up a Reading, Pennsylvania, lawyer named Darlington Hoopes, not because the White House was in sight but mostly to buttress the municipal tickets in Reading and Milwaukee. Getting only 20,189 votes, Hoopes did worse than any previous Socialist candidate for the presidency, even running behind the candidate for the Prohibition party. The palpable weakening of the left also facilitated the formation of a right-of-center consensus.

The spectrum of reputable opinion narrowed, shriveling the framework within which realistic political choices were entertained. "Americans live in fundamental agreement concerning certain long-range aims and principles," *Fortune* magazine proclaimed in 1951, adding that "never have left-wing ideologies had so little influence on the American labor movement as they have today." The proof was George Meany, who presided over the combined American Federation of Labor-Congress of Industrial Organizations (AFL-CIO), which had merged in 1955. Far from trying to exacerbate class conflict, Meany resembled a big-shot lobbyist instead, taking a chauffeur-driven Cadillac to an office that overlooked the White House, golfing with cabinet officers at his country club, and living in the suburb of Bethesda, Maryland, rather than in a working-class neighborhood. What he did at the office was to apply the dogmas of the Cold War, which few public figures accepted more fully (or had adhered to longer). The eccentric view of Senator Barry Goldwater (R-Ariz.) that Walter Reuther of the United Auto Workers was "more dangerous than . . . anything Russia might do" was not said of Reuther's chief rival.

The shrunken distance between the two political parties included the question of civil rights. Eisenhower showed no sympathy for black aspirations for equal rights, considered the appointment of the liberal Earl Warren to the Supreme Court as his biggest mistake, and hoped for a slow implementation of the racial desegregation that *Brown* v. *Board of Education* (1954) required. Stevenson also failed to grasp black impatience with the national failure to enforce the guarantees of the Constitution. Before the 1956 campaign, he was booed by a black audience in Los Angeles for saying that "we must proceed gradually, not upsetting habits or traditions that are older than the Republic." Stevenson's ostensible support of civil rights legislation had to be weighed against picking as a running mate in 1952 an Alabama senator who opposed it, and also against his bizarre remarks in Richmond that "anti-Southernism" was just as unpleasant as "anti-Negroism." No wonder that satirist Mort Sahl concluded: "Eisenhower says he's for integration but gradually; Stevenson says he's for integration but moderately. It should be possible to compromise between those extremes."

The struggle for civil rights, which became conspicuous in the fifties, aroused the suspicion of those who inferred from the evidence that Communism was loathsome the conclusion that anything loathsome was Communism. As early as 1942 Martin Dies (D-Tex.), the chairman of HUAC, deplored "the fact that throughout the South today subversive elements are attempting to convince the Negro that he should be placed on social equality with white people, that now is the time for him to assert his rights." For Albert Canwell, who chaired the Washington State Legislative Fact-Finding Committee on Un-American Activities, any awareness of imperfections in American society was suspect: "If someone insists that there is discrimination against Negroes in this country, or that there is inequality of wealth, there is every reason to believe that person is a Communist." That person, unlike the colonial printer John Peter Zenger in New York, could not have summoned truth as a defense.

The FBI was especially quick to connect a commitment to racial justice with political subversion. Bureau attitudes were faithfully reflected in a Warner Brothers film, *I Was a Communist for the FBI* (1951), which shows the Party taking credit for race riots in Harlem and Detroit in 1943. "To bring about Communism in America," one of its leaders announces to his comrades, "we must incite riots." The blacks who have died in these outbreaks of violence, an FBI agent in the film explains, "never knew that their death warrants were signed in Moscow." The FBI had trouble imagining racial change as anything but troublesome and interpreted ordinary decency as extraordinarily radical. *Parting the Waters* (1988), Taylor Branch's Pulitzer Prize-winning saga of Martin Luther King, Jr., reported that "FBI agents spotted white Communists by their ease and politeness around Negroes, or by the simple social fact that they socialized with Negroes at all." Of course, Party members and fellow travelers held no franchise in the civil rights struggle, but many were actively involved in the implementation of interracial ideals.

Indeed, so insensitive were most white Americans to systematic bigotry, in the era before racism became a common mode of social analysis, that segregationists were not entirely wrong in suspecting that a dedicated opposition to racial discrimination *was* often Communist-inspired. "Concern for such things as human rights for American blacks came, ironically, to be regarded as *prima facie* proof of a person's communist inclinations," journalist Nicholas von Hoffman wrote, "because so few non-Communists in positions of power and influence cared to do anything about the problems of caste and deprivation." Not even President Roosevelt had bothered to support an antilynching bill. But by 1961 his son James was lamenting that the various investigating committees "have helped to create such a general atmosphere of fear that all social reformers—including advocates of racial justice—tend to be frightened into silence. When the committees succeed in equating social reform with Bolshevism, it is to be expected that some people will confuse the Fourteenth Amendment with *The Communist Manifesto.* To avoid being called Reds, they will be sure not to talk like integrationists."

Even though HUAC was willing to certify the National Association for the Advancement of Colored People (NAACP) as "a non-Communist organization" in late 1954, various official committees in states like Alabama, Arkansas, Florida, and Louisiana summoned "expert witnesses," preferably ex-Communists, to brand the NAACP as an instrument of the international conspiracy. In a few states such investigations led to the outlawing of the organization, and the attendant publicity may have helped stifle criticism of Jim Crow. It mattered little to segregationists that the largest black organization in the country was not the NAACP, nor a Communist front like the National Negro Congress, but the National Baptist Convention, and that the ratio of black churches to churchgoers was double that of whites. It was therefore natural for King and other ministers who formed the Southern Christian Leadership Conference in 1957 to advertise their piety to the black community. But the Cold War was also taken into account. To include the word "Christian" in the name of the organization was also to demonstrate that, though the SCLC was consecrated to civil rights, it was not Communist-inspired.

The highest appellate court in the country lacked such camouflage. For its appreciation of the egalitarian implications of the Fourteenth Amendment, the Supreme Court after 1954 was also accused of susceptibility to Communism—especially in the South. A footnote in *Brown* v. *Board of Education* had cited the most influential scholarly account ever written about race relations, Gunnar Myrdal's *An American Dilemma* (1944); the citation gave segregationists the opening that they craved (even if they did not need it). Though Herbert Aptheker, a Communist historian and pamphleteer, had ferociously assaulted Myrdal's classic in 1946, right-wing and racist attacks on his book as Communist became common in the following decade. Myrdal was tagged a "notorious Swedish Communist" (he was in fact anti-Communist), a "Red psychologist," and an "alien anthropologist" (he was in fact an economist). He was often called "Dr. Karl Gunnar Myrdal," the full name that he never used, because the first name was the same as Dr. Marx's. By such acrobatics Senator James O. Eastland (D-Miss.) was able to charge, after *Brown* v. *Board of Education*, that the Supreme Court had dared "to graft into the organic law of the land the teachings, preachings and social doctrines [of] Karl Marx."

Because an intense concern with unsolved social problems may have betrayed Soviet influence, policy options thinned. Consider, as one example, the issue of health. When Truman proposed a plan of national health insurance in his State of the Union address in 1948, the American Medical Association (AMA) bitterly attacked it, warning that a "monstrosity of Bolshevik bureaucracy" would result. Faking a quotation from Lenin that "socialized medicine is the keystone to the arch of the Socialist State," an AMA pamphlet noted that the Communist party also championed "compulsory health insurance." Truman's proposal was spiked, and the United States remained the only Western democracy to deprive its population of guaranteed medical care.

Truman's successor made no effort to revive the notion that the government itself should uphold such a principle, perhaps because Eisenhower's experience and ideology were too limited. As Senator James E. Murray (D-Mont.) noted, a lifetime of army service had included "complete medical-care service, provided, without charge, by the American taxpayer. . . . In short, since President Eisenhower has been getting free, socialized medicine almost all his adult life, it is obvious there is no reason why he personally would have developed any real understanding" of how average American families had to pay for health care. His first secretary of Health, Education and Welfare, a millionaire named Oveta Culp Hobby, objected strongly to the free distribution of the polio vaccine that Dr. Jonas Salk had developed for children, and which the government declared safe in 1955. Such free dissemination would be tantamount to "socialized medicine" by "the back door," which she apparently dreaded even more than the epidemic itself.

Mrs. Hobby's views were too extreme for the right-of-center consensus, and she was eased out of the cabinet. The president nevertheless acceded to the stance of the AMA, which demanded that the Salk polio vaccine be distributed commercially, like any other drug. Had the government given the National Foundation for Infantile Paralysis $100 million for its clinics, all the elementary school children in the nation might have been vaccinated. With another $40 million, everyone under the age of twenty-one could have been spared the plague. But Eisenhower asked Congress to appropriate only $30 million, to reimburse state governments for vaccinating the indigent. Private practitioners expecting fees for services were thereby protected, and socialized medicine was avoided.

The political culture of the 1950s thus looks bizarre from the perspective of European social democracies, which managed to distribute welfare benefits—and to accept the legitimacy of Communist parties—without succumbing to the fears that damaged so much of the American ambience. The historian is also compelled to record how odd public discourse looks from a later perspective as well. The virulence of the Cold War largely spanned two administrations. The Republicans succeeded the Democrats in part because accusations of softness stuck to an administration that, in the summation of historian Stephen E. Ambrose, had "forced the Russians out of Iran in 1946, come to the aid of the Greek government in 1947, met the Red Army's challenge at Berlin and inaugurated the Marshall Plan in 1948, joined the North Atlantic Treaty Organization in 1949, and hurled back the Communist invaders of South Korea in 1950, all under the umbrella of the Truman Doctrine, which had proclaimed American resistance to any advance by any Communist anywhere."

The Truman and Eisenhower administrations had also applied extensive security programs that demoralized much of the civil service, using flexible criteria of loyalty and shifting the burden upon employees to prove their innocence. In the entire postwar period, not a single American Communist was caught committing espionage or even trying to engage in sabotage. In the teaching profession, Communists were supposed to be under orders to indoctrinate in the classroom, which is why philosopher Sidney Hook in particular insisted that they show cause why they should *not* be fired. Not a single case of such indoctrination ever came to light, but well over a hundred faculty members were dismissed for political reasons, though Hook himself did not alter his views. Such a loss of the sense of proportion, such an eclipse of rationality, was among the signatures of the Cold War.

So too was hypocrisy. When it became necessary to explain to the Russians what made American society so praiseworthy, even rabid anti-Communists were compelled to highlight the civil liberties that they themselves had sought to curtail. The Bill of Rights that Vice-President Nixon claimed abroad was operating in the United States was not a document that he and his allies sought to reinforce when he was at home. Yet in an address that he delivered in Moscow in 1959, printed in full in both *Pravda* and *Izvestia*, he noted that the material achievements of the American economy coincided with liberty, such as the freedom to criticize the president (a daily occurrence), freedom of worship and information, and freedom of movement: "Within our country we live and travel where we please. . . . We also travel freely abroad." Such misrepresentations were endemic to the global struggle, in which Cold War contrasts were heightened and the proclivity for self-righteousness went unchecked. The actual distinctions were real enough, without having to confirm Alexis de Tocqueville's observation of over a century earlier: "It is impossible to conceive of a more troublesome or more garrulous patriotism; it wearies even those who are disposed to respect it."

2

SEEING RED:
THE STIGMA

The most consequential of the postwar political trials was not for
treason or espionage but for perjury, and its importance derived not
from the weightiness of the indictment or the length of the sentence
but from the stature of the defendant. In March 1951, when news
photographers clamored around Alger Hiss as he headed for the penitentiary where he would spend the next forty-four months, the common criminal to whom he was handcuffed covered his own face
with his hat in shame. The scene was an extraordinary denouement
to an illustrious career. Suave and polished, Hiss had been a favorite
student of Professor Felix Frankfurter's at Harvard Law School, afterward a law clerk to Supreme Court justice Oliver Wendell
Holmes, Jr., and then in turn a crackerjack government attorney
during the New Deal, a top State Department bureaucrat, a member
of the American delegation at the Big Three conference at Yalta, the
secretary general of the inaugural meeting of the United Nations,
and, since 1947, the president of the Carnegie Endowment for International Peace. One item was missing from this résumé, however; for Alger Hiss was also a Soviet agent.

The evidence is virtually conclusive that, in the mid-1930s, he
had passed classified documents to Whittaker Chambers, who had
broken with the Soviet military intelligence system by 1938 and
had become a senior editor of *Time* magazine. The totality of what
Hiss actually transmitted—and its usefulness—to the Soviets is not
fully known, of course, because the archives of espionage agencies

have not adopted a policy of open stacks. Though sociologist Edward A. Shils could find "no reason to believe that the documents transferred by Alger Hiss had weakened the United States," the opposite conjecture is equally true. Some of the State Department material was "strictly confidential." Yet Hiss's value to Moscow may be gleaned from one curio in the annals of diplomacy: in 1945, Andrei Gromyko, the Soviet ambassador in Washington, nominated Hiss as a suitable temporary secretary general of the United Nations. It was astonishing for a Soviet diplomat to propose an American for what was then the UN's highest and most sensitive diplomatic post.

In 1949, Hiss was tried twice for perjury, because the statute of limitations prevented his prosecution on more serious charges. Though a second jury considered the evidence of his guilt beyond a reasonable doubt, the implications still seemed incredible. "I know Alger Hiss," Walter Lippmann reassured another journalist that year. "He couldn't be guilty of treason." But such faith left unexplained how someone of Hiss's status could be made suitable for framing. As the details of the case sank in, "the problem of Communist espionage became dramatized . . . in a new framework," historian John P. Roche explained. For "Hiss wore no beard, spoke with no accent, moved casually in the best circles. . . . The stereotype of the Communist agent was irremediably shattered. Hiss looked like the man down the block in Scarsdale or Evanston, the man in the office across the hall on Wall Street or State Street. If this man could be a spy, anybody could."

The political fallout for the Democratic party—and for the fate of liberalism—was immediate. Because Hiss had been a New Dealer, the thrust of social reform became discredited, progressives felt further beleaguered, and Roosevelt's wartime policies toward the Soviet Union and Eastern Europe were open to venomous interpretations. Because HUAC had ferreted out Hiss's treason, thanks primarily to the enterprise and skill of first-term congressman Richard Nixon, partisan initiative shifted to the right, as the case was transferred from the criminal courts into the electric field of political iconography. Nor did Dean Acheson's involvement in the defense of his friend and associate help the Democrats. On the day of Hiss's sentencing, the secretary of state (and also son of an Episcopal bishop) cited the Gospel according to St. Matthew 25:34 as a model of Christian loyalty while vowing: "I do not intend to turn my back on Alger Hiss."

Nixon's first reaction was to brand Acheson's statement "disgusting," adding that the secretary of state suffered from "color blindness—a form of pink eye toward the Communist threat in the

United States." Nixon's general statement on the Hiss case included several recommendations: (1) support of the FBI; (2) extension of the statute of limitations on espionage cases from three years to ten; (3) "wholehearted support" of HUAC by Congress; (4) a complete "overhaul [of] our system of checking the loyalty of Federal employees"; and (5) an educational program against Communism. Most of what he recommended was already in place or was quickly added to the order of battle of the Cold War. Though Nixon had lamented that membership on HUAC was "probably the most unpleasant and thankless assignment in Congress," a whopping 185 out of 221 Republicans felt that duty beckoned and, when the Eighty-third Congress opened in 1953, asked to serve on that committee.

Only two weeks after Hiss was sentenced to Lewisburg Penitentiary, the Lincoln Day orator for the Republican Women of Wheeling, West Virginia, Senator Joseph McCarthy (R-Wis.) claimed to have in his hand a list of 205 Communists who were still working under Acheson. Four days later, on February 13, the Department of State replied to such charges by summarizing the results of its own internal loyalty investigations and by declaring that "it knows of no Communists who are presently employed." But the damage had been done. A single perjury conviction was to have enormous repercussions in aggravating the public concern that growing Soviet power had already provoked.

In the 1950 Democratic senatorial primary in Florida, a pamphlet entitled *The Red Record of Senator Claude Pepper* was distributed throughout the state. For a Southerner, Pepper had indeed compiled an unusually liberal record, refusing to participate in filibusters, opposing the poll tax, voting for antilynching bills, calling for an Equal Rights Amendment, and advocating national health insurance tied to Social Security. Beginning in 1948, Pepper also supported Truman's firm foreign policy as well as his domestic programs, but voting for NATO as well as the peacetime draft did not prevent his opponent from warning that "the people of our state will no longer tolerate advocates of treason." Challenger George Smathers often mentioned his pride in wearing the orange and blue colors of the University of Florida. "Thank God," he exulted, "I don't have to wear the crimson of Pepper's and Felix Frankfurter's Harvard Law School. Alger Hiss is no classmate of mine." He wasn't the incumbent's either, having graduated five years after "Red" Pepper, who badly lost the primary anyway.

The following year, a Louisiana arch-segregationist named Leander Perez orchestrated the opposition to the gubernatorial candidacy of moderate Hale Boggs. The device that Perez, an attorney, used was a state law prohibiting Communists from appearing on the ballot. How Boggs, a Democrat, became encumbered with that incubus was ingenious. Without calling a single witness and without producing any evidence, Perez contrived a syllogism: "Alger Hiss denied having communist connections. Congressman Boggs has denied communist connections. Therefore, Congressman Boggs is as dangerous as Alger Hiss." Few Louisiana voters were trained in Aristotelian logic; and Boggs, who was knocked out of the runoff, thereafter suspected that Perez's daffy insinuation contributed to his defeat.

The Hiss case was injected into partisan politics outside the South as well. In 1952, one winner of a Republican congressional primary in Illinois was Phyllis Schlafly, whom the *St. Louis Globe-Democrat* described as an "attractive Alton housewife." She campaigned with the warning that "only a Republican victory this year will end the striped-pants diplomacy of the New Deal, including the vertical stripes worn by Dean Acheson and the horizontal stripes now worn in jail by his good friend, Alger Hiss." Though Schlafly lost the general election, her party finally gained the White House in a year in which the Democratic presidential candidate was compelled to devote a campaign speech to Hiss, for whom Stevenson had testified as a character witness.

The situation had been delicate. When rumors of Hiss's subversion had been reported to John Foster Dulles, who served as chairman of the board of the Carnegie Endowment, he had found "no reason to doubt Mr. Hiss's complete loyalty to our American institutions." After Hiss's indictment, when the board of the Carnegie Endowment had voted not to accept his resignation, trustee Dwight D. Eisenhower had not publicly objected to this gesture of confidence in Hiss. And so, when Stevenson had accurately testified in 1949 that Hiss's reputation was good, the Democratic nominee could later insist that he had only done his duty: "It will be a very sad day for Anglo-Saxon justice when any man, and especially a lawyer, will refuse to give honest evidence in a criminal trial for fear the defendant may eventually be found guilty. What would happen to our whole system of law if such timidity prevailed?" In fact, the deposition had been voluntary, though Stevenson took further evasive action by adding, " 'Thou shalt not bear false witness' is one of the Ten Commandments, in case Senator Nixon has not read them lately." During the campaign the Republican vice-presidential candidate had nevertheless interpreted Stevenson's deposition as "going down the line for the arch traitor of our generation." Senator McCarthy contributed to his party's crusade by including the Democratic presidential nominee in the "Acheson-Hiss-[Owen] Latti-more group" that had advanced the interests of Communism, and cackled maliciously after making a deliberate slip of the tongue ("Alger—I mean Adlai—Adlai in 1952").

Thus, liberalism was forced onto the defensive. A single criminal conviction had encouraged the inference that *anyone* might be a Communist, and that any Communist in government might be a traitor. In March 1951, the conviction of Julius and Ethel Rosenberg further suggested that any Communist might be an atomic spy.

Until their arrest in the summer of 1950, the Rosenbergs had led obscure lives. Both had been born into Jewish immigrant families in New York and, despite the pressures of poverty that the Great Depression exacerbated, were upwardly mobile. Julius had gradu-ated from the City College in electrical engineering, served in the Army Signal Corps during World War II, and was discharged from the army in 1945 for being a Communist—a political affiliation that he vehemently denied. But the evidence is indisputable that he and Ethel were deeply enmeshed in Stalinism. In the winter of 1943–44, for example, Party authorities on their own canceled the Ro-senbergs' subscription to the *Daily Worker*, perhaps to detach them from Popular Front Communism while they were engaged in un-derground work for the Soviet Union. When the German-born phys-icist Klaus Fuchs was arrested in Britain early in 1950 for having passed atomic secrets to Russia during and immediately after World War II, the FBI followed the trail to Fuchs's courier, Harry Gold, then to another of Gold's contacts, a former army machinist named David Greenglass, and then to Greenglass's brother-in-law, Julius Rosenberg, and Greenglass's sister, Ethel Rosenberg. Gold and Greenglass, as well as Greenglass's wife, Ruth, cooperated with the FBI. The Rosenbergs did not, and they were tried and convicted of conspiracy to commit espionage in transmitting atomic secrets to the Soviet Union.

In sentencing the Rosenbergs to death, Judge Irving R. Kaufman believed that the defendants had committed a crime "worse than murder." They were accused of "denial of the sanctity of the indi-vidual and [of] aggression against free men everywhere instead of serving the cause of liberty." The judge blamed the Rosenbergs for the American combat deaths in Korea and continued that, were atomic war to break out, "who knows but what that millions more innocent people may pay the price of your treason. Indeed, by your betrayal, you undoubtedly have altered the course of history to the disadvantage of our country." Kaufman momentarily forgot that the charge had not been "treason," which requires exacting standards of evidence—including the testimony of two separate witnesses to all overt acts cited in the charge. Nor could the prosecution have easily proved treasonous *intent*, since the Soviet Union had been an ally in World War II.

But such excesses as Kaufman's were built into the atmosphere of their trial, though not even J. Edgar Hoover had claimed that Greenglass had given his brother-in-law "the" secret of the atomic bomb. Curiously, the FBI director's article on the subject in the *Reader's Digest* (May 1951) does not even mention the couple. The technical details that Rosenberg had apparently received from Greenglass were considered of far less value than what Fuchs had passed on to the Soviet Union, though Greenglass's sketch of the lens mold of the bomb may well have corroborated the physicist's information. The indictment of Ethel Rosenberg represented an unsuccessful effort to extract a full confession from her husband; the failure of such pressure left their two sons orphans. Co-defendant Morton Sobell was never accused of getting, stealing, or transmitting classified information; nor was any evidence presented that he had ever committed atomic espionage. He still received a thirty-year sentence—double the punishment of the cooperative Greenglass.

Never before had capital punishment been imposed on anyone convicted in peacetime of espionage, and an international outcry resulted in a campaign for executive clemency. The *Daily Worker*, which had been silent during the trial (probably because the Party was unsure whether the defendants would confess to espionage and implicate others), waxed indignant thereafter at the prospect of martyrdom. Throughout the world the Communist and pro-Communist press orchestrated a major drive to protest the verdict as a frame-up, even though Julius and possibly Ethel were guilty as charged. "When two innocents are sentenced to death, it is the whole world's business," Jean-Paul Sartre exclaimed, defining Fascism not "by the number of its victims but by the way it kills them." The French philosopher added that the execution of the Rosenbergs was "a legal lynching that has covered a whole nation in blood." By coincidence, on the same day that the Rosenberg defense committee was founded in France, eleven former leaders of the Czech Communist party were executed in Prague. Eight of those hanged were Jews, but there ended similarities with the Rosenbergs. Since Rudolf Slansky and the others had abjectly "confessed," no judicial appeal could be presented. Since all the Czech defendants were executed overnight, defense committees had no time to form anyway. Nor did mass outrage erupt in front of Soviet or Czech embassies. Pablo Picasso sketched no portraits of the victims, and Sartre was silent. The Rosenberg protests were not, however, confined to the Communists and their allies. Even Pope Pius XII intervened, asking President Eisenhower to temper justice with charity. Eisenhower did not comply, fearing that clemency would be considered weakness. The couple was executed in June 1953.

The impact of such cases was registered in such widely assigned American history texts as Bragdon and McCutchen's *History of a Free People* (1954), which undoubtedly multiplied the number of suspicious minds. "Unquestioning party members are found everywhere. Everywhere they are willing to engage in spying, sabotage, and the promotion of unrest on orders from Moscow," high school students were told. "Agents of the worldwide Communist conspiracy have been active inside the United States. Some of them have been trusted officials of the State Department, regularly furnishing information to Russia. Others have passed on atomic secrets; still others have even represented the United States in the UN." The plural here is puzzling, since the authors did not specify which conspirators *besides* Hiss served in the State Department and at the United Nations. But the demonology of the Cold War was amplified. Transposing the genuine evil that emanated from abroad to domestic politics, influential voices then magnified the danger that American Communism represented and made democratic norms seem like luxuries that the crisis could not permit.

As liberal impulses became suspect, as sensitivities to constitutional safeguards were coarsened, the axis of American politics spun toward the primitive, the intolerant, the paranoid. In 1952, for example, the Supreme Court upheld in *Carlson* v. *Landon* a lower court decision to hold five aliens without bail, while the question of their deportation was under review. None had been convicted of—or even charged with—any crime. Refusing to grant the aliens bail, the district judge explained, "I am not going to turn these people loose if they are Communists, any more than I would turn loose a deadly germ in this community." Anti-Communism was expected to be visceral. Though George Kennan, the diplomat who devised the strategy of containment, had compared Communists to a "swarm of rats" whose abandonment of Western civilization was a "sacrilege" that "someday must be punished as all ignorant presumption and egotism must be punished," that was not good enough for James Burnham, an especially hard-boiled egghead. "Although George Kennan is unquestionably anti-Soviet and from a rational standpoint anti-Communist, nowhere in his published writings does one ever find expressed in the texture of his style a powerful emotion concerning Communism, a hatred of Communism," the philosopher complained. "The analysis and rejection, which are there, are always pale and abstract."

Locked in ultimate combat with the domestic apostles of totalitarianism, the polity readjusted itself to bear greater resemblance to the foe outside. Insisting on the rigid distinction between "Americanism" and Communism, some ardent patriots risked paying the sincerest form of flattery. "We are facing an implacable enemy whose avowed objective is world domination by whatever means and at whatever cost," the Doolittle study group on foreign intelligence reported to President Eisenhower. Discussing the work of the Central Intelligence Agency, this committee explained that "there are no rules in such a game. Hitherto acceptable norms of human conduct do not apply. We must develop effective espionage and counterespionage services and must learn to subvert, sabotage and destroy our enemies by more clever, more sophisticated, and more effective means than those used against us."

The rules of political conflict at home needed revision as well. To help expose the duplicitous intrigue of Communist infiltrators, the public could turn to the testimony of ex-Communists and FBI agents. Their memoirs—Louis Budenz's *This Is My Story* (1947), Angela Calomiris's *Red Masquerade* (1950), Elizabeth Bentley's *Out of Bondage* (1951), Chambers's *Witness* (1952), and Herbert Philbrick's *I Led Three Lives* (1952)—were serialized in popular magazines or adapted for the movies and television. Such testimony depicted Communists as primed to commit espionage, as pursuing the violent overthrow of the government, as capable of submitting to a harsh mental discipline. Budenz wrote that "the ordinary American has no idea of the alien world . . . whose leadership works secretly in the shadows." Party operations "cannot be conveyed to a normal American mind," which therefore had to confront an unprecedented danger.

1

One response can be explored at the murkier edges of popular sensibility, the locale of novelist Mickey Spillane. His *oeuvre* requires the cultural historian to discard aesthetic sensitivities, however, and to ignore, at least momentarily, the poet W. H. Auden's critical standards of "nuance and scruple" for the sake of listening to one of the most stridently representative and sensationalist voices of the era. Of the top ten fictional bestsellers of the decade of the 1950s, Spillane wrote an astounding six of them: number three, *The Big Kill* (1951); number five, *My Gun Is Quick* (1950); number six, *One*

Lonely Night (1951); number seven, *The Long Wait* (1951); number eight, *Vengeance Is Mine* (1950); and number nine, *Kiss Me, Deadly* (1952). This catalogue does not count his most popular novel, *I, the Jury*, which had been published prior to the decade. By 1953, the New American Library had sold seventeen million paperbacks of his first six novels, which meant that having Spillane on the firm's list of authors was like a license to print money.

I, the Jury (1947) introduced a private investigator named Mike Hammer, a World War II veteran of such magnanimity that he harbors no hostility toward Nazis. Though he chose not to become a cop because a "pansy" bureaucracy was emasculating policemen with its rules and regulations, his real contempt is reserved for the professional and intellectual classes, for homosexuals, and above all for swarthy criminals like "the Mafia. The stinking slimy Mafia. An oversized mob of ignorant, lunk-headed jerks who ruled with fear and got away with it because they had the money to back themselves up." In *I, the Jury*, a character named Charlotte Manning, who is endowed with a beauty that Hammer admires as "Nordic" or "Viking," is easily overwhelmed by the force of his machismo. But she is also a psychiatrist who, rather implausibly, uses her professional practice to run a heroin ring. As a female intellectual criminal, Dr. Manning must ineluctably die at his hands. Hammer is not entirely a misogynist, however. In this novel, like the others, the presence of Velda, his secretary and fiancée, proves his capacity for love. Though Velda is readily used as a sexual decoy, and though he asserts his sexual claims upon other women, Hammer expects her to remain chaste.

The detective's hairy-chested heroics would have made such novels enormously popular even if they had been devoid of any explicit politics, but the overt anti-Communism of Spillane's fiction engraved it with the signature of the period. Two decades earlier, Hammer might have combated only organized criminals spawned in the lower depths; two decades later, the adversaries would have been a cabal of Third World terrorists. In the early 1950s, however, the Red Scare required his special skills. For the comrades and conspirators in *One Lonely Night*, Hammer has reserved kicks that can shatter bone on impact, bursts of lead from his .45, and the sadistic pleasures of strangulation.

In that novel, which sold more than 3 million copies, the detective seduces a millionaire's estranged granddaughter, whom boredom has driven to Communism. At first Hammer cannot fathom why Ethel Brighton, despite her early exposure to the attractions of capitalism, can embrace the twisted creed of Bolshevism. He suspects that she needs only the substitute of *his* embrace. Confident that his virility can transform her politics, he has her spend one night in his apartment, and concludes, "Now that she had a taste of life[,] maybe she'd go out and seek some different company for a change." He is wrong—or at least seems to be, and realizes that Ethel Brighton has continued to associate with the scum and perverts who comprise the Communist movement. So he strips and whips her. Eventually Hammer poses as a member of the Soviet intelligence apparatus; since no one in this supposedly very clandestine organization thinks of challenging his credentials, he considers these conspirators as "dumb as horse manure." These malignant dreamers of world conquest "had a jackal look of discontent and cowardice." When they are not merely credulous cretins, they are either vicious hypocrites or else clinically insane. The supreme villain in *One Lonely Night* is Oscar Deamer, who is both a Communist and a psychopath. Hammer tells this master criminal, just before choking him to death: "You were a Commie, Oscar, because you were batty. It was the only philosophy that would appeal to your crazy mind. It justified everything you did and you saw a chance of getting back at the world." The explanation for the appeal of Communism is, apparently, insanity.

In destroying such motiveless, psychopathic malevolence, Hammer personifies the rejection of liberalism. The cure for the plague of Communism cannot be the diffusion of New Deal programs to relieve economic misery, or the extension of the Four Freedoms to amplify the meaning of an open society, or more resonant calls to lighten the burden of social injustice. The solution, the creator of Hammer seems to fantasize, is violent prophylaxis. After the detective has saved his naked fiancée from hysterical Bolshevik flagellants, he murders them all, and then—in an act of ritual purification—torches the abandoned building where Velda was stripped and lashed, thus making it impossible to recover the corpses of his dishonorable foes. "I killed more people tonight than I have fingers on my hands," he later boasts. "I shot them in cold blood and enjoyed every minute of it. . . . They were Commies. . . . They were red sons-of-bitches who should have died long ago. . . . They never thought that there were people like us in this country. They figured us all to be soft as horse manure and just as stupid." Such violence is presented as redemptive and even sacrificial, sinuously finding its source—however preposterously—in Christian ethics. For the feat of rescuing Velda in *One Lonely Night* has enabled Hammer to understand "why my rottenness was tolerated and kept alive. . . . I lived only to kill the scum and lice. . . . I lived to kill so that others could live. . . . I was the evil that opposed other evil, leaving the good and the meek in the middle to live and inherit the earth."

To appraise the literary significance of such fiction would be utterly irrelevant, to sermonize against such appalling crudeness equally pointless. What needs underscoring is that, at least in the night battles of the Cold War for which Spillane recruited more Americans than any other author, the procedural rules and legal guarantees that helped make a civil society worth defending were treated with savage contempt. Justice was imagined as coming from the barrel of a pistol, and cruelty was not confined to Party headquarters but was exalted in the exploits of Mike Hammer. Because of the official limitations under which formal authority chafed, vigilante ruthlessness was the only effective antidote to unmitigated evil. The end appeared to justify the means, so that it is almost too obvious to insist upon the analogy between the stigma that Spillane's fiction described and the methods that McCarthyism employed. To be sure, the junior senator from Wisconsin had no *political* rival, journalist Richard Rovere observed, in gaining "access to the dark places of the American mind." But lurking beneath the civility of so much of American life in the early 1950s was nightmarish territory that Spillane had already penetrated, a realm of subterranean turmoil that was ripe for a "fighting Irish Marine [who] would give the shirt off his back to anyone who needs it—except a dirty, lying, stinking Communist. That guy," Senator Herman Welker (R-Idaho) announced, "he'd kill."

2

"What do we find in the summer of 1951? The writs of Moscow run to . . . a good 40 percent of all men living. . . . How do we account for our present situation unless we believe that men high in this government are concerting to deliver us to disaster? This must be the product of a great conspiracy, a conspiracy on a scale so immense as to dwarf any previous such venture in the history of man. A conspiracy of infamy so black that, when it is finally exposed, its principals shall be forever deserving of the maledictions of all honest men."

Welcome to the paranoid world of Joe McCarthy, in which the most preposterous concoctions and fantasies blended with a canny sense of what would inflame his followers and snare the headlines. In that world, the failures of foreign policy were not due to misjudgment, contingency, ignorance, and error but to deliberate disloyalty—or to a willingness to countenance disloyalty. In fighting

Communism, the opposition party did not offer an alternative approach but was instead "the administration Commiecrat Party of Betrayal." By 1952, the five terms of Roosevelt and Truman did not represent the ambiguous achievements of the New Deal and the Fair Deal but were reduced to "twenty years of treason."

Only in 1954, after McCarthy referred to "twenty-one years of treason," did his own party lose its reluctance to dislodge him. But by switching the terms of the debate from "treason" to "traitors," this boorish thug decisively altered the nature of the anti-Communist crusade and dominated national politics more fully than any other demagogue in American history. "He scraped the raw nerve of the nation's anxiety and turned it into a neurosis," journalist Cabell Phillips wrote. "He spit in the eye of constituted authority, undermined public confidence in the government and its leaders, and tore at the nation's foreign policy with the indiscriminate ferocity of a bulldozer. He used lies, slander, and innuendo to smash his opponents and to build his own image of invincibility. He made cowards of all but a handful of his fellow Senators, and he kept two Presidents angrily and helplessly on the defensive in nearly everything they did."

McCarthyism, a term that the cartoonist Herblock invented at its very birth, did not require that the traitors be identified with any pretense to exactitude. On March 19, 1950, the senator explained on *Meet the Press* that "when you talk about being a member of the Communist party, I'm not so much concerned about whether they have a card in their pocket saying, 'I am a member of the party.' I'm concerned about those men who are doing the job that the Communists want them to do." Such a standard was so amorphous that, because McCarthy so discredited the democratic process of fair play and so traduced the established institutions of American self-government, he himself could be considered a Communist. His mischievous brutality certainly befouled the anti-Communist cause and injured the reputation of his country abroad. Even Chambers kept his distance, considering him "irresponsible," a "raven of disaster."

The senator never found a real Communist on his own, and indeed a United Press reporter who covered him once quipped that McCarthy "couldn't find a Communist in Red Square." But because he liked to shoot from the hip ("my gun is quick"), it took a while for the public to realize that he was only firing blanks. Ironically, the negligible domestic influence that Communism exercised had already receded before McCarthy discovered the advantages of excoriating it. Its power had been broken with the crashing failure of the Henry Wallace campaign and with the expulsions of Communist-dominated unions from the CIO. This demagogue had nothing to with defeating Communism, but he had much to do with *defining* it. He made its demonization central to Republican arch-conservatism (and a rebuke to liberalism), and with such a shift to the right the definition of evil became cynically loose.

The extremely dubious scope of his inquisitions, his casual disregard for whatever actual security threat confronted the United States, can be gauged from critic Dwight Macdonald's 1954 summation: "Like Gogol's Chichikov, McCarthy is a dealer in dead souls. His targets are not actual, living, breathing Communists but rather people who once were or may have been but were not but may be made to appear to have possibly once been Communists or sympathizers or at any rate suspiciously 'soft' on the question." Especially after his coarse assault on General Marshall, the architect of victory in World War II, "as an instrument of the Soviet conspiracy," virtually no one could be exempted from the aura of suspicion that McCarthy amplified more cleverly and more viciously than anyone else. After belles-lettrist E. B. White published a satiric piece in the *New Yorker* suggesting that, if McCarthy had known of Thoreau, the Concord writer would have been denounced as a security risk, McCarthy's classiest defender, William F. Buckley, Jr., rebutted: "Thoreau *was*."

Perhaps in a similarly remorseless spirit, the State Department hoped to deflect McCarthy's young minions—Cohn and Schine— by issuing a directive that prohibited from its overseas libraries all materials, including paintings, by "any controversial persons, Communists, fellow-travellers, et cetera." The vagueness of a phrase like "controversial persons" aroused such strong criticism that the International Information Administration eliminated the category, but that adhesive "et cetera" remained in effect. Yet not even the experts could agree on who the Communists and fellow travelers were. HUAC's list of subversive organizations, for example, was five times longer than the attorney general's list, which interdicted seventy-eight groups when it was first promulgated in 1948. The National Lawyers Guild (NLG) was only on HUAC's list; and when McCarthy decided to go for the jugular during the 1954 army hearings, he identified one former NLG member as Fred Fisher, a young Hale & Dorr associate of army special counsel Joseph N. Welch. Had McCarthy stuck to the attorney general's list, which had omitted the organization that McCarthy called "the legal arm of the Communist Party," Welch's rebuttal of June 9, 1954, would not have struck with such magnum force: "Until this moment, Senator, I think I never really gauged your cruelty or your recklessness."

Because McCarthy bore so much responsibility for shifting the meaning of the stigma, he also helped certify the authenticity of anti-Communism, which he considered incompatible with liberalism. Indeed, liberal anti-Communism was a self-contradiction. James Wechsler, for instance, had helped to found the vigorously anti-Communist Americans for Democratic Action. As editor of the *New York Post*, the city's most liberal daily, he had run a devastating exposé of McCarthy's career in September 1951. Two years later (and sixteen years after Wechsler had quit the Young Communist League), he was called to Washington, where McCarthy charged, in the editor's recollection, "that I not only was but still am an agent of the communist conspiracy; that the numberless anti-communist words I have written and spoken in the last fifteen years—from the age of twenty-two to thirty-seven—have been elaborately designed to conceal my true allegiance; and that the proof of my continuing sin is that I have shown no reverence for committees such as his and offered no testimony that has resulted in anyone's indictment."

McCarthy told him: "Your paper, in my opinion, is next to and almost paralleling the *Daily Worker.* . . . You have done exactly what you would do if you were a member of the Communist Party, if you wanted to have a phony break and then use that phony break to the advantage of the Communist Party. I feel that you have not broken with Communist ideals. I feel that you are serving them very, very actively. . . . [You are] still very, very valuable to the Communist Party." Wechsler felt that he had no choice but to name names, but he concluded his testimony by telling McCarthy that, "under the standards you have established here this afternoon, the only way that I could in your view prove my devotion to America and the validity of my break with communism would be to come out in support of Senator McCarthy. This I do not plan to do."

Like Wechsler, Professor Arthur M. Schlesinger, Jr., had been an unalloyed voice of anti-Communism before McCarthy discovered how to score with it. That record of steadfast opposition did not prevent the senator from smearing the liberal Harvard historian— and Stevenson adviser—on television during the 1952 campaign. The liberal writers who condemned McCarthy's malicious methods in the leading Roman Catholic weekly were known as "*Commonweal* Catholics." To McCarthy, however, they were *Commonweal* Communists. "I feel that you have done and are doing a tremendous disservice to the Catholic church and a great service to the Communist Party," he lectured its editors in 1953. For a magazine that "falsely and dishonestly masquerades under the title of being a mouthpiece for the Catholic Church can perform unlimited service to the Communist movement." The crime of the magazine was not sympathy for Stalinism, which it vehemently criticized; it was antipathy to a senator who valued no anti-Communism other than his own capricious version.

This proprietary claim was advanced through his appeal to a "Loyal American Underground" within the executive branch—even when it was under the auspices of his own Republican party—to bootleg classified documents about possible Communist infiltration. For a pro-McCarthy rally late in 1954, thirty-five hundred loyalists purchased admission tickets that requested the ushers at Constitution Hall to "Admit One Anti-Communist." Indeed, immediately after the Senate censured McCarthy in December 1954, he felt compelled to "apologize" to his fellow citizens for having promised them in 1952 that a GOP administration would make a "vigorous, forceful fight against Communists in government. . . . I was mistaken." His thinking resembled the response of Emperor Franz Josef I, when assured that a junior officer who was about to be promoted was "a patriot." "Yes," the Habsburg ruler asked, "but is he a patriot for me?"

Politically dead with the senatorial rebuke for the indignity that he inflicted upon his colleagues (no one else), McCarthy suffered a fatal attack of acute hepatitis—or inflammation of the liver—three years later. The eponym did not fade away. But the obsession with the stigma receded by the end of the 1950s, and the preoccupation with security risks that had earlier gripped mainstream opinion largely evaporated. Wisconsin voters even elected a Harvard-educated Democrat to succeed McCarthy in the Senate. Roy Cohn, who had been committee counsel and the demagogue's indispensable aide, returned to New York in 1954 to set up a lucrative law practice. G. David Schine, the former "chief consultant," married a Miss Universe from Sweden the following year and devoted himself to the family's hotel business as well as to movie production in Los Angeles. The national emergency would thus have to be addressed without them.

Since the wildest suspicions that marked the culture of the Cold War could not be easily extinguished, however, the paranoia simply moved further to the right. Entrenching itself on the margins, the woolly logic of McCarthyism reached its terminus in the John Birch Society. Named in memory of an army captain and Baptist missionary who was killed during an encounter with Chinese Communists soon after World War II, the society was founded in 1958. Its guiding spirit was a retired candy baron, Robert Welch, Jr., who announced, "Our enemy is the Communist—nobody else." Five years later he had attracted forty thousand members, though the ubiquity of "Communist infiltrators" prevented adherence to "so-called democratic processes" in the more than three hundred chapters of the John Birch Society.

Welch memorialized McCarthy as the victim of "smears by his enemies" and thus a martyr to the bloodthirsty malevolence of the Communists. But the founder of the society was more than faithful to the senator's memory, for Welch extended the fears of Communist penetration even farther than the Grand Inquisitor had dared to go. If someone like Hiss could be a Soviet agent, McCarthy had reasoned in 1951, why couldn't General Marshall be part of the conspiracy? And if so, Welch wondered, why not the general whom Marshall had promoted to command Allied forces in Europe in World War II? The initial version of Welch's book, *The Politician* (1958), therefore charged that the president of the United States was "a dedicated, conscious agent of the Communist conspiracy," "a political front man" for the Party. And since Eisenhower had often praised the astuteness of his brother, who served as president of the Johns Hopkins University, Welch conjectured, "The chances are very strong that Milton Eisenhower is actually Dwight Eisenhower's superior and boss within the Communist party." How else could one account for Ike's continuation of the policies of the "Communist-directed Truman Administration"? The Republican president was therefore "knowingly accepting and abiding by Communist orders, and [had been] consciously serving the Communist conspiracy for all of his adult life." Welch stretched the consensus of the 1950s so far that he had the rulers of the Kremlin wearing "I Like Ike" buttons in their lapels.

But the conspiracy was even more insidious than that. "For many reasons and after a lot of study," he proclaimed, "I personally believe [John Foster] Dulles to be a Communist agent." But surely the Central Intelligence Agency . . . No, Welch insisted, the CIA remained quite simply "on the Communist side." To promote such warnings of an "imminent . . . danger of the physical enslavement of the whole world, including ourselves," the John Birch Society was annually spending over $5 million. The organization thus exemplified what the historian Richard Hofstadter termed "the paranoid style," which deduced from the truism that history contains conspiracies the quite different belief that "history *is* a conspiracy, set in motion by demonic forces of almost transcendent power." The rambling and ragged definitions of Communism enunciated at the dawn of the Red Scare had by the end of the decade passed over into the twilight zone.

3

In an era that fixed so rigidly the distinction between Communist tyranny and the Free World, and which prescribed that men were men and women were housewives, perhaps only one peril seemed, if anything, worse than Communism. "The overriding fear of every American parent," a visiting English anthropologist noticed in 1950, was that a son would become a "sissie." Such anxieties were also reflected in bigotry and discrimination, especially in employment, even as homosexual acts between consenting adults remained against the law, however haphazardly enforced. In the early 1950s, police in the District of Columbia usually arrested about a thousand men annually on homosexual charges. To protest against the invasion of personal freedom, the Mattachine Society was organized as a civil rights group in Los Angeles in 1951. Its founder, Henry Hay, had quit the Communist party because its requirements of control and discipline were seen as incompatible with his own growing emphasis on his sexual orientation. Both perpetrators and victims of the Red Scare could agree on one subject, and stigmatized homosexuality.

If only through innuendo, nothing in the political arena in the 1950s was more convenient than establishing some sort of connection between political and sexual "perversion." Occasionally, even the liberal imagination yielded to such temptations of conjuncture. In *The Vital Center* (1949), Schlesinger contrasted "the new virility" of the leaders of postwar reform with the "political sterility" of those to their left and right. Lest readers still not catch Schlesinger's drift, the book described Communism as "something secret, sweaty and furtive like nothing so much, in the phrase of one wise observer of modern Russia, as homosexuals in a boys' school." But seeing lavender was mostly a proclivity of the right. Senator Kenneth Wherry (R-Neb.), whose preference for the heartland over port cities had been indelibly expressed in his 1943 pledge that "we will lift Shanghai up and up, ever up, until it is just like Kansas City," advocated laws to secure "seaports and major cities against sabotage through conspiracy of subversives and moral perverts in government establishments." Wherry explained to a liberal journalist that "you can't . . . separate homosexuals from subversives. . . . I don't say every homosexual is a subversive, and I don't say every subversive is a homosexual. But a man of low morality is a menace in the government, whatever he is, and they are tied up together."

Sexual "deviants," it was assumed, were so readily equated with security risks because they were so readily susceptible to seduction and then subject to blackmail, or—since they were so bereft of will power or moral control anyway—they were easily drawn to subversive organizations on their own. A 1950 Senate report, *Employment of Homosexuals and Other Sex Perverts in Government*, confidently asserted, for example, that "those who engage in overt acts of perversion lack the emotional stability of normal persons. . . . One homosexual can pollute a Government office." The Department of State was especially vulnerable. This haven for "cookie pushers" came under special attack shortly before the 1950 congressional elections. John O'Donnell, the top political commentator of the tabloid *New York Daily News*, considered "the primary issue" of the campaign to be "the charge that the foreign policy of the U.S., even before World War II, was dominated by an all-powerful, super-secret, inner circle of highly educated, socially highly placed sexual misfits in the State Department, all easy to blackmail, all susceptible to blandishments by homosexuals in foreign nations." In 1952, Senator Everett M. Dirksen (R-Ill.) promised to kick "the lavender lads" out of the State Department, once the GOP regained control of the executive branch. Vice-presidential candidate Nixon, whom *Time* magazine would later hail as "the personification of a kind of disciplined vigor that belied tales of the decadent and limp-wristed West," rejected a "nicey-nice little powder-puff duel" with the Reds, who were expected to shrink from the truculence that he tried to project.

McCarthy himself vowed that year that, if only permitted to board the Stevenson campaign train with "a slippery-elm club, I will use it on some of his advisors," and thus make of the Democratic candidate "a good American" (translation: a real man). The exaggerated masculinity with which McCarthyism went about its business always implied a contrast with the effete delicacy of the "striped pants boys in the State Department." When Cohn and Schine, investigating the International Information Administration, had been assigned a double room in Munich, Cohn slyly protested to the room clerk, "Hey, we're not the State Department." (A couple of decades later, it was revealed that Cohn himself was a homosexual. He died of AIDS in 1986.) Citing "rumors," Dulles wanted Charles E. Bohlen, whom the Senate had confirmed as ambassador to the Soviet Union early in 1953, to travel there on the same flight as his wife, which would somehow prove that the urbane diplomat was normal enough to have wed a woman. Though neither such ferocious anti-Communists as J. Edgar Hoover or Francis Cardinal Spellman was a family man, their followers were paradoxically reassured if our representative in Moscow was. The connection between subversion and perversion was sanctified when the Reverend Billy Graham praised Capitol Hill inquisitors "who, in the face of public denouncement and ridicule, go loyally on in their work of exposing the pinks, the lavenders, and the reds who have sought refuge beneath the wings of the American eagle."

4

The wickedness ascribed to domestic Communism not only allowed Americans to indulge in forbidden desires of demolishing it outside the rules, but the demonic peril that the Party incarnated also warranted its destruction *within* the law. Because the Communists could exploit the Constitution, all three branches of the federal government united to destroy their political freedom, paying the Stalinist apparatus at least the tribute of sneaky imitation. Thus Andrei Vishinsky's notorious 1938 treatise on Soviet law, which denied the legitimacy of political opposition, came to be adopted by American anti-Communists, who abandoned the Jeffersonian faith in the ultimate wisdom of the electorate.

Confidence in the suffrage was widely jettisoned. Alabama not only kept blacks from voting but also kept Reds from running, and in 1947 it became the first state to honor the call of the American Legion to outlaw the Communist party. Other states and localities found increasingly imaginative ways to immunize themselves against the bacillus. In a state like Texas, a Communist was more likely to be exotic than dangerous. Its legislature nevertheless made Party membership a felony, for which the punishment could be twenty years' imprisonment. Governor Allan Shivers was reluctant to sign the bill because he disagreed with the penalty, which he thought should be death. With even more subversives living in New York, a loyalty oath was imposed there on applicants who wanted to fish in municipal reservoirs. Indiana also forced professional wrestlers to take a loyalty oath.

Ordinances in Jacksonville, Florida, and McKeesport, Pennsylvania, required Communists and even fellow travelers to be out of town within forty-eight hours. Perhaps it is surprising that other communities did not take that step, though the city council of New Rochelle, New York, limited itself to an ordinance in 1950 that obligated Communists living there or "regularly passing through" to register. One law-abiding citizen on the morning train for Manhattan got off to present himself at the New Rochelle city hall, where he was reassured that the registration was for Communists—not commuters. In March 1947, a member of Truman's cabinet, Secretary of Labor Lewis B. Schwellenbach, became the first national politician to demand that the Communist party be outlawed. In the Republican primaries the following spring, the "liberal" ex-governor of Minnesota, Harold Stassen, echoed that call; and Senator Arthur H. Vandenberg (R-Mich.) warned, "We are suicidal fools if we do not root out any treason at home which may dream of bringing world revolution to the United States."

The most powerful national instrument for the political elimination of Communism was a law that bore the name of Congressman Howard W. Smith (D-Va.). Mr. Smith had gone to Washington in 1940 and convinced Congress to pass its first sedition act in almost a century and a half. The genesis of its use against the Communist party was the Truman administration's need to demonstrate its sensitivity to national security, when GOP attacks encouraged the Department of Justice to reconcile the Soviet peril that the foreign policy of the Democrats recognized with the nearby danger that Stalin's disciples posed at home. Indeed, a possible case against the Party had been built within the administration as early as the summer of 1945.

Enforcement of the Smith Act was the anticipated responsibility of the FBI, which would round up Americans whose loyalty was highly questionable, in the event of war with the Soviet Union. This "Custodial Detention Program" would require the compilation of names, based not on previous criminal conduct but on beliefs and associations. Because such an emergency was unprecedented and only potential, the FBI recommended early in 1948 that the Communist leadership be prosecuted under the Smith Act to establish a constitutional basis for future use. Then, if the Cold War were to escalate into a superpower military conflict, Party members could be legally arrested as "substantive violators" of the Smith Act. The public also had to be persuaded to sanction the unprecedented notion of an emergency Custodial Detention Program. The FBI's educational crusade was therefore designed to explain how imminent and serious a danger domestic Communism represented.

When Hoover presented Attorney General Tom Clark with the brief that became the case against the Party, the bureau did not bother to present evidence that any individual member had actually committed illegal acts. George Kneip, the Justice Department attorney who was instructed to draw up the case for prosecution based on the FBI brief, acknowledged that "the Government will be faced with a difficult task in seeking to prove beyond a reasonable doubt, in a criminal prosecution, that the Communist Party advocates revolution by violence." Section 11, the conspiracy provision of the

Smith Act, enabled the Department of Justice to go after the Party itself rather than any particular individuals, about whom the department knew so little that, when it was about to indict them, the FBI was asked for the names of the current leaders of the Communist party.

Their threat to the Republic was wildly overestimated, especially against the backdrop of the extremely close 1948 election campaign. But the FBI was certainly right to question their loyalty. In Europe the Communist leaders of Italy and France, Palmiro Togliatti and Maurice Thorez, issued a joint declaration that, in the event of war, their parties would come to the aid of Soviet troops (in resisting "aggression"), even if within the national borders of their own countries. Four American apparatchiks wanted to issue a similar statement, but in early March 1949 the National Committee hammered out a compromise that proclaimed: "If, despite the efforts of the peace forces of America and the world, Wall Street should succeed in plunging the world into war, we would oppose it as an unjust, aggressive, imperialist war, as an undemocratic and anti-Socialist war." By then the Party leaders were already on trial, though the jury had not yet heard the evidence—much less reached a conclusion—when President Truman found the defendants guilty of something worse than the conspiracy for which they had been indicted: "I have no comment on a statement made by traitors." The repression that ballooned into the Red Scare was manifestly bipartisan.

One scholarly history of American Communism notes that "conviction was almost a foregone conclusion." The eleven leaders who went on trial in February 1949 in Foley Square in New York were charged with intending to conspire to advocate violence sometime in the future. Because the Smith Act made *words* treasonable, much depended on their exegesis—especially since the director of the New York Public Library testified that all the Marxist texts that the government introduced as evidence were available in the general circulation division of his library. Interpretation of those classics was the role of the thirteen "expert" witnesses for the prosecution, who explained the "Aesopian language" of the Communist party. Budenz, for example, read into the record passages from Lenin's *Imperialism: The Highest Stage of Capitalism* and *State and Revolution*, Stalin's *Foundations of Leninism*, the *History of the Communist Party of the U.S.S.R.*, and other works that sanctioned or promoted revolutionary violence. One section of the constitution of the American Communist party nevertheless required the immediate expulsion of any advocate of such violence, a contradiction that the former managing editor of the *Daily Worker* resolved by applying the appropriate critical method: If Marxist-Leninist texts preached the violent extinction of the ruling class, the words were to be taken literally. But if a peaceful transition to socialism was expected, they were to be distrusted as deliberately misleading.

Yet even the government's first witness, Herbert Philbrick, an undercover agent in the Party since 1940 who had risen to its middle ranks, had never reported to his FBI superiors any violent or criminal acts among his Marxist-Leninist comrades. (He also conceded that he had never met the eleven leaders on trial.) The absence of any overt acts among these conspirators enabled defense attorney Abraham Isserman to claim that the Department of Justice had failed to prove a "clear and present danger," which was Justice Holmes's test of the limits of free speech in *Schenck* v. *U.S.* (1919). That particular standard was too strict for the prosecution even to try to meet during the nine-month trial, and Judge Harold R. Medina ruled that the Smith Act need not be so interpreted for the jury to find the defendants guilty. Medina thus scrapped Holmes's celebrated test, instructing the jury that "there is a sufficient danger of a substantive evil that the Congress has a right to prevent to justify the application of the statute under the First Amendment." The eleven defendants were duly convicted. For good measure Medina imprisoned all five defense attorneys (plus Eugene Dennis, who defended himself) for contempt of court. A six-months' jail sentence thus alerted other members of the bar to the risks of vigorous representation of Communist clients.

The *New York Times* editorially applauded the verdict and reported on its front page that the defendants had been "convicted of secretly teaching and advocating, on secret orders from Moscow, overthrow of the U.S. Government and destruction of American democracy by force and violence." The *Times* got it wrong: the charge had been the looser legal test of *conspiracy* to advocate revolution by violence. The following year the Court of Appeals unanimously upheld the Smith Act convictions, though Chief Judge Learned Hand altered Medina's "substantive evil" to "grave evil" and wondered "how one could ask for a more probable danger, unless we must wait till the actual eve of hostilities." The Supreme Court agreed, even though Chief Justice Fred M. Vinson conceded that the Party was too small and weak to overthrow the government and that its leadership had not attempted to put revolutionary theory into practice during the period (1945–48) in question. Only Hugo L. Black and William O. Douglas dissented in *Dennis* v. *U.S.* (1951). Justice Black clearly wrote for posterity: "Public opinion being what it now is, few will protest the conviction of these Communist petitioners. There is hope, however, that in calmer times, when present pressures, passions and fears subside, this or some later Court will restore the First Amendment liberties to the high preferred place where they belong in a free society."

Not all liberals agreed. Former attorney general Francis Biddle believed that the Party leadership had been properly convicted of "the secret teaching of a preparation for sabotage and espionage" and of plans "to act violently when the time comes." Stevenson's valiant opposition to McCarthyism was compromised when he supported the Smith Act itself and then extolled Truman for having "put the leaders of the Communist Party . . . where they belong—behind bars." Professor Schlesinger urged the repeal of the provision of the Smith Act that penalized advocacy, but he proposed new legislation outlawing the Communist party as "a criminal conspiracy systematically utilizing perjury and espionage in the interests of a foreign totalitarian power" (even though perjury and espionage were already illegal). Traditional civil liberties would thus be safeguarded by denying them to the conspiratorial movement that would have destroyed them, were it ever to seize power. Perhaps somewhat inconsistently, Schlesinger opposed any further prosecutions under the act. By the end of 1952, another thirty-three Communists had nevertheless been convicted, three others had been acquitted, and further trials were scheduled. One hundred twenty-six Party leaders were eventually indicted, of whom ninety-three were convicted. Four of the original Foley Square defendants also jumped bail, fearing the imposition of what they called an American fascism. These paranoids had real enemies, however. Hoover, the chief official responsible for rounding them up, concurred that a war emergency was imminent; and the FBI was indeed making plans to arrest and "detain" them.

Other legislation was designed to weaken American Communism even further. Over a Truman veto in 1950, Congress passed the Internal Security Act, which established concentration camps in Pennsylvania, Florida, Oklahoma, Arizona (two), and California. A Subversive Activities Control Board was also charged with registering Communists and Communist fronts. Such organizations could be fined up to ten thousand dollars and its officers imprisoned for five years as well. The Communist Control Act of 1954, which Senator Hubert H. Humphrey (D-Minn.) championed, defined Communism itself as "a clear, present and continuing danger to the security of the United States" and deprived the Party itself of "all rights, privileges, and immunities attendant upon legal bodies."

The ADA had long opposed treating Communists like other political groups because the Party did not compete openly in the marketplace of ideas, because its methods were secretive rather than persuasive. Humphrey's law blocked the possibility of open competition by barring Communists from seeking political office. Forcing the Party underground of course reinforced the accusation that it was an underground organization. The Loss of Citizenship Act, also passed in 1954, compounded the penalties already imposed under the Smith Act by adding one that had been historically reserved for those convicted of treason. Also, through tax liens of four hundred thousand dollars, the Department of Justice sought to extinguish the *Daily Worker,* which ran an annual deficit of two hundred thousand dollars.

Such pressures guaranteed that, by 1956 at the very latest, this minuscule movement was twisting slowly, slowly in the wind. Party membership had skidded from eighty thousand immediately after World War II to about five thousand—of whom so many were FBI operatives that Hoover considered taking control of the Communist Party, simply by massing his informants behind one faction at the national convention scheduled for early 1957. The proper dialectical approach, the FBI concluded, was "middle of the road" because, if the bureau's own cadres swung too openly to a losing faction, they risked expulsion from the Party. But they did wreak further internal havoc by raising vexing questions about Soviet Premier Nikita S. Khrushchev's de-Stalinization campaign as well as his invasion of Hungary. And beginning in 1956, the FBI's Counter Intelligence Program (COINTELPRO) conducted an aggressive demolition campaign that spread disruptive rumors about individual comrades and engaged in various "dirty tricks" to deepen the apprehensions and distrust that already rippled through the Party.

Such clandestine influence did not, however, make the director of the FBI more realistic about the "masters of deceit" who menaced the Republic. After 1956, when the Federal Bureau of Prisons closed the detention camps that had been set up six years earlier, Hoover complained about the "growing public complacency toward the threat of subversion." The Party was not a subject of disinterested assessment; anti-Communism had become an addiction. Other right-wingers expressed alarm as well, showing reluctance to awaken from their nightmares—or to abandon the repressive instruments that vigilance required. "I am not willing to accept the idea that there are no Communists left in this country," Senator Goldwater remarked in 1959. "I think that if we lift up enough rocks, we will find some."

Hoover in particular could hardly have been pleased when the

Supreme Court began gutting the Smith Act. In *Yates* v. *U.S.* (1957), the Warren Court ruled that a criminal prosecution for advocacy had to be of some future *action*, not for belief that something in the future was *desirable*. By holding that the testimony of the FBI's paid informers had to be made available to the defense, the Court in *Jencks* v. *U.S.* (1957) forced the government to retry the cases of several Communists—or drop the prosecutions. *Pennsylvania* v. *Nelson* (1956) brought to a halt state prosecutions for sedition. Other decisions also signaled that the Court was giving civil liberties greater weight on the scales of justice, as Black had hoped his brethren would. Recognition of the rights of Communists convinced Eisenhower that Chief Justice Warren was not the political moderate whom the president thought he had appointed to the Court. Warren's memoirs disclose that, while traveling with the ex-president to Churchill's funeral in 1965, he was asked about "those Communist cases" of the previous decade. Warren wondered which particular decisions. "All of them," Eisenhower answered. The former president candidly acknowledged that he had not read the opinions (despite the oath he had twice taken to "preserve, protect and defend the Constitution of the United States"), though he claimed familiarity with the contents of the Supreme Court rulings. Warren explained that, like other citizens, Party members deserved equal justice under law, and asked him how he would have dealt with Communists. Eisenhower's reply virtually lip-synched Mike Hammer: "I would kill the S.O.B.'s."

3

ASSENTING: THE TREND
OF IDEOLOGY

"Patriotism," Adlai Stevenson told an unsympathetic American Legion convention during the 1952 campaign, "is not the *fear* of something; it is the *love* of something." The fear intensified the love, however, just as the love reinforced the fear. But what was the object that truly loyal citizens were supposed to love? And how was that "something" to be explained to foreigners? "Those who do not believe in the ideology of the United States," Attorney General Tom Clark warned in 1948, "shall not be allowed to stay in the United States." But what was the ideology to which aliens were compelled to subscribe?

The search to define and affirm a way of life, the need to express and celebrate the meaning of "Americanism," was the flip side of stigmatizing Communism; to decipher the culture of the 1950s requires tracing the formulation of this national ideology. It was not invented but inherited, and some of its components were intensified under the political pressures of the era. The belief system that most middle-class Americans considered their birthright—the traditional commitment to competitive individualism in social life, to the liberal stress on rights in political life, and to private enterprise in economic life—was adapted to the crisis of the Cold War. An uncritical patriotism often shaped the interpretations of the past. Faith was strengthened in the institutions of authority as the best preservatives of national values, and the esteem for business achievements became perhaps the most common vindication of American life. But since "materialism" was presumably the special philosophical province of the enemy, respect for religion became pervasive—so much so that it merits a chapter of its own.

To advance this argument is to run against the thinking of the 1950s. Its paradigmatic intellectuals did not view ideology as a trend to be analyzed but as an end to be welcomed. In *The True Believer* (1951), the longshoreman Eric Hoffer fired the opening salvo against the political fanaticism that was animated by an internally consistent world-view. Typical opponents of ideology were social scientists and publicists who were themselves abandoning the radical movements of the 1930s and 1940s. They found that the power of utopianism had largely dissolved in postwar America and Western Europe, and that such a condition was not only demonstrable but desirable. "We no longer feel the need for a comprehensive, explicit system of beliefs," Professor Shils avowed. "We have seen not only the substantive errors of totalitarianism and extremist enthusiasm, but we have also seen the wrongfulness of the type of ideological orientation which once constituted its attraction." Even as traditional class antagonisms were becoming far less intense, and as the differences between left and right were narrowing, such intellectuals endorsed the resort to the pragmatic resolution of conflict as essential to the health of a democracy.

In his programmatic statement on the national past, historian Daniel J. Boorstin identified *The Genius of American Politics* (1953) as antimetaphysical, a blank slate that was devoid of susceptibility to the "philosophies" of Nazism, Fascism, and Communism. American politicians were supposed to arrange deals, not articulate ideals. European leaders lacked the democratic advantage of birth in log cabins but were, at their worst, "garret-spawned" agitators like Hitler, Mussolini, and Lenin. That is why the danger of McCarthy was exaggerated, conservative intellectual Will Herberg argued: "The totalitarian demagogue operates with something positive, with some idea or cause, which he himself believes in." The senator from Wisconsin was simply a wrecker without a blueprint, a bully without a creed. The ineptness with which President Eisenhower handled ideas was therefore comforting, and his struggle to define the philosophy of the new administration ("dynamic conservatism," "progressive, dynamic conservatism," "progressive moderation," "moderate progressivism," "positive progressivism") was quaintly touching rather than embarrassing. Ike was not even a conservative, political theorist Russell Kirk conceded (with regret); "he is a golfer." Perhaps that was because no authentically conservative ideas *could* be extracted from the American political heritage, literary critic Lionel Trilling asserted—only "irritable mental gestures."

Though the ideas in general circulation may not have added up to a coherent *Weltanschauung*, large numbers of Americans did inhabit a recognizable mental world. That ideology was not a lever with which the politically informed could act; it was more like a lounge chair in which they could repose. For change had to be gradual and incremental, since the fundamental virtue and value of the American experiment was taken for granted. That mental universe could be shown in the view of the past that became ascendant.

1

The conservative mood partly accounted for the vogue of Arnold J. Toynbee's multivolume, 3,488-page work, *A Study of History*. Professor Allan Nevins's blurb put Toynbee on a metaphoric Mount Everest, and *Time* put him on its cover (March 17, 1947), proclaiming that, by making civilizations rather than nations the basic unit of study, "Toynbee had found history Ptolemaic and left it Copernican." Nor, presumably, was history Marxist any longer, for the British scholar had "shattered the frozen patterns of historical determinism and materialism by again asserting God as an active force in history." The senior editor who wrote this profile, the ubiquitous Chambers, put Toynbee's magnum opus in the context of the Cold War, for the United States had to become conscious of its mission as "the champion of the remnant of Christian civilization against the forces that threatened it." The historian himself had not prophesied how the crisis would be resolved—only that "here is a challenge which we cannot evade, and our destiny depends on our response." It can be doubted how many of Toynbee's admirers actually read those first six volumes, or completed the last four (which appeared in 1954), or even read the abridged *Study* (of which a stunning quarter of a million copies were sold). Yet the scholar crisscrossed the United States on lecture tours and was treated as a secular prophet rather than as a mere historian.

The analyst of the 1950s can also discover the uses of the past in an even more widely diffused historical interpretation, though confined to merely one nation: the texts assigned in the public schools, which best revealed the lineaments of consensus. Intellectuals who wrote obituaries for ideology in the 1950s either used the term in a restrictive sense (referring to the eclipse of socialism among themselves) or had not examined the American history texts that public schools adopted.

Here, as the journalist Frances FitzGerald noted, the belief system to be transmitted to the young constituted a seamless vision of how Americans commonly conceived their past and present. "Inside their covers, America was perfect: the greatest nation in the world, and the embodiment of democracy, freedom, and technological progress. For them, the country never changed in any important way: its values and its political institutions remained constant from the time of the American Revolution." This vision was akin to what the French historians Fernand Braudel and Emmanuel Le Roy Ladurie were then calling *l'histoire immobile*. She added that "these texts appeared permanent just because they were so self-contained. Their orthodoxy, it seemed, left no hand-holds for attack. . . . There was, it seemed, no point in comparing these visions with reality, since they were the public truth and were thus quite irrelevant to what existed and to what anyone privately believed. They were— or so it seemed—the permanent expression of mass culture in America." This is a matter of some importance, for the only version of the past that most citizens will ever know is what they picked up in the textbooks of their childhood, fixed at one possibly impressionable moment.

The 1950s version differed from the history that had been disseminated to schoolchildren two decades earlier. Consider, for example, *An Introduction to Problems of American Culture* (1930), a series written by Harold Rugg of Columbia University Teachers College. Though he did not advocate socialism, his text mentioned it—and did endorse national economic planning. Beginning in 1939, Professor Rugg was accused by the Advertising Federation of America, the National Association of Manufacturers, and the American Legion of advocating socialism and Communism. Such criticism was so devastating that sales dropped from 289,000 copies in 1938 to 21,000 copies in 1944; and soon *An Introduction to Problems of American Culture* disappeared from the market. During that decade, similar texts fell into disfavor as well. By 1950, the grievances of business and right-wing groups against liberalism had been redressed so completely that history had become the version that the National Association of Manufacturers deemed suitable for the young. Perhaps only the Texas legislature remained unappeased. That state required a loyalty oath from all writers of school texts, then passed a resolution urging that "the American history courses in the public schools emphasize in the textbooks our glowing and throbbing history of hearts and souls inspired by wonderful American principles and traditions." The legislature thus hoped, no doubt, to counter what the Communists had supposedly monopolized: "propaganda."

In the sanitized texts that remained, FitzGerald noted, words like "we" and "our" made frequent appearances. *The Story of America* and *The Story of Our Republic* encouraged students to infer that they were expected to "identify with everything that has ever happened in American history." A word like "democracy" ceased to be, as in the texts of the 1930s, "a call to social action"; it became instead a synonym for the status quo and "the opposite of Fascism and Communism—which are not themselves very well defined." The "American way of life" was not presented diachronically but was extolled as fixed and stable, as so entrenched that it could not have been changed with a lug wrench.

Though drumbeats of praise punctuated descriptions of the economic system, the word "capitalism" was rarely applied to it. The term may have sounded vaguely pejorative. "Conceivably, the authors feared that it was not really a free-enterprise system," FitzGerald speculated, "or perhaps they thought that any precise description of it . . . would imply the existence of alternatives." Income-distribution figures were rarely provided in such texts, nor was any deviation from full equality—whether economic, political, or racial—acknowledged. Though such books lavished far more enthusiasm upon free enterprise than upon the freedoms guaranteed in the Bill of Rights, "they never actually explained how the American economy worked, or how it had changed over time." The structural transformation of the economy over the previous century and how this process affected politics are not recounted in such texts, so that the pupils who were required to read such books "remained wholly ignorant of the virtues as well as the vices of their own economic system."

The history of foreign relations bore little resemblance to views widely held outside the United States. The texts depicted American foreign policy as motivated by philanthropy and disinterested good will in dealing with other peoples. Unique in its altruism, the United States waged war against disease, poverty, and ignorance; and except for a brief period of isolationism, the United States in the twentieth century helped save other continents from the scourges of Fascism, Communism, and militarism. Bragdon and McCutchen's *History of a Free People* quoted some anonymous Oxford scholars as saying, after World War II, "We are too little astonished at the unprecedented virtuousness of U.S. foreign policy, and at its good sense."

Such an interpretation was so marred by smugness that readers would have been ill prepared for the far more ambivalent and even hostile sentiments of many foreigners. And in a world in which whites made up a minority, these histories did not reveal that their readers were living in a multiracial society. Yet for all their boost-erism and hyper-patriotism, such books emitted several warnings. American schoolchildren were often vaguely instructed to defend their liberties, lest they disappear; and readers were advised to train themselves to recognize—of all things—propaganda. The culture of the Cold War often shaped such histories into mere preludes of the contemporary crisis—the threat that international Communism posed. For example, Bragdon and McCutchen's text concluded with a celebration of the rewards of liberty not for its own sake but primarily because of its advantages in the struggle against the Soviet Union.

Occasionally, professional historians and scholars were urged to enlist in the Cold War. In 1949, the president of the American Historical Association declared that the challenge of totalitarianism had invalidated the ideal of neutrality. "We must clearly assume a militant attitude if we are to survive. The antidote to bad doctrine is better doctrine, not neutralized intelligence," Professor Conyers Read announced. "Discipline is the essential prerequisite of every effective army whether it march under the Stars and Stripes or under the Hammer and Sickle. We have to fight an enemy whose value system is deliberately simplified in order to achieve quick decisions." The University of Pennsylvania historian argued that the world had radically changed and that the status of the detached civilian had become a luxury: "The liberal neutral attitude . . . will no longer suffice. . . . Total war, whether it be hot or cold, enlists everyone and calls upon everyone to assume his part. The historian is no freer from this obligation than the physicist." Read added that "freedom can survive only if it goes hand in hand with a deep sense of social responsibility. . . . This need not imply any deliberate distortion of the past in the interests of any ideology. . . . But we need something more than an intellectual commitment. We need an act of faith . . . [in] our democratic assumptions."

2

If even academicians could face conscription into the culture of the Cold War, the emphasis placed upon the acceptance of authority lent a special aura to the two institutions that seemed least susceptible to a "liberal neutral attitude." If a president of the guild of professional historians could think of the Cold War as "total war," then the impulse to place inordinate trust in the military and the FBI becomes intelligible.

The military enjoyed tremendous prestige and was largely unchallenged in the 1950s, which was the only decade of the twentieth century in which a general was elected president. His young successor campaigned in 1960 in part on the complaint that *not enough* had been spent on defense. In the 1950s, the only politician bold enough to take on the army was McCarthy. Because a World War II hero like General Ralph W. Zwicker had not blocked the automatic promotion from captain to major of a leftist army dentist named Irving Peress, McCarthy reviled him: "You are a disgrace to the uniform. You're shielding Communist conspirators. You're not fit to be an officer." But such viciousness was so disturbing that soon thereafter the overreacher was himself destroyed.

When Stevenson challenged the necessity of conscription and of nuclear testing during the 1956 campaign, he exceeded the perimeters of respectable opinion, raising doubts about his eagerness to be president. Small pacifist organizations like the War Resisters League and the Fellowship of Reconciliation got even smaller in the 1950s, and ministers of the gospel told activist A. J. Muste that peace could not be introduced in their sermons, because the subject was considered communistic. Major General Claire L. Chennault, the retired former chief of the United States Air Force in China who headed the CIA's Civil Air Transport Company on Taiwan, was so well known that he endorsed Camel cigarettes in magazine advertisements. The military stress upon authority, leadership, and strength was reinforced with other patriotic associations—as the first line of defense against Communism (and atheism too) and as a bulwark of order against subversion and chaos.

In the spring of 1951, when Truman announced that General Douglas MacArthur had been dismissed for insubordination, the press conference was sneaked in after midnight. Shock and anger were nevertheless widespread. The Michigan state legislature passed a resolution which began, *"Whereas,* at 1 a.m., of this day, World Communism achieved its greatest victory of the decade in the dismissal of General MacArthur . . ."* By the time the startling news reached Los Angeles, the city councillors were so upset that they adjourned for the day. Old Glory was flown at half-mast. McCarthy called the general's removal "the greatest victory the Communists have ever won," ignoring such minor historical episodes as the Bolshevik seizure of power in Russia in 1917 and the Maoist victory in China in 1949. According to Senator William E. Jenner (R-Ind.), the dismissal proved that "agents of the Soviet Union" were actually running the Democratic administration: "Our only choice is to impeach President Truman to find out who is the secret invisible government." Others were more temperate than Jenner, merely demanding the resignation of the commander in chief.

Over two out of every three Americans told pollsters of their opposition to the firing of the five-star general, whose landing at Inchon, Korea, in September 1950 was the last consequential American military victory of the century. Billy Graham, who called the general "one of the greatest Americans of all time," put the dismissal in an otherworldly perspective: "Christianity has suffered another major blow." When New York City gave MacArthur a far bigger ticker-tape parade than Charles A. Lindbergh had received after returning from Paris in 1927, members of the crowd were seen crossing themselves as the limousine passed. Eighteen New Yorkers were also hospitalized for hysteria. Until his wife finally muzzled the general, he rumbled ominously about "Communist influences" in the executive branch and continued to insist that the very nature of warfare allowed "no substitute for victory." But Truman's policy of no wider war was sustained; and, true to MacArthur's own prediction at a joint session of Congress, he soon faded away.

In that same year, the popularity of a novel demonstrated the esteem that military authority enjoyed during the Cold War. The winner of the Pulitzer Prize in 1952, *The Caine Mutiny* sold about three million copies within three years of its publication. Herman Wouk's novel was translated into seventeen foreign languages, and his stage version of the forensic climax, *The Caine Mutiny Court-Martial*, sold out the house for two seasons on Broadway. In World War II, the author had served as a lieutenant in the Naval Reserve, and he had risen to become an executive officer (second in command) of a destroyer-minesweeper. "No topic is more popular in officers' clubs throughout the wide Pacific than 'Captain Bligh' stories of this war," Wouk noted in a memorandum; he later dedicated his play to its Broadway director, Charles Laughton, who had played Bligh so famously in M-G-M's *Mutiny on the Bounty* (1935). Yet a prefatory note in Wouk's novel insists upon an ideological point: American naval annals disclosed no mutiny during the previous three decades. The invocation of Regulations 184, 185, and 186 in *The Caine Mutiny* was therefore completely fictional and was not intended to reflect badly on the U.S. Navy. The author added that both captains under whom he had served were "decorated for valor."

But what if a commander is not brave at all, and scarcely capable of exercising leadership? Willie Keith, who matures in two years on the *Caine* from a callow civilian to a good sailor, realizes, "Once you get an incompetent ass of a skipper—and it's a chance of war—there's nothing to do but serve him as though he were the wisest and the best, cover his mistakes, keep the ship going, and bear up." But what if the skipper is, like Philip Queeg, mentally unbalanced, exhausted, tending toward paranoia? Is mutiny, under conditions of peril to the entire ship and crew, justified? That is the moral dilemma posed by the novel. Though attorney Barney Greenwald wins acquittal for the mutineers by forcing Captain Queeg to break down, he berates his clients at the celebration afterward, turning Queeg into the hero, Lieutenant Steve Maryk into a dupe, and Lieutenant Tom Keefer into the villain.

As journalist William H. Whyte, Jr., pointed out in *The Organization Man* (1956), the twist is not what gives the plot its punch, and the enormous popularity of *The Caine Mutiny* was due to Wouk's silken narrative abilities, not to the ending. But Greenwald's rearrangement of moral categories was not accidental or peripheral to his creator's purposes; it was essential. For Wouk wrote in his journal that "the crux of the tale will come in the realization of Maryk and Keith that the mutiny was a mistake even though Maryk was acquitted." Thus, as Wouk told an interviewer in 1972, what had begun as a panoramic war novel switched into "a novel about authority versus responsibility." This counterpoint is puzzling. For Wouk seemed to take the side of authority *against* responsibility, leaving unexplained why—in defense of democracy—blind obedience warranted a higher priority than individual conscience and independent judgment during a crisis. *The Caine Mutiny* implies that losing the ship in a typhoon is better than challenging a skipper whose powers of command have failed.

This was a message that millions of readers did not seem to reject or resist, a message at variance with the novels that became famous in the aftermath of World War I. Hemingway's *A Farewell to Arms*, Dos Passos's *Three Soldiers*, and Remarque's *All Quiet on the Western Front* were antimilitary or pacifist. Other post–World War II bestsellers, like Norman Mailer's *The Naked and the Dead* (1948) and James Jones's *From Here to Eternity* (1951), echoed earlier grievances against the army for crushing the spirit of individuality. What can be inferred from the runaway success of *The Caine Mutiny* is how smoothly popular taste could accommodate an authoritarian ideology, justifying submission to a demented superior. Maryk, a career man, is punished in Wouk's navy by realizing that he will never be promoted.

By presenting the intellectual as the villain, *The Caine Mutiny* diverged further from other American novels of the two world wars. Keefer has succeeded Queeg as captain of the minesweeper, confines himself to writing in his cabin, and then, when a kamikaze plane hits the *Caine*, jumps overboard like a coward. Before meeting his clients, Greenwald imagines the instigator of the mutiny as "slight, thin, nervous, dark, and with the self-satisfied expression of a petty intellectual." The persona of Maryk fails to sustain this prejudice, but Keefer confirms it. Upon discovering that a novel had been written aboard the *Caine*, the attorney sardonically conjectures what sort of book it must be: "I'm sure that it exposes this war in all its grim futility and waste, and shows up the military men for the stupid, Fascist-minded sadists they are . . . throwing away the lives of fatalistic, humorous, lovable citizen-soldiers." This is the novel that wins a thousand-dollar publisher's advance, enabling Keefer to subsidize the party for the acquitted mutineers, whom he has cleverly manipulated. It is also the novel that Keefer's creator had deliberately chosen not to write.

The joke, however, was soon on Wouk. Though he had composed *The Caine Mutiny* as a valentine to the navy, the service at first adamantly refused to cooperate with any film studio seeking to transfer his sizzling property to the screen. Again, the navy insisted that it had never suffered a mutiny, and two studios that tried to adapt Wouk's novel gave up. Warner Brothers, for example, was informed that *The Caine Mutiny* was "extreme" and "derogatory." It took independent producer Stanley Kramer a year and a half to secure an agreement; in the end, he had to go all the way up to the secretary of the navy. In 1954, two years after the chief of naval operations gave his approval, Columbia Pictures released the movie, which explicitly assures audiences (again) that no mutiny had ever marred naval annals. The edgy skipper (Humphrey Bogart) still turns out to be the hero after all—a misunderstood, unappreciated professional. Though the navy had cooperated, permitting the filming of actual ships, its help could not be directly acknowledged in the lapidary final credits: "The dedication of this film is simple: To the United States Navy." *The Caine Mutiny* was also an early directing assignment for an emeritus of the Hollywood Ten, Edward Dmytryk, who emerged from prison to recant his Communist past and testify voluntarily before HUAC.

In this era, Soviet culture was notoriously strait-jacketed by official dogma, completely constrained by censorship, throttled by political and moral vigilance. But perhaps it was a little too easy for Hollywood to feel superior to it, when the producers of American popular art freely and willingly subjugated themselves to state controls as well. The champions of free enterprise saw nothing contradictory in submitting to such governmental interference. For the American motion picture industry had long relied on the military to provide technical expertise and personnel, as well as equipment and locales, in order to convince audiences of the verisimilitude of its stories. It was virtually unthinkable in the 1950s to proceed without the cooperation of the Pentagon, which exercised script approval—and therefore censorship.

The aesthetic analyses of the Department of Defense were crude, and its reaction to criticism was oversensitive; and of course it was under no obligation to assist the studios. But what is striking is how eager the producers were to be co-opted into the military system, to relinquish the independence that they sometimes praised on the screen. Though Kramer ran his own production company and cultivated a reputation for maverick liberalism, he apparently never considered filming *The Caine Mutiny* over the objections of so touchy an institution as the navy. And when Fred Zinnemann was hired to adapt *From Here to Eternity*, the director claimed that he would have resigned from the project had the army not cooperated. It was convenient that Zinnemann did not consider James Jones's novel "anti-army." If it had been critical of the military, a movie version would have been not only intolerable but, in the 1950s, also inconceivable.

At least *The Caine Mutiny* recorded no episodes of violence or brutality, contained no obscenity, and described no acts of adultery. Indeed, Willie Keith's girlfriend, Marie Minotti, is so pure that the impression Wouk's readers got of her sleeping habits with a bandleader turned out to be false. The public relations problem that Queeg gave the officer class seemed simple compared to that contained in *From Here to Eternity*, a novel which Postmaster General Arthur Summerfield—a slow reader—declared nonmailable in 1955, four years after it had perched on top of the bestseller list. The Washington representative of Columbia Pictures even warned the studio's president, Harry Cohn, that *From Here to Eternity* incorporated "a lot of apparent Communist doctrine," though Jones dedicated this first novel not to his loved ones but to the U.S. Army. Both Warner Brothers and Twentieth Century-Fox dropped plans to adapt the bestseller because of resistance from the Pentagon, which claimed that conditions described in the novel were no longer true. The misleading impression that *From Here to Eternity* gave, the Department of Defense insisted, would hamper recruiting efforts—an argument that would not have dissuaded, say, Aristophanes from writing *Lysistrata*.

But Cohn was undeterred, demanding numerous script changes to win military approval. The barracks profanity as well as the stockade violence was entirely eliminated, and the house of prostitution was transformed into a sort of U.S.O. club. In the novel, the sadistic Captain Holmes is promoted; in the film, he is removed from the army. His wife, Karen Holmes, suffers from gonorrhea in the novel; violation of the Seventh Commandment in the movie results in a miscarriage instead. The bestiality of Fatso, the bruising sergeant, is somewhat tamed. No wonder that the army professed to be "delighted" with the changes, and after the release of *From Here to Eternity* in 1953 purchased prints for showing on its bases. So did the air force, though the navy broke ranks, banning the film from its ships and its shore installations as "derogatory to a sister service." Zinnemann's film won eight Oscars, overruling the objections of the *Los Angeles Times* that *From Here to Eternity* "goes all out in making the military situation look its worst, and could probably be used by alien interests for subversive purposes if they happen to want to make capital of this production." If the concealment of military imperfections had become a new cinematic test of patriotism, even the Dean Martin and Jerry Lewis service comedies of the era might have flunked. But such alarm bells could still clang when most American men—even G. David Schine, even Elvis Presley—were expected to take one step forward and perform military service.

3

McCarthy had foolishly tried to squeeze off a few rounds against the army; but for all his anti-establishmentarian recklessness, he never dared to criticize the one institution that was immune to "security risks" a priori. The FBI became a kind of prep school for the investigators whom McCarthy hired, and J. Edgar Hoover provided information from his bureau's files to McCarthy and his staff (probably in the guise of "reports" based on the files rather than the actual "raw" files themselves). The senator and the FBI director had been on good terms since 1946, and when they stayed at the same California hotel in 1953, Hoover told a reporter that "the investigating committees do a valuable job. They have subpoena rights without which some vital investigations could not be accomplished." He considered McCarthy "a friend and [I] believe he so views me. Certainly he is a controversial man. He is earnest and he is honest. He has enemies. Whenever you attack subversives of any kind . . . you are going to be the victim of the most extreme vicious criticism that can be made."

No imprimatur was more authoritative in the 1950s, which Hoover later regarded as the best and happiest of the forty-eight years—

two-thirds of his own life—during which he headed the FBI. The nation's most famous gangbuster had become Washington's most durable bureaucrat, as well as the very symbol of the stable way of life that Americans cherished and wished to defend against Communism. And Hoover transformed himself into its most obdurate enemy. His office on Pennsylvania Avenue became the headquarters of the domestic Cold War, and his way of addressing the challenge of Communism was absorbed into folklore. The FBI became more than a police agency delegated with powers of investigation and arrest. It exemplified the square-jawed ideology of Americanism; its director stamped upon his fiefdom the traditional verities that he projected to the nation, stressing personal rectitude, family unity, and social respect for patriotism and piety.

In the foreword that he provided for journalist Quentin Reynolds's *The F.B.I.* (1954), a Landmark Book aimed at adolescent readers, Hoover claimed that "when a young man files an application with the F.B.I., we do not ask if he was the smartest boy in his class. We want to know if he was truthful, dependable, and if he played the game fair. We want to know if he respects his parents, reveres God, honors his flag and loves his country." Among the applicants whom the bureau nevertheless rejected was a 1937 graduate of Duke Law School named Richard Nixon, who was considered lacking in "aggressiveness." Long afterward Nixon had occasion to hail the FBI director as "one of the nation's leaders of morals and manners and opinion"—a curious job description for a policeman, but an apt label for the role that Hoover elected to play during the Cold War.

To complement his reputation as an expert in criminology, Hoover added a flair for sermonizing. To cope with the rising tide of homicide, he offered the moral absolutes of homiletics. He worried that somehow American society was no longer inculcating the proper moral education in the young, who were growing up with fewer wholesome influences from parents, schools, churches, and government. The revolution in values that modernity had instigated was so destructive of tranquillity and order that crime festered; and the battle against it would fail without the revitalization of the family and of authority, without the pressure of public opinion based on "the laws of Moses," which "must remain . . . our National Creed." He told a unit of the Michigan Bar Association that "America is strong because she is good," but only if goodness were strengthened would crime be eradicated.

If crime represented the most violent expression of hostility toward the traditional moral order, then socialism, "pseudo-liberalism," and especially Communism were the most dramatic variations on that theme. Russian agents were also agents of change, and their American comrades were the latest edition of the public enemies whom Hoover had defeated during the Great Depression. But the Communists were more dangerous than Pretty Boy Floyd. For they were extensions of a foreign power, a "Trojan snake" to be fought with a more diverse repertoire than tommy guns—or even undercover agents and the infiltration of Party operations and the smashing of spy rings. Public enlightenment was necessary too. The G-man would become an educator.

The earliest Cold War foray into mass culture was *I Led Three Lives*, a television series of 117 half-hour episodes that ran from 1953 until 1956. Local sponsors of the syndicated series received promotional material informing them that they were members of "the businessman's crusade" against international Communism. The program was based on the "exploits" of Herbert Philbrick, the key witness in the Smith Act trial in 1949. But *I Led Three Lives* offered viewers little insight into the motives that drove adult Americans toward allegiance to the Soviet Union, little information into the actual extent of espionage and subversion, and less reassurance of how enfeebled the Party had become. Later a columnist for the *New York Herald Tribune* as well as a professional anti-Communist writer and lecturer, Philbrick was closely involved in the production of *I Led Three Lives*, reviewing scripts for historical accuracy and for consistency with the practices of the bureau. As he later explained, "I knew of the things that the Bureau does and doesn't do, and the things that Mr. Hoover liked, and the things he didn't like. So, that was my job, to kind of make sure that they [the FBI] didn't have to take care of this." The bureau was not officially involved in the production of *I Led Three Lives* because it did not need to be.

In 1956 an authorized history entitled *The F.B.I. Story* was published, with Hoover's introduction. On its dust jacket he permitted use of the FBI seal which, beginning two years earlier, had been protected against unauthorized commercial infringement, like Smokey the Bear. The author of *The F.B.I. Story* was Don Whitehead, a two-time Pulitzer Prize-winner who headed the Washington bureau of the *New York Herald Tribune*. Although the chief of the Crime Records Division had persuaded Whitehead to write this sympathetic history, and though the bureau gave him material and checked his manuscript, it did not apparently edit it. Even after *The F.B.I. Story* was serialized in 170 newspapers, the enormous public appetite was not sated. In 1957 Whitehead's saga outsold all other works of nonfiction, except for *Kids Say the Darndest Things!* by television interviewer Art Linkletter. After thirty-eight weeks on the bestseller lists, the film rights to *The F.B.I. Story* were sold at a meeting that both Louis B. Nichols, head of FBI public relations, and Hoover himself attended.

Two years later, when Warner Brothers released the film, a striking transformation in Whitehead's history had occurred. Director-producer Mervyn LeRoy injected a fictional hero to thread the historical episodes together and establish narrative coherence, so that *The F.B.I. Story* became the story of upright Special Agent Chip Hardesty (Jimmy Stewart), who solved all the bureau's most challenging cases. His career spanned decades so easily that he could confound Nazis, Communists, and airplane terrorists as skillfully as he had cornered John Dillinger. Indeed, Hardesty is so good at his job that the only dramatic tension is provided by that necessary adjunct to 1950s heroism, the reason why the defense can never rest: the family. His wife is Lucy Hardesty (Vera Miles), who doesn't like guns, doesn't welcome Chip's transfers to places without churches or schools, doesn't fathom the darned inconvenience of World War II. The perils that the nation confronted over three decades and that summoned the resources of the FBI are reduced in the film to family crises, so that history has become housebroken. Only as a gray-haired grandmother back in their home in Nashville does Lucy become fully reconciled to the responsibility that she assumed in marrying a G-man. Whitehead's *The F.B.I. Story* had become something that the *Saturday Review* called "One F.B.I. Man's Family."

A movie focusing more on domestic travail and bliss than on gangsters and saboteurs was a little too disorienting to meet universal acceptance. "The F.B.I. agent is presented as a pillar of the American home, as much as—or even more than—a pillar of law enforcement and protection against Communist spies," the *New York Times* reviewer complained. The G-man had become a paragon of virtue, an aging devotee of bourgeois comfort—indeed, an ideal scoutmaster—rather than an adventurous lawman who could face down desperadoes on the mean streets of modern cities. But the switch reflected Hoover's anxiety that the traditional home had to rebuild its ramparts against the unsettling disorder of crime and Communism. Warner Brothers may have produced the screen adaptation of the bestseller; but the real *auteur* was Hoover himself, who influenced the film's director so much that Hoover and his associates "controlled the movie." LeRoy added: "Everybody on that picture, from the carpenters and electricians right to the top, everybody, had to be okayed by the FBI. . . . I had two FBI men with me all the time, for research purposes, so that we did things right." Whatever revisions were made of the book, especially the relocation of the G-man from the crossroads of history to the center of the middle-class family, were apparently certified by the bureau itself.

Chip Hardesty and Hoover himself were shown rounding up Reds in the immediate postwar period because Communism "threatened labor and management, church and home." Between the hardcover and screen versions of *The F.B.I. Story*, Hoover consolidated his reputation as a crusader against domestic Communism with *Masters of Deceit*, the number four nonfiction bestseller of 1958. It was the biggest publishing coup of his career, selling a quarter of a million copies in hardback and another two million in paperback, and going through twenty-nine printings over the next dozen years. Ghostwritten primarily by Nichols, though carefully edited by his boss, *Masters of Deceit* "was written on government time by government employees," Hoover's biographer reports, though the director and his fellow public servants "split the money among themselves." To have objected to the impropriety of fleecing the taxpayers would only have deflected attention from the crisis.

"Communism is more than an economic, political, social, or philosophical doctrine," *Masters of Deceit* announced. "It is a way of life; a false, materialistic, 'religion.' It would strip man of his belief in God, his heritage of freedom, his trust in love, justice, and mercy. Under communism all would become, as so many already have, twentieth-century slaves." It was satanic, and yet its diabolical power could be defeated by the shining goodness of spiritual resources. In *Masters of Deceit*, Hoover asserted that "all we need is faith, *real faith*. . . . The truly revolutionary force of history is not material power but the spirit of religion." His own files, for instance, were replete with accounts of ex-Party members who claimed that coming across one of Hoover's own anti-Communist articles had emancipated them from their own illusions and enabled such readers to find their way back to "the truths which have eternally guided civilized man."

ABC bought the rights to *Masters of Deceit* but never filmed it. The network did, however, facilitate Hoover's last significant stab at mass culture, Quinn Martin's production of *The F.B.I.*, which was inaugurated each season with a guest appearance by the director of the bureau. Each episode opened and closed with a shot of the FBI seal, and the credits at the end of each episode expressed gratitude to "J. Edgar Hoover and his associates for their cooperation in the production of this series." This TV program was so nonviolent that its star, Efrem Zimbalist, Jr., could not recall "kill[ing] anybody,

I think, the last two or three years." Of course, there was no hint of sex, either. "Perhaps we are inclined toward Puritanism in an increasingly permissive world," Hoover conceded in *TV Guide* in 1972, "but foremost in our minds from the beginning episode has been the fact that *The F.B.I.* is telecast into American homes at a 'family hour' on a 'family evening.'" ABC and Quinn Martin had pledged to give the bureau complete power to approve scripts, personnel, and sponsorship. Glavlit, the Soviet censoring agency, could hardly have demanded fuller compliance.

4

What the Department of Defense and the Federal Bureau of Investigation were supposed to protect was, above all, a lifestyle intimately associated with the blessings of prosperity. Above all the American experiment meant—at home and abroad—abundance, which was the firmest proof of manifest destiny. The enlargement of wealth ensured the democratic promise and was indeed the primary American mission in the world. Two centuries earlier Benjamin Franklin had invited immigrants to cross the Atlantic to enjoy "a happy mediocrity"—in contrast to the extremes of luxury and misery, the inordinate disparities of opulence and poverty that he associated with Europe. But by the mid-twentieth century, the United States was enjoying the world's highest living standard, a bounty that tempted foreigners as well as its own population with the glamour and comforts of wealth. To historian David Potter, Americans had long been a "people of plenty"—the title of his 1954 interpretation of the national character. The treadmill of poverty no longer seemed inevitable. According to radical theorist Herbert Marcuse's *Eros and Civilization* (1955), utopian thinking had become urgent because, with material impediments largely surmounted, new social relations needed to be imagined in the leap from the realm of necessity to the realm of freedom.

Pride in the blessings of private enterprise induced an air of sanctity. When the average annual growth rate dropped from 4.3 percent in the last six years of Truman's presidency to 2.5 percent under Eisenhower, and Stevenson observed that the economy had become sluggish, Nixon's response was wrathful: "Mr. Stevenson has been guilty, probably without being aware that he was doing so, of spreading pro-Communist propaganda as he has attacked with violent fury the economic system of the United States." Objections to Democratic party blasphemy had a statistical basis. Six percent of the world's population lived in the United States, which by the mid-

1950s was producing and consuming over a third of the goods and services of the planet. American industry used half of the world's steel and oil, and three-fourths of all the cars and appliances on earth were consumed in the United States. Real gross national product (GNP) increased from $206 billion in 1940 to more than $500 billion in 1960. With productivity rising by more than 2 percent annually for most of the postwar decade, American workers bore much of the responsibility for this extraordinary growth and earned more with which to buy the goods streaming from their factories. In 1945, average weekly earnings in manufacturing were $44. In 1963, such wages had jumped to $97—a 50 percent increase even after making allowance for inflation, which was modest. Indeed, when Eisenhower took his oath of office, real personal income was half again the average of what it had been when Herbert Hoover became president at the end of the prosperous 1920s. Total income in the country was growing twice as fast as the population, fulfilling much of Roosevelt's promise of freedom from want.

Despite the huge gaps in income that persisted, riches were becoming more equitably distributed in the postwar decade. Those occupying the highest brackets (which *Fortune* magazine measured in terms of earning more than $7,500 per year in 1953 dollars) had more than doubled from 1929, but their proportion of the total national income had fallen. Although the government did not bother to formulate an official poverty line until 1960, the absolute number of poorest families dropped from 15.6 million to 11.7 million. In the solid middle class ($4,000–$7,000 in annual 1953 dollars), the 5.5 million families in this category in 1929 had more than tripled to 17.9 million by 1953. In that year, such families represented 35 percent of the population and earned 42 percent of the national income, making somewhat more truthful Franklin's description of the achievement of a happy mediocrity. Even demography conspired in favor of greater material ease. The lowest birthrate in American history had been recorded during the decade of the Great Depression, which marked the smallest growth in absolute population since the Civil War. Because of World War II, birthrates had also remained low during the first half of the 1940s. The result, as journalist Thomas Hine noted, was that by the 1950s, "there was more wealth to go around and a decline in the number of people to share it. Nothing like it had ever happened before, and nothing like it has happened since."

But if problems of production had been solved on so unprecedented a scale, how could the cornucopia of goods be purchased when the absolute number of consumers did not keep pace? For sociologist

David Riesman, such a disparity largely explained a shift in the social character of the middle class, from inner-direction (steered by parents toward individual accomplishment) to other-direction (picking up cues in taste from peers and mass media). For economist John Kenneth Galbraith, such a disparity accounted for the growth of advertising. Styling changes were required to make products sell more often; here autos, with their annual models and lavish publicity, set the pace.

Having been encouraged in the nineteenth century to produce, Americans of the mid-twentieth century were urged to consume. Credit cards were launched with the first Diners Club card in 1950, repudiating the ancient commandment of frugality and encouraging immediate gratification instead, thus upending the wise advice in *Poor Richard's Almanac* to avoid being a borrower or a lender. The bounties pouring forth from American factories and laboratories, made available in such profusion in stores and markets, had become perhaps the chief ideological prop—the most palpable vindication—of "the American way of life." Success and virtue were so easily equated that, after *Life* magazine published *The Old Man and the Sea* (1952), the industrialist who became Eisenhower's secretary of the treasury was puzzled by the popular fascination with Hemingway's story. "Why would anybody be interested in some old man who was a failure," George M. Humphrey wondered, "and never amounted to anything anyway?"

Such assumptions help account for Barbie (b. 1958), the most popular doll in history. With her own national fan club, she received five hundred letters a week. Eleven and one-half inches tall, this late adolescent was endowed with a three-and-one-quarter-inch bust that smashed an anatomical taboo in the toy market. But what made her something of an icon of the Cold War were the fantasies of consumption that she evoked. Barbie came cheap: three dollars. But her full wardrobe cost more than one hundred dollars, and her appetite for more was insatiable: party dresses and casual attire, prom gowns and eventually a wedding ensemble (her boyfriend's name was Ken), outdoor outfits, professional uniforms. Barbie lived in a split-level house, patronized a beauty parlor, drove a Corvette. She "seemed to be only a product," one scholar concluded, "but she turned out to be a way of life," an affirmation of national supremacy. The capitalist "fetishism of commodities" that Marx found so repellent had advanced to the first line of defense.

Because the foreign policy of containment had seemed so passive and frustrating, and because domestic patterns of consumption seemed so obvious a manifestation of American supremacy, Riesman was inspired to twin and then tweak these attitudes in a satiric 1951 essay entitled "The Nylon War." Imagining an alternative to the arms race called Operation Abundance, the sociologist began as follows:

> Today—August 1, 1951—the Nylon War enters upon the third month since the United States began all-out bombing of the Soviet Union with consumers' goods, and it seems time to take a retrospective look. Behind the initial raid of June 1 were years of secret and complex preparations, and an idea of disarming simplicity: that if allowed to sample the riches of America, the Russian people would not long tolerate masters who gave them tanks and spies instead of vacuum cleaners and beauty parlors. The Russian rulers would thereupon be forced to turn out consumers' goods, or face mass discontent on an increasing scale.

The author recalled a decade later that "when 'The Nylon War' was first published, I began to get letters and telephone calls asking me if the 'war' (whose fictional date had then been passed) had actually gotten under way! People have asked for references to the New York *Times* or periodical literature where they could catch up on these events. I was reminded of the 'Invasion from Mars' broadcast. . . . That my tale could be taken for literal fact was a sign of the remoteness of the inquirers from the current of what was probably so." Riesman speculated that "it seems clear that satire is too playful and perhaps too snobbish a mode, save in cartoon form, to combat the combination of fright and self-righteousness of many Americans, who would accept the *fait accompli* of a Nylon War if the authorities ordered it." Perhaps it was easier for the public to appreciate *Silk Stockings* (1957), the musical update of the 1939 film *Ninotchka* that showed even apparatchiks swooning before the temptations of capitalist luxury.

The usefulness of consuming passions as proof of national grandeur was fully revealed in the summer of 1959, when the United States and its chief enemy exchanged exhibitions in Moscow and New York, respectively. Two years earlier, sputnik had shaken American confidence in its technological superiority and educational advantages, but here was an opportunity to trump an economic system that was organized according to different principles. The exchange was therefore more than a chance to show off wares; it took on ideological significance and symbolic meaning as well. Anticipating the combat of commodities, *Newsweek* called it "a contest of two diverse ways of life—of modern capitalism with its ideology of political and economic freedom and Communism." Despite the shock of sputnik, the outcome of the contest was not in doubt. For with Americans purchasing so many fabulous conveniences, spending with such unprecedented extravagance, and using up such a vast array of products with so many different brand names and variations in style, how could the United States lose to a backward economy like the Soviet Union?

To underscore the political importance of the exchange, Ike's vice-president and heir apparent opened the American National Exhibition in Moscow. It was one of Nixon's six crises, requiring conscientious preparation. According to his 1962 political memoir, he sought the help of a former ambassador to the Soviet Union, who warned him: "We are idealists. They are materialists. You can no more describe Khrushchev or any other Communist as being sincere than you can describe that coffee table as being sincere." Whatever the aptness of the ex-diplomat's phenomenology, or of his dichotomy of national styles (addressed, ironically, to a politician afflicted with a fragile reputation for sincerity), the vice-president was not coming to Moscow to scorn the perquisites of materialism. In his formal speech at the exhibition, Nixon managed to transcend his country's proclivity for idealism by referring to the 44 million families in the United States who owned 56 million cars, 50 million television sets and 143 million radios. Three-fourths of these families, he added, owned their own homes. (Such real estate records were especially bracing because, as suburban builder William Levitt asserted, "No man who owns his own house and lot can be a communist. He has too much to do.") The country that the vice-president represented "comes closest to the ideal of prosperity for all in a classless society." (Nixon thus ignored the disparity that Professor Paul Samuelson noted in the most authoritative economics text of the era: "If we made an income pyramid out of child's blocks, with each portraying $1,000 of income, the peak would be far higher than the Eiffel Tower, but almost all of us would be within a yard of the ground.")

But what made Nixon's visit indelible was the "kitchen debate," conducted in the rather unprepossessing model suburban home that a Long Island builder had put up in Sokolniki Park, where the exhibition was held. Strolling through the six-room, ranch-style house, the vice-president and the Soviet premier argued back and forth, accompanied mostly by about a hundred American photographers and reporters. Khrushchev repeatedly predicted that the Soviet Union would soon overtake the American economy and win the brass ring of world influence. Nixon preferred to focus on the fetishism of commodities and tried to steer the conversation to color television sets. The vice-president's persistence paid off when the debaters reached the model kitchen, and washing machines became apropos. Nixon praised the freedom of choice among American housewives. Khrushchev countered that one kind of washing machine would be sufficient, if it worked. "Isn't it better to talk about the relative merits of washing machines than the relative strength of rockets?" Nixon inquired. "Isn't this the kind of competition you want?" The Soviet premier angrily replied that America was pursuing both types of competition, which Nixon did not deny.

Oddly enough for a Marxist, Khrushchev did not seize the occasion to mention that the same capitalist enterprises were dependent for their profits on both washing machines and rockets. Those who controlled the means of production were also intimately involved in the means of destruction. The push buttons that were designed to make housework easier came from the same laboratories as the push buttons for guided missiles. In a class by itself was General Motors, which by 1952 had become the nation's leading defense contractor. Its president, "Engine" Charlie Wilson, was the highest-paid American citizen; he became Eisenhower's secretary of defense without breaking stride. Wilson had informed the Senate Armed Services Committee of his long-held view that "what was good for our country was good for General Motors, and vice versa." He did not find it dizzying to be running the world's largest planned economy outside the Soviet Union. For the assets of GM were greater than Argentina's, its revenues eight times larger than the state of New York's, its cut of the American car and truck market equal to all of its competitors combined. By 1955, when GM became the first company to earn a billion dollars in a single year and rolled its fifty millionth car off the assembly lines, Americans had spent sixty-five billion dollars on automobiles—a fifth of the gross national product. Wilson's successor as president, Harlow Curtice, Time's "Man of the Year" in 1955, ceased bothering to talk in terms of GM's percentages of the car market. He spoke instead of his corporation's share of the GNP.

Chrysler, General Electric, Goodyear, and Westinghouse were also major Pentagon contractors; for all of their pride in their consumer wares, these companies lavished much of their advertising budgets—especially in the late 1950s—on promoting the necessity and efficiency of their military weaponry. Enlarging the defense budget, Goodyear ads claimed, would also result in more durable and safer tires for the family automobile. What enhanced the home was not unrelated to what protected the homeland. Indeed, the secretary of defense at the time of the "kitchen debate" was Neil McElroy, who had previously headed Procter & Gamble. Nor was it coincidental that Ronald Reagan was then serving an eight-year stint as a good-will ambassador for General Electric, perfecting his hawkish foreign policy views while honing his opposition to interference in "the private sector."

Khrushchev may not have realized that, in Nixon's own southern California, over half of the economic growth between 1947 and 1957 was due to defense contracts. In San Diego and its immediate vicinity, 70 percent of *all* gainful employment stemmed from military spending. Taking indirect as well as direct effects into account, the figure was 59 percent for all jobs in the Los Angeles area, and slightly less than that for gainful employment in California generally. It might be added that the author of "The Nylon War" had hoped, by 1962, to discover "not only moral equivalents for war but also economic equivalents for the arms race and political equivalents for the use and threat of force." But Riesman did not explicitly consider how deeply engaged the same large corporations were in the arms race and its economic equivalents. Indeed, the "relative strength of rockets" had more to do with prosperity than the "relative merits of washing machines," but in Moscow the vice-president preferred to talk about the various options in color television sets.

The American journalists flocking around the exhibition did not pause to analyze Khrushchev's anger at competition in both defense hardware and domestic software. It was much more photogenic to show the two politicians fiercely jabbing fingers at one another, and many Americans were reassured that the vice-president had stood tall against the Soviet ruler's bare-knuckle intimidation. With an election coming up, the news photos were raw meat hurled at Nixon's carnivorous constituents from one of the triumphant institutions of capitalism: the middle-class suburban home. "The images that resulted were very powerful, largely because they seemed to confirm what many Americans believed," Thomas Hine concluded. "The way they lived, with their comforts and conveniences, was shown as an essential part of the American way of life. Not only was it worth defending, but it was a defense in itself because its richness challenged every other political system . . . to do the same for its citizenry."

But the technological advantage that the exhibition seemed to validate could not disguise the growing dissatisfaction with material satisfaction, the moral uneasiness with physical ease. One sign was the bestsellerdom (number two) accorded to *The Affluent Society* (1958), which traced the diminished quality of life that an unchecked "private sector" betokened. Professor Galbraith's most famous observation can bear further quotation:

> The family which takes its mauve and cerise, air-conditioned, power-steered and power-braked automobile out for a tour passes through cities that are badly paved, made hideous by litter, blighted buildings, billboards and posts for wires that should long since have been put underground. They pass on into a countryside that has been rendered largely invisible by commercial art. . . . They picnic on exquisitely packaged food from a portable icebox by a polluted stream and go on to spend the night at a park which is a menace to public health and morals. Just before dozing off on an air mattress, beneath a nylon tent, amid the stench of decaying refuse, they may vaguely reflect on the curious unevenness of their blessings.

A year after the kitchen debate, Galbraith became an adviser to the presidential candidate who defeated Nixon. John F. Kennedy campaigned in part against the complacency that abundance had generated, for it has "weaned and wooed us from the tough condition in which, heretofore, we have approached whatever it is we have had to do. . . . A nation, replete with goods and services, confident that 'there's more where that came from,' may feel less ardor for questing." Kennedy's campaign reflected the same anxiety that the representative of an earlier Massachusetts political family had articulated. "Will you tell me," John Adams had asked Jefferson in 1819, "how to prevent riches becoming the effects of temperance and industry? Will you tell me how to prevent riches from producing luxury? Will you tell me how to prevent luxury from producing effeminacy, intoxication, extravagance, vice and folly?" Such were the cultural and moral contradictions of capitalism that loomed just over the horizon of the Cold War itself.

4

PRAYING:
GOD BLESS AMERICA

Two days after President Truman's disclosure of the loss of nuclear monopoly, a Protestant revival opened in Los Angeles in an atmosphere that was apocalyptic. "Do you know the area that is marked out for the enemy's first atomic bomb?" the thirty-one-year-old preacher asked. "New York! Secondly, Chicago! And thirdly, the city of Los Angeles!" The choice of Los Angeles was not due to the presence of industrial or military targets, but because it was a "city of wickedness . . . known around the world because of its sin, crime, and immorality," meriting destruction as much as Sodom and Gomorrah. Also decisive to the threat hovering over Los Angeles in the fall of 1949 was Bolshevism: "Do you know that the Fifth Columnists, called Communists, are more rampant in Los Angeles than any other city in America?" How such details could have been known, and where the evidence was drawn from, were left unexplained. But no warning could have been more dramatic: "God is giving us a desperate choice, a choice of either revival or judgment. There is no alternative! . . . The world is divided into two camps! On the one side we see Communism . . . [which] has declared war against God, against Christ, against the Bible, and against all religion! . . . Unless the Western world has an old-fashioned revival, we cannot last!"

Despite so tense a moment in the Cold War and such charged rhetoric about "God's last great call," this revival attracted little significant interest until its fourth week, when the reactionary publisher William Randolph Hearst sent his editors a pithy memo from his home: "Puff Graham."

Such patronage might have struck Billy Graham as sordid. For the yellow journalism that had kept Hearst so rich depended upon popular fascination with wickedness and sin, and the publisher's own longstanding liaison with a blonde actress had openly flouted the vows of holy matrimony. But the provenance of such intervention did not seem even in retrospect to bother Graham, who was "convinced that God uses the press in our work, and it has been one of the most effective factors in sustaining public interest through the years." The evangelist's vigorous anti-Communism appealed to Hearst, who was pivotal in making him the most famous churchman of the postwar era. By the time the crusade folded its tent in Los Angeles late that year, attendance had reached 350,000, of whom 4,200 had made their way to the sawdust kneeling ground in front. Cecil B. De Mille, the fervently anti-Communist film director whose biblical epics were enlivened with steamy depictions of the sins that required repentance, even offered Billy Graham a screen test.

Certainly, his influence was to outlast the Cold War, and he probably remained the most consistently and deeply admired American of his time. But Graham's rise to prominence is unintelligible outside of the milieu of dread and anxiety in which he emerged. A preacher became more publicized than any American other than the president because of the message that he delivered—mixing the fear of Armageddon with the assurance of redemption. The concerns that he addressed, perhaps more than the solution that he provided, made Graham a phenomenon who seemed uncommonly attuned to the *Zeitgeist*.

In South Carolina, where his first revival after Los Angeles was held, the occasion was so exigent that Governor J. Strom Thurmond as well as James M. Byrnes, who had been secretary of state when the atomic bombs were dropped on Japan, made a point of attendance and endorsement. Magazine publisher Henry R. Luce flew down to Columbia to meet Graham and, over the next half decade, put the evangelist on the cover of *Life* four times. By the time the Graham crusade reached New York, the ground zero of wickedness, theologian Reinhold Niebuhr felt compelled to take into account "the evidence of 'mass' conversions under the ministrations of popular evangelists who arouse the religious emotions and elicit religious commitments with greater success than at any time since the days of Billy Sunday." Niebuhr clearly had the "Salesman of the Year" in mind.

When The Billy Graham Evangelistic Association was incorporated in 1950, only one secretary was employed in a one-room office. Within eight years a staff of two hundred was headquartered in a four-story office building in Minneapolis, where it became the largest user of the local post office, receiving and answering ten thousand letters each week and collecting and disbursing over two million dollars every year. Graham's weekly television program began in 1952, and his newspaper column was syndicated in 125 newspapers. He regularly landed near the top of the ten-most-admired lists as well as on the covers of *Newsweek* (half a dozen times) and *Look* (ditto). Preaching in a staccato manner first modeled on the machine-gun delivery of the radio gossip-monger Walter Winchell, Graham injected a strident urgency all his own into a mostly traditional message. Echoing evangelists like Dwight Moody and Billy Sunday, he insisted that allegiance to the divinely ordained village code of nineteenth-century America remained valid for all human beings, always and everywhere. Drinking, smoking, card playing, dancing, swearing, reading salacious magazines and books, and skipping church remained sins. The Bible was to be read literally for signs of the Lord's eternal plan, which dwarfed in significance the designs of mortals. "Many people are confident that legislation will solve our problems," Graham announced. "Our problem is deeper than that. It is the constant problem of the sinner before God," for which the immediate and only cure was conversion.

Praying to a deity of mercy as well as justice, reading the Scriptures, saving other souls from the perils of damnation—how tempting for historical scholarship to see in Graham's solutions little more than an escape route from the post-Hiroshima world, where fear could be shown in a handful of dust. Indeed, he did proclaim that the old verities were still in force and that divine intervention might restore the world to its former coherence and meaning. "Billy Graham is a personable, modest[,] and appealing young man who has wedded considerable dramatic and demagogic gifts with a rather obscurantist version of the Christian faith," Niebuhr observed in 1956. "His message is not completely irrelevant to the broader social issues of the day but it approaches irrelevance." Such an interpretation missed, however, the extent to which Graham's crusades broke with the pietist tradition of his predecessors and were pitched explicitly to the culture of the Cold War. For Graham was neither otherworldly nor apolitical. Indeed, an early biography noted that "scarcely one of his Sunday afternoon sermons over a nine-year period has failed to touch on communism[,] and in his regular revival sermons he constantly refers to it to illustrate his doctrinal points. . . . Almost every time he mentions the need or value of a revival[,] he does so in connection with the spread of communism. And several times he has devoted a whole sermon to the death-duel between Christian America and atheistic Russia."

As early as 1947 Graham was denouncing Communism, for he doubted that his country was sufficiently vigilant in combating the Antichrist. Twice he delivered over the air, and distributed as a pamphlet, a sermon on "The Sin of Tolerance," which noted that "the word 'tolerant' means 'liberal,' 'broad-minded.'" And though such adjectives do not seem *les mots justes* in describing American policy toward the Soviet Union in the 1950s, Graham applied the term to appeasement of his country's Cold War adversary, reflecting "the easy-going compromise and tolerance that we have been taught by pseudo-liberals in almost every area of our life for years." Though a registered Democrat, Graham subscribed to the Republican critique of the conduct of foreign policy under Roosevelt and Truman, who were accused of betrayals at Teheran, Yalta, and Potsdam, and of leaving China's Chiang Kai-shek and South Korea's Syngman Rhee in the lurch. The evangelist exuded a pit-bull aggressiveness, urging the Republican administration to encourage armed rebellion in the "people's democracies" behind the Iron Curtain and hoping that Chiang and his "crack troops" might be unleashed against the Maoist regime on the mainland.

The Antichrist also posed a danger *within* the United States. In the winter of 1950–51, Graham warned against "over 1100 social sounding organizations that are communist or communist operated in this country. They control the minds of a great segment of our people." Indeed, "the infiltration of the left wing . . . both pink and red into the intellectual strata of America" had become so advanced that American "educational [and] religious culture is almost beyond repair." In an article in the *American Mercury* in 1954, Graham amplified the charge: "The mysterious pull of this satanic religion is so strong that it has caused some citizens of America to become traitors, betraying a benevolent land which had showered them with blessings innumerable. It has attracted some of our famous entertainers, some of our finest politicians, and some of our outstanding educators." He backed Senator McCarthy's demand that witnesses before his committee not be permitted to shield themselves behind the Fifth Amendment.

Graham's economic views also coincided with the conservative Republican vision of "the American way of life." He shared a concern with the financial corruption and political ambition of the labor movement and opposed "government restrictions" that might obstruct "freedom of opportunity." Graham's description of the Garden of Eden departed somewhat from the text of the Book of Genesis: the paradise of Adam and Eve had "no union dues, no labor leaders, no snakes, no disease." Like virtually all other evangelists, Graham assumed that Christianity and capitalism are as inextricably connected as the spiritual conversion of souls and their worldly success as selves.

Were this the substance of Graham's ideology, he would have been indistinguishable from the more transparent publicists for the National Association of Manufacturers and the Chamber of Commerce. Were his hostility to the appeasement of Communism the heart of his views, Christian faith would not have been necessary to share them; nor does a Christian commitment to personal salvation even require involvement in social affairs. What made Graham so special among the conservative anti-Communist voices of the 1950s was the root cause that he ascribed for the evil that the country confronted. "My own theory about Communism," he revealed in September 1957, "is that it is master-minded by Satan. . . . I think there is no other explanation for the tremendous gains of Communism in which they seem to outwit us at every turn, unless they have supernatural power and wisdom and intelligence given to them."

A 1953 sermon had also reported that "almost all ministers of the gospel and students of the Bible agree that it [Communism] is master-minded by Satan himself." In 1948, Chambers had written an article for *Life* magazine, "The Devil," but even the witness who had not returned empty-handed from Hell was unable to make so certain an identification. Graham's solution was nevertheless compelling: "Only as millions of Americans turn to Jesus Christ at this hour and accept him as Savior, can this nation possibly be spared the onslaught of a demon-possessed communism." For Graham, only Christianity could resist such a force, and only revivalism could save America itself. "If you would be a true patriot, then become a Christian," he advised. "If you would be a loyal American, then become a loyal Christian." An "old-fashioned Americanism" that was equated in 1954 with "the way of the Cross" was Graham's proposal for the most effective shield against "Satan's version of religion," which was Communism.

Yet the very act of transcending the premillennial pessimism in which revivalism was grounded landed Graham in logical inconsistencies. As an evangelist he stressed the turpitude to which America had succumbed, a sinfulness so pervasive that only a "heaven-sent, Holy Ghost revival" could offer hope of redemption. But operating within a political culture of self-righteousness, Graham was compelled to transform such wickedness into goodness. For with Armageddon approaching and the Antichrist to be defeated, it was obvious that "we were created for a spiritual mission among the nations." If Los Angeles and New York were not sinful, there would be no point to revival meetings and crusades like his own. But if Los Angeles and New York were not good, then the divine plan that such revivals promised to explain would have no meaning.

It is hard to see how these contradictory messages could be reconciled. And if the only hope lay in individual salvation, then the strong military policy that Graham persistently championed was as irrelevant as a weak defense, and a green light for the Nationalist Chinese forces on Formosa was as insignificant as a leash. If the Cold War could be understood only in terms of supernatural powers, the scope for American action, ingenuity, and will was drastically reduced—perhaps almost entirely. And if the policies of the Kremlin were literally diabolical, then the hope for permanent, successful opposition virtually evaporated. If changes in the hearts of individuals could solve not only personal problems but also all international and national crises, as Graham claimed, why then did he offer policy prescriptions to statesmen and legislators?

Any effort to resolve such internal contradictions might have confused or alienated audiences who heard his warnings and shared his fears. Any interest in challenging—much less ridiculing—popular superstitions about the devil might well have shocked many of his constituents. Any attempt to modulate his right-wing patriotism— or to apply Arthur Koestler's incisive formulation that "we are fighting against a total lie in the name of a half-truth"—would have cost Graham his patronage as well. Indeed, those logical tensions emerged only because the premillennial tradition from which he came became so loaded with the contemporary obsession with Communism as the locus of evil. The resolution of such contradictions could not be achieved—only evaded, thanks to Graham's manifest dedication, integrity, and fervor. His wholesomeness could melt even the cynical Hearst. Formerly a Fuller Brush salesman, Graham had unloaded more from his sample case during a three-month high school vacation than any other salesman in North Carolina. "I believed in the product," he explained, and later revealed the secret of his influence: "Sincerity is the biggest part of selling anything— including the Christian Plan of Salvation."

1

Salvation was in enormous demand during the Cold War. But though atheists had apparently absented themselves from the foxholes of

World War II, the antecedents of the religious revival cannot be traced only to that conflict. For the United States was unique among Western nations in experiencing so dramatic an upsurge of postwar piety. It is more likely that certain historic traits reasserted themselves, such as the tendency to equate faith with individual success and prosperity, and the assumption that national well-being was a sign of divine approval. What intensified such beliefs was the need to combat a political system that was, above all, defined as godless.

Thus, church membership and a highly favorable attitude toward religion became forms of affirming "the American way of life" during the Cold War, especially since the Soviet Union and its allies officially subscribed to atheism. And conspicuously active church membership became the most effective shield against the suspicion of subversiveness. Reverence was so irreproachable that even the junior senator from Wisconsin could insert in his Wheeling, West Virginia, speech—the birth certificate of McCarthyism—a reference to the "final, all-out battle between Communistic atheism and Christianity. . . . The war is on." With the American Legion also sponsoring and organizing a "Back to God" movement, it was no wonder that in 1953 Professor Boorstin tried to convince HUAC that he had repudiated his youthful Communism by affirming support of the Hillel Foundation at the University of Chicago.

Religious affiliation was indeed rising. In 1910 and 1920, church membership in the United States had held steady at 43 percent of the population. By 1940 it had risen to 49 percent, then 55 percent by 1950, 62 percent by 1956, and 69 percent by the end of the decade; it then fell again to under 63 percent by 1970. In the twentieth century, formal church affiliation had never been as high as it was in the 1950s, and it would never be as high again. A 1954 survey revealed that nine Americans in ten believed in the divinity of Christ, and almost two in three accepted the existence of the devil. Though no decennial census had ever inquired into particular religious beliefs or practices, the Current Population Survey of 1957 discovered that 66.2 percent of Americans professing a religion were Protestant, 25.7 percent were Catholic, and 3.2 percent were Jewish. When pollsters asked which group was "doing the most good for the country," the answers lifted religious leaders from third place in 1942 (after government and business leaders) to first in 1947. The proportion of Americans who thought that clergymen were the most useful citizens went up from 32.6 percent to 46 percent over the next decade.

Churches were by far the most trusted institution in American life—ahead of schools, radio and newspapers, and the government itself. Moreover, a staggering 26.5 million copies of the *Revised Standard Version of the Bible* (1952) were sold within a year of its publication. Such was the prestige of religion that this particular bestseller was listed under the category of nonfiction, though such a status was dubious even by the most indulgent historical and scientific criteria. It was also symbolic of the 1950s that copies of G. David Schine's *Definition of Communism*, a preposterous six-page syllabus of errors that *Time* magazine called "remarkably succinct," were placed next to Gideon Bibles in the hotels his family owned.

In an era when admissions to mental hospitals were nearly doubling, when by 1956 mental patients were occupying more hospital beds than all other patients combined, and when over a billion tranquilizer pills were annually consumed, the most popular therapist of the age of anxiety was a man of the cloth: Norman Vincent Peale. His *Guide to Confident Living* was the number ten bestseller in 1947. Five years later came *The Power of Positive Thinking*—probably the most popular nonfiction book of the decade (other than the Bible itself). Peale's volume was number six on the charts in 1952 and rose to number two for the next two years (right behind the Bible). By 1955, *The Power of Positive Thinking* had skidded to third place (with the Revised Standard Version still first). But in 1957 the Reverend Peale was back, offering the sound advice to *Stay Alive All Your Life;* it ranked third that year. Peale assured his readers that "a Higher Power . . . can do everything for you. . . . This power is constantly available. . . . This tremendous inflow of power is of such force that it drives everything before it, casting out fear, hate, sickness, weakness, moral defeat . . . restrengthening your life with health, happiness, and goodness." It is noteworthy that the personal problems that prayer could lick derived from no social causes that readers might consider or confront.

Peale's success as an author was hardly freakish in an era when the most popular novels included Fulton Oursler's *The Greatest Story Ever Told* (1949), Henry Morton Robinson's *The Cardinal* (1950), and Thomas B. Costain's *The Silver Chalice* (1952), and when readers were especially drawn to works of spiritual biography like Thomas Merton's *The Seven Storey Mountain* (1948), Catherine Marshall's *A Man Called Peter* (1952), and Jim Bishop's *The Day Christ Died* (1957). Nineteen fifty-nine was the first year in which *no* religious books reached the top ten in either the fiction or the nonfiction category.

One of the curios on the shelves of religious works of the 1950s, though not a bestseller, was *The J. Edgar Hoover You Ought to Know*, written—as its cover announces—by "His Pastor," Edward

L. R. Elson. Himself a Presbyterian, the director of the FBI had informed a conference of Methodist ministers in 1947 that crime was ultimately caused by secularism, of which the terminus was—no extra credit for guessing correctly—Communism. "The danger of Communism in America," he had concluded by 1953, "lies not in the fact that it is a political philosophy but in the awesome fact that it is a materialistic religion, inflaming in its adherents a destructive fanaticism. Communism is secularism on the march. It is a moral foe of Christianity. . . . The two cannot live side by side." In his own formidable bestseller, *Masters of Deceit,* Hoover urged regular attendance for children in church and Sunday School and dreamed: "Suppose every American spent a little time each day . . . studying the Bible and the basic documents of American history, government[,] and culture? The result would be a new America, vigilant, strong, but ever humble in the service of God. . . . All we need is faith, real faith." The transition in Hoover's persona impressed his biographer to write as though "the nation's no. 1 G-Man had dropped his machine gun and picked up the cross," switching from public defender to defender of the faith.

Signs of spirituality were everywhere. By early 1952, even Mickey Spillane had found religion. Leaving Mike Hammer with a body count of forty-five corpses in six novels, the literary purveyor of such mayhem became a Jehovah's Witness. Seen handing out tracts and participating in baptisms by immersion, Spillane stopped writing for nine years. When he made a comeback in 1961, his piety had not ruined his popularity. Actress Jane Russell described in a magazine article her own path to the Lord, leading to the discovery that "when you get to know Him, you find He's a Livin' Doll." Upon becoming president of Harvard University in 1953, Nathan Pusey announced as his top priority the revival of the Divinity School and quickly raised five million dollars for the study of God. Hollywood also tried to cash in on holiness. In M-G-M's *The Next Voice You Hear* (1950), a fractious family in a California suburb tunes in on the radio to God's advice to appreciate the blessings of middle-class America. The family becomes harmoniously whole. And the Deity chooses sides in the Cold War in a United Artists movie entitled *Red Planet Mars* (1952), even speaking on the Voice of America to Russian peasants, who are so inspired by an abbreviated version of the Sermon on the Mount that they rip their portraits of Stalin from their walls. A rebellion follows, as Christians in the Soviet Union replace the Politburo with a new government. Churches are reopened, while the Western alliance pays homage to "a nation finding its soul."

America risked the loss of its own soul, however, to judge by the concerns that religious figures often articulated. There was, for example, a rampant rise in and fear of juvenile delinquency, in which wild ones revving up their "cycles of outrage" might tear up a town; and the rock 'n' roll that teenagers made their own seemed merely spasms of libidinous abandon. Frank Sinatra tapped such adult anxieties in 1958 by informing congressmen that rock 'n' roll was "the most brutal, ugly, desperate, vicious form of expression it has been my misfortune to hear," for it was written and sung "for the most part by cretinous goons," and "by means of its almost imbecilic reiterations and sly, lewd—in plain fact dirty—lyrics . . . [it] manages to be the martial music of every side-burned delinquent on the face of the earth."

Yet such music could also be incorporated into the proclivity toward piety. In the same year as Sinatra's sanctimonious testimony, Paul Anka, George Hamilton IV, and Johnny Nash recorded a song entitled "The Teen Commandments," a ten-point "code for today's teens." Its couplets included instructions to "be humble enough to obey / you will be giving orders yourself someday," and "choose a date who would make a good mate." Here is how *Time* described nineteen-year-old Tommy Sands, who starred in "The Singing Idol" on NBC in 1957 and in Twentieth Century-Fox's *Sing, Boy, Sing!* in 1958: "As uncomplicated as most of the songs he sings, Tommy neither drinks nor smokes, lives with his mother in a four-room Hollywood apartment, drives a red Ford convertible and, he says, reads philosophical and religious books 'to find out what makes people tick.' Tommy explains, his brown eyes watering, 'I think all religions are the greatest.'" Pat Boone, who was marketed as a square rival to Presley, refused for religious reasons to kiss his leading ladies on screen, thus deflating the romantic power of films like *April Love* (1957) and *Bernadine* (1957). Even Presley cut a Christmas album; and the kinetic Little Richard, whose raunchy songs got on television only because the network censor could not understand the enunciation of the lyrics, repudiated "the devil's music" after a religious experience.

Such evidences of the Holy Spirit bore little resemblance to the revivals that had punctuated earlier periods of American history. The 1950s did not constitute another Great Awakening. Peale and his confreres promised peace of soul and mind, not convulsive frenzy. Few religious passions were unleashed, few lives transformed by the imperatives of faith, few works composed that enlarged and ennobled the heritage of Christendom. What was revived was not so much religious belief as belief in the *value* of religion. The benefits of devotion were not seen as mystical and metaphysical, nor existential, and less psychological or ethical than political and social. The faith of the fifties often took its cues from the "piety on the Potomac."

2

The theology of the fifties was based far less on, say, Aquinas's proofs for the existence of God than on the conviction that religion was virtually synonymous with American nationalism. Such a conception was irresistible to conservative politicians; in that form it had little to do with faith as such, as when Edward Martin (R-Pa.) argued for a peacetime draft on the Senate floor in 1950 by proclaiming that "America must move forward with the atomic bomb in one hand and the cross in the other." Nuclear weapons could be rattled at the Russians; but what America lacked, Dulles wrote in 1950, was a "righteous and dynamic faith." Liberals joined in too. In his 1952 campaign, Stevenson urged the electorate to adopt a militant faith, because Communism "seeks even to dethrone God from his central place in the Universe. It attempts to uproot everywhere [that] it goes the gentle and restraining influences of the religion of love and peace."

With such stark conceptions of how the Soviet threat was to be defined and resisted, it was not illogical for a leading District of Columbia clergyman to call an American atheist "a contradiction in terms." One consequence was the discrimination to which nonbelievers were subjected. A dozen states barred atheists and even agnostics from serving as notary publics, and in many other states as well agnostic couples were not allowed to adopt children. Religious agencies were given the responsibility of screening refugees and of determining their suitability for entry. Though public life had earlier contrived to find a place for those who did not believe in God, such as Justice Holmes and attorney Clarence Darrow, such "free thinkers" had disappeared by the 1950s. When Judge Kaufman sentenced the Rosenbergs to death, their "devoting themselves to the Russian ideology of denial of God" was apparently held against them, as though unbelief were itself shameful. For as even that ornery liberal, Justice William O. Douglas, observed in *Zorach* v. *Clauson* (1952), Americans were "a religious people whose institutions presuppose a Supreme Being."

In 1957, when the Census Bureau asked, "What is your religion?" an astonishing 96 percent of the populace could cite a specific affiliation. But one American who could not have done so five years earlier was Eisenhower, who had confided to Billy Graham during the campaign that, in his career as a soldier, his own worship had been lax. Nevertheless, Eisenhower told Graham, "I don't believe the American people are going to follow anybody who's not a member of a church." The candidate conceded that he was not a member of any denomination, though his parents were River Brethren. Graham guessed that the denomination was close to Presbyterianism and recommended two particular Presbyterian churches in Washington because their pastors were supporting the GOP. Ike told Graham that for appearances' sake he did not wish to join until after the election, which did not prevent the Republican National Committee from identifying its candidate as "the spiritual leader of our times." He became the first president ever to be baptized in the White House and then, after some doctrinal instruction, was formally accepted into the Presbyterian church. It was the first time as an adult that he had joined a church.

Through both terms he kept on his bedside table the Bible that Graham had given him, and the president's first foreign policy speech inspired Graham to compare it to the Sermon on the Mount. At the first cabinet meeting, Eisenhower permitted Ezra Taft Benson, the secretary of agriculture who was also one of the Twelve Apostles of the Mormon church, to deliver an opening prayer. The cabinet voted to pray at all subsequent meetings. The chief executive also inaugurated a series of national "prayer breakfasts." But when Dr. Elson boasted in the Washington Post that his was the church of presidents, Eisenhower yelled to his press secretary an even more direct invocation of the Deity: "You go and tell that goddam minister that if he gives out one more story about my religious faith I won't join his goddam church."

The president thus sought to exemplify the faith that was so urgent during the Cold War, and in that spirit he gave perfect expression to the latitudinarianism that has historically characterized American religion: "Our government makes no sense unless it is founded on a deeply felt religious faith—and I don't care what it is." Since his interpretation of the origins of American democracy would have surprised a secular rationalist like Franklin or an anticlerical champion of deism like Jefferson, and since the connections between the Enlightenment and the varieties of religious experience were never elaborated, Eisenhower also found it difficult to explain this system of self-government to Soviet marshal Georgi Zhukov. "Since at the age of fourteen he had been taken over by the Bolshevik religion and had believed in it since that time," Ike recalled, "I was quite certain [that] it was hopeless on my part to talk to him about the fact that our form of government is founded in religion."

The president and his wife were in the pew of a Presbyterian church in Washington early in 1954 when its pastor, the Reverend George M. Docherty, reached what he termed "a strange conclusion" about the Pledge of Allegiance: "That which was missing was the characteristic and definitive factor in the American way of life. Indeed, apart from the mention of the phrase 'the United States of America,' it could be the pledge of any republic. In fact, I could hear little Moscovites [sic] repeat a similar pledge to their hammer-and-sickle flag in Moscow with equal solemnity. Russia is also a republic that claims to have overthrown the tyranny of kingship. Russia also claims to be indivisible." Docherty therefore suggested the addition of "one nation under God"—a slight paraphrase of the Gettysburg Address, in which Lincoln had hoped "that this nation, under God, shall have a new birth of freedom."

This sermon aroused Congress to action: seventeen new bills were swiftly dropped into the hopper. Louis Rabaut (D-Mich.), the first congressman to propose the expansion of the Pledge of Allegiance, reminded his colleagues that the Soviet Union "could not . . . place in its patriotic ritual an acknowledgment that their nation existed 'under God.'" Senator Homer Ferguson (R-Mich.) added that "this modification of the pledge is important because it highlights one of the real fundamental differences between the free world and the Communist world." And though such a theological declaration would exclude millions of American nonbelievers, the president signed the pledge bill into law on Flag Day, June 14, 1954. He expressed satisfaction that schoolchildren would henceforth be affirming daily "the dedication of our Nation and our people to the Almighty," especially in a world where so many others were "deadened in mind and soul by a materialistic philosophy of life," and where "the prospect of atomic war" hovered so perilously.

Although the Senate Judiciary Subcommittee on Constitutional Amendments eventually rejected the proposal of Ralph Flanders (R-Vt.) to put explicit recognition of the law and authority of Jesus Christ into the Constitution, a nonsectarian prayer room was constructed on Capitol Hill in 1955. A year later, all first- and second-class mail had to be canceled with a die bearing the nondenominational request to "Pray for Peace." Also in 1956, Congress ordained as the nation's official motto a phrase used on coinage since the end of the Civil War: "In God We Trust." When the phrase was put on a red-white-and-blue eight-cent postage stamp, the president as well as the secretary of state put in a public appearance to celebrate the occasion. In the fervor with which the public was expected to embrace such formulaic reverence, it is hard to miss a note of anxiety, however, which forces the historian to wonder whether the devout politicians of the era were aware of the contradictions lurking beneath the surface.

For Graham had concluded his enormously successful Washington revival in 1952 by warning that Americans were "a desperately wicked people" whom God was about to destroy (unless they repented), since the Lord could not "long abide our sins of materialism." Yet it was the flood of material goods, pouring out in such huge quantities and advertised in such alluring ways, that the Republican administration was promising the citizenry. (To signify the importance of maintaining prosperity, the president granted a fixed weekly appointment to only one official: the chairman of the Council of Economic Advisors. He was, ironically, an unobservant Jew, a foreign-born intellectual named Arthur Burns.) An administration pledged to taking care of business offered not self-sacrifice or abnegation but increasing creature comforts. If, as Eisenhower told the Reverend Graham, "Billy, I believe one reason I was elected President was to lead America in a religious revival," why provide further temptations to sin? The chief executive never explained how endless consumer products were adding to the spiritual strength of the nation. And contrary to the Sermon on the Mount, the poor were not considered blessed in the 1950s. Indeed, they were rarely considered at all.

Though Eisenhower was very fond of words like "spiritual" (in contrast to Soviet materialism) and called "spiritual weapons . . . our country's most powerful resource, in peace or in war," such talk ceased when his administration asked Congress for military appropriations. During his two terms, the Department of Defense spent $313 billion—in fact, $354 billion when the costs of atomic energy, military aid, and strategic stockpiling were factored into the budget. The volume of Pentagon business exceeded *all* the profits that American businesses earned during those same years. No wonder that Marshal Zhukov would have been baffled had Ike stressed the spiritual roots of the American polity, and this believer in "the Bolshevik religion" might well have been skeptical about turning swords into ploughshares when capitalist investors were plowing shares into defense industries. Kremlin analysts of the national faith would have been misled by the decade's hottest nonfiction bestseller, in which the Reverend Peale called prayer "the most tremendous power in the world."

Given such obvious contradictions and such subterranean worries, the need for a holy alliance had to be fervently invoked, the quest for divine blessing conspicuously pursued, and the evidence for the superiority of the American creed eagerly sought. In 1947, Bill Mauldin drew a cartoon that depicted an unkempt young couple sitting beneath a picture of Stalin. "Two magazines are competing for exclusive serial rights," says one to the other, "if we convert." Indeed, ex-Communists were perhaps especially strong advocates of spiritual combat, hoping that the West would understand that the foe, though godless, was tenacious in its effort to make its ideology operational. Only a more powerful faith could dare to hope to defeat the creed that Chambers and Herberg had repudiated. "The Communist vision is the vision of Man without God," Chambers intoned. "It is the vision of man's mind displacing God as the creative intelligence of the world." Herberg, a self-made existentialist theologian, argued that "only a transcendental faith that finds its absolutes *beyond* the ideas, institutions, or allegiances of the world could meet the challenge of the demonic idolatry of Communism without falling into idolatry itself." Dedication to the ideals of human dignity inherent in democracy was not enough, for the West could be saved only by faith "in something more ultimate."

3

The faith that could most unequivocally present itself as combat-ready was itself one that Sidney Hook called "the oldest and greatest totalitarian movement in history." Roman Catholicism considered Communism the Antichrist itself, and a papal encyclical (*Nostis et Nobiscum*) had denounced the movement as early as 1849—soon after publication of *The Communist Manifesto*. The Communist desire to abolish private property challenged the papal assumption that property was integral to an orderly society. The violence of Communist methods and the reductive materialism of "scientific socialism" were an affront to the Catholic affirmation of transcendent love. The explicit godlessness of the Marxist movement directly challenged the worldly power and the salvific claims of the church. In the 1930s, Catholicism openly allied itself with the Fascists during the Spanish Civil War, intensifying opposition to its atheist rival for bodies and souls. It was then that Orwell located the "sin" of the left intelligentsia in having been "anti-Fascist without being anti-totalitarian." But the church was anti-Communist without being antitotalitarian. Pope Pius XII never excommunicated any Nazis, never stifled their hopes of salvation after they had perpetrated genocide. But after July 1949 he excommunicated Catholics who voluntarily "profess, defend and spread" Communist tenets, which were described as "materialistic and anti-Christian."

For American Catholics, the persecution of their co-religionists behind the Iron Curtain heightened not only their own anti-Communism but made their patriotism more impassioned as well. By inflating a historic hostility to Communism into the primary issue, they could embrace American nationalism and formulate an authentic Catholicism too. In 1946, two years after becoming archbishop, Richard J. Cushing of Boston told the Holy Name Society that the United States needed Roman Catholicism "as one of the greatest bulwarks against the inroads of Communism." A minority that had been subjected to a century of bigotry in Protestant America thus took out final citizenship papers. Cushing, an early ecumenicist, even felt it necessary that same year to warn against regarding the campaign against Communism as "an exclusively *Catholic* one." For "although Red Fascism threatens us Catholics and our institutions, it threatens with equal violence and fatal purpose all others who love God or seek to serve Him."

The most relevant sign of the Catholic investment in the culture of the Cold War was McCarthyism. The *Brooklyn Tablet*, for example, was the Catholic newspaper with the largest circulation in the United States. In June 1950, an editorial on its front page was boldly entitled, "PUT UP OR SHUT UP." Readers of the weekly were informed that "the presence of close to a hundred perverts in the State Department—even though Hiss has been forced out and convicted and the perverts fired—justify [sic] a complete and thorough search for further evidence of the Communist conspiracy within the departments of our government." Editor Patrick Scanlon, whose flair for sensationalism earned the admiration of Hearst himself, added that "it is time to put the direct question to each Congressman and Senator: 'What are YOU doing about getting rid of Communists in our government? It is YOUR job as well as Senator McCarthy's. What are YOU doing about it?'"

In 1954, there were over 920,000 members of the Knights of Columbus; though the organization gave no formal endorsement, its monthly magazine, *Columbia*, was pro-McCarthy. In January of that year, 58 percent of Catholics told pollsters that they approved of McCarthy, while only 23 percent said they disapproved of the senator's activities. In 1954, the Catholic War Veterans of New York City also bestowed upon him their "Americanism" award. After his death, the same organization gave to his widow, whose wedding had received papal blessing, a plaque that compared the late senator to the Savior. For when the Lord "saw fit to send us Joseph R. Mc-

Carthy, He showed His love for us. . . . Greater love than this no man hath—that a man lay down his life for his friends" in the struggle against "the menace of Atheistic Communism." To memorialize him, the Catholic War Veterans, which boasted over 200,000 members, established its annual Senator Joe McCarthy Gold Medal Americanism Award in 1957. It was to be given to a Catholic War Veteran who best represented the spirit of patriotism. Fittingly enough, the first winner had scoured the shelves of a high school library in Baltimore, and the discovery of some subversive and obscene books led him to organize a municipal campaign for their immediate removal.

But the decisions of the Catholic War Veterans to discontinue awarding such a gold medal and to stop celebrating its annual New York City mass for McCarthy suggest that Catholic support for McCarthyism can be overstated. Catholics generally remained Democrats even in his heyday, and polls did not demonstrate that Catholics were overwhelmingly more anxious about Communism than the rest of the population. Catholics serving in Congress were *less* likely to vote for the Mundt-Nixon Bill (1948), which required registration of the Party and its fronts with the Department of Justice, and for pro-HUAC legislation than was the House of Representatives as a whole. Eugene McCarthy (D-Minn.), who had once lived in a Benedictine monastery, claimed to be the first congressman to condemn the methods of Joe McCarthy; and the first university president to denounce him was also a Catholic, George N. Shuster of Hunter College.

The auxiliary bishop for the archdiocese of Chicago, Bernard J. Sheil, proved that one could be notably anti-McCarthy as well as vigorously anti-Communist. Sheil's most famous condemnation, an April 1954 speech to the United Auto Workers, asserted that "anti-Communism is a serious business," not "a game to be played so [that] publicity-mad politicos can build fame for themselves." The church, he added, had to speak out against "lies, calumny, the absence of charity and calculated deceit." Though the *Brooklyn Tablet* sneered that Sheil's speech had lifted the *Daily Worker* to a state of "high glee," and though he was forced out as director of the Catholic Youth Organization that he founded, the ghosting of the bishop's speech by John Cogley, the executive editor of *Commonweal*, accentuated the consistent anti-McCarthyism that the magazine itself voiced.

McCarthy's deliberate "Alger—I mean Adlai" slur in a televised speech late in the 1952 campaign outraged the editor of *America*, Father Robert Hartnett, who happened to be very pro-Stevenson. Indeed, the Jesuits' magazine opposed McCarthy so vehemently that

St. Patrick's Cathedral canceled its subscription. Hartnett himself had to be silenced from Rome, which transmitted a direct order from the Father General of the Jesuits, who followed the injunction of St. Ignatius Loyola against exposure of church disputes. The Catholic liberalism that Cogley and Hartnett championed cherished civil liberties even amid the struggle against Communism, but its case was overshadowed by more truculent voices. The "shrill hyper-patriotism" that *Commonweal* attributed to the *Brooklyn Tablet* was far more representative of the Catholic press, even if Catholic attitudes in general were more tolerant and liberal. But because only 44 percent of Catholics told pollsters that they customarily read a Catholic newspaper or periodical, the church's leading historian of McCarthyism was not surprised that "the overwhelmingly McCarthyite Catholic press failed to have so little influence on the Catholic readership in America."

In making McCarthyism respectable and acceptable, the most powerful church prelate of the era deserves special attention for personifying the ardent ideological enmity of Catholicism toward Communism. Operating from a New York chancery that was nicknamed "the Powerhouse," unable—or unwilling—to scuttle speculation that he was destined to be the first American pope, Francis Cardinal Spellman did not need the Hiss case, or the Rosenberg case—much less the Wisconsin senator—to make him recoil before the specter of domestic Communism. More than anyone else, he was the chaplain of the Cold War. By 1946, Spellman was urging Catholic military chaplains to "protect America against aggression of enemies within her borders," and he conjectured that anti-Catholic bigotry—despite its ancient lineage in the United States—could be traced to the Communists.

"His language may have been clumsy and repetitive," Jesuit historian Donald F. Crosby concluded, "but no one could claim that his message was obscure." Whether in speeches throughout the country or in magazines like *Cosmopolitan* and *Good Housekeeping*, Spellman emphasized the menace of Communist infiltration within America and the destruction of the church abroad. The cardinal was a frequent guest on the explicitly anti-Communist radio programs that the Knights of Columbus broadcast over 226 stations in 1947. For him, patriotism and anti-Communism were synonymous. "A true American," he thundered in 1946, "can be neither a Communist nor a Communist condoner, and we realize that the first loyalty of every American is vigilantly to weed out and counteract Communism and convert every American Communist to

Americanism." Only later would the difficulty of squaring that "first loyalty" with civil liberties become more obvious.

Spellman's commitment to anti-Communism went beyond exercising his own freedom of expression. According to his biographer, he agreed to cooperate with the FBI in alerting employers to Communists in the ranks of labor unions. An FBI memo reported that on February 19, 1946, two days before his own elevation to the Sacred College of Cardinals, Archbishop Spellman approved the plan to provide a service to employers, presented in the form of a legitimate business, that showed how Communists could be eliminated from their union employees. Spellman was antagonistic to labor unions anyway, believing them to harbor men "who are afraid of work" as well as Communists. He agreed to help "ferret out and eliminate the Communists and fellow-travelers who are in positions of control in labor unions," the FBI memo stated, only if his own role were concealed—since such cooperation violated the principle of separation of church and state.

Such a principle did not govern Roman Catholic politics in Europe, where the fate of the church under Communist domination certainly haunted and angered him. In 1946, the regime of Marshal Josip Broz Tito inflicted a sixteen-year-jail term upon Aloysius Stepinac, the archbishop of Zagreb and Roman Catholic primate of Yugoslavia who had been a German collaborator and councillor of the Croatian dictatorship of Ante Pavelić during World War II. Spellman described his fellow prelate as "one of thousands of martyrs of every faith whom corrupt, ruthless dictators daily betray and befoul as they wield poisoned power."

Two years later, Joseph Cardinal Mindszenty was arrested in Budapest, where a secret police major stripped him of his clothes and had the cardinal dressed in the costume of a clown, while the jailers and other secret police officers shouted obscenities at him. When Mindszenty initially refused to sign a confession, he was put back in his cell and was beaten until he fainted. For a month he was interrogated, hit, reviled, and humiliated. In February 1949, a People's Court convicted the cardinal of treason, misuse of foreign currency, and conspiracy, and sentenced him to life imprisonment. Spellman was so disturbed by this particular persecution that he spoke from the pulpit of St. Patrick's Cathedral for the first time since V-E Day. "Unless the American people . . . unite to stop the Communist floodings of our own land," he warned, "our sons, for the third and last time, shall be summoned from the comforts, tranquility and love of their own homes and families to bear arms against those who would desecrate and destroy them." Having served as military vicar of the U.S. armed forces, Spellman asked his parishioners to "help save civilization from the world's most fiendish, ghoulish men of slaughter."

The sense of imminent catastrophe close to home seems to have pervaded the Powerhouse, and, with the intertwining of Catholicism and Americanism, the front lines seemed near. In *Is This Tomorrow?*, the four-color comic book printed by the Catechetical Guild, a horde of crazed Reds was shown attacking St. Patrick's and nailing an angelic-looking cardinal to the front door of the cathedral. Because His Eminence feared the possibility that it *could* happen here, biographer John Cooney claimed that Spellman's private solution to the problem of domestic Communism was encapsulated in Spillane's *One Lonely Night*, which Spellman urged priests to read. The cardinal was taken with Mike Hammer's prescriptions: "Don't arrest them, don't treat them with the dignity of the democratic process of the courts of law . . . do the same thing they'd do to you! Treat 'em to the inglorious taste of sudden death." Addressing the annual dinner of the Friendly Sons of St. Patrick's in 1948, with President Truman on the dais, the cardinal warned that "America is no safer from mastery by Communism than was any European country. There we witnessed the killing and enslavement of whole peoples by Communists, who, with the shedding of blood, became as if drunk with it!" He added that "it is not alone in defense of my faith that I condemn atheistic Communism, but as an American in defense of my country. We stand at a crossroads of civilization, a civilization threatened with the crucifixion of Communism."

So persistent an overestimation of the Communist threat *within* the United States led to Spellman's public endorsement of Senator McCarthy. In the spring of 1953, McCarthy went to mass with New York City policemen at St. Patrick's, where the police chaplain eulogized the senator at the communion breakfast of the force's Holy Name Society. Then Spellman himself entered the ballroom, warmly grasped the hand that had held a list of names, turned to the policemen in the audience, and grinned as they screamed their approval. He sat at the head table near the senator and followed him to the podium, again to the cops' rousing applause and interruption. As Spellman explained to journalists, "He is against communism and he has done and is doing something about it. He is making America aware of the dangers of communism." McCarthyism had gotten an imprimatur.

Two months later, in Brussels, Spellman defended "Congressional inquiries into Communist activities in the United States." Such investigations were "not the result of any mad legislative whim," the prelate claimed. "We thank God that they have begun while there is still time to do something about it." For "Americans . . . desire to see Communists exposed and removed from positions where they can carry out their nefarious plans. . . . No American uncontaminated by Communism has lost his good name because of congressional hearings on un-American activities." Such claims led President Eisenhower to the farfetched suspicion, according to his attorney general, that Spellman wanted to catapult McCarthy into the White House. In any event, the cardinal never repudiated the demagogue or expressed regret for encouraging him, and the "McCarthy Mass" at St. Patrick's was held every year on the anniversary of his death.

For all the savvy that guided the operations of the Powerhouse, Spellman could overplay his hand. Contrary to his own intentions, he helped expel the crime of blasphemy from constitutional law, and in the process demonstrated the extent to which his thought was fixed within the culture of the Cold War. The rigidity of his stance compelled him to view greater freedom of thought and expression as a danger to the social fabric rather than as a justification for resisting tyranny. In 1951, Roberto Rossellini's film *The Miracle* was released in the United States. Its subject was a demented woman (Anna Magnani) who, enveloped in religious frenzy, imagines that St. Joseph has seduced her. The mocking villagers convince her that the conception of her child, to whom she gives birth alone in a deserted church, is miraculous. *The Miracle* won the New York Film Critics award for best foreign film, which His Eminence had not bothered to see. But he ordered the drafting of a pastoral letter that condemned the movie and that was read during every mass in St. Patrick's Cathedral as well as from the pulpits of the four hundred parishes around the archdiocese of New York. All Catholics were expected to boycott *The Miracle*. After the cardinal's appeal, the Holy Name Society picketed outside the Manhattan theater showing the film, shouting the ultimate deprecations of shame: "This is the kind of picture the Communists want!" and "Don't be a Communist—all the Communists are inside!" The Catholic War Veterans swelled the ranks to an estimated thousand, protesting the "Insult to Every Woman Not to Mention Children."

Virtually every resource was deployed to prevent others from seeing *The Miracle*. The fire commissioner suddenly issued a number of violations against the theater, which the police raided several times as well, claiming bomb scares. The New York Board of Regents, which supervised the licensing of movies, voted unanimously to hold a hearing in which the distributors of the film had to explain why *The Miracle* should not be banned as "sacrilegious." When critic Frank Getlein gave the movie a favorable review in the *Catholic Messenger*, he was fired from his faculty teaching post at Fairfield University. "Spellman must have picked up the phone," Getlein later conjectured, since the Catholic university had offered him no explanation for his dismissal. After Professor William P. Clancy criticized the censorship of *The Miracle* as "semi-ecclesiastic McCarthyism" in the liberal Catholic journal *Commonweal*, Notre Dame University fired him from its English department.

Even the Vatican did not seem sufficiently wary of the peril that tolerance of *The Miracle* portended. When it was learned that *L'Osservatore Romano* had given the movie a mixed review, Spellman was furious. "Satan alone would dare such perversion," he wrote in a pastoral letter. "To those who perpetrate such a crime as *The Miracle* within the law[,] all that we can say is: How long will enemies of decency tear at the heart of America? . . . Divide and conquer is the technique of the greatest enemy of civilization, atheistic communism. God forbid that the producers of racial and religious mockeries should divide and demoralize Americans so that the minions of Moscow might enslave this land of liberty." Beginning with the morally correct stance that Communism was repugnant, he had sniffed Communism in *whatever* was repugnant.

The cardinal's overreaction transformed *The Miracle* into a *cause célèbre*. Never before had a foreign film benefited from so prominent and indefatigable a publicist. Until Spellman had called for a boycott, the Manhattan theater that had booked the film was doing little business. After the Powerhouse swung into action, however, the lines for every showing of *The Miracle* stretched around the block. And in 1952 the Supreme Court erased blasphemy from the criminal code. Citing both Getlein and Clancy, Justice Frankfurter's concurring opinion in *Burstyn* v. *Wilson* found the vague notion of "sacrilege" inconsistent with the First Amendment, for such censorship was "bound to have stultifying consequences on the creative process of literature and art."

Perhaps, in the cardinal's mind, the defense of Catholic sexual values had assumed an even larger significance than the political and military threat that Communism posed. Or perhaps the distinction between the two issues had blurred beyond recovery. In any event, on December 16, 1956, Spellman mounted the pulpit during mass for the first time since his denunciation of the jailing and torture of Cardinal Mindszenty in 1949. This Sunday, the target was *Baby Doll*, a movie which, though not yet released, "has been responsibly judged to be evil in concept and which is certain to exert an immoral and corrupting influence on those who see it." Thus was inaugurated perhaps Spellman's biggest campaign of censorship ever. Priests were assigned to the lobbies of theaters where *Baby Doll* was showing and were expected to write down the names of parishioners attending it, under "pain of sin" for their movie-going tastes. Though Spellman himself had not seen the film, the reviewer for *Time* magazine had, and called *Baby Doll* "just possibly the dirtiest American-made motion picture that has ever been legally exhibited." Though the advertisements showed actress Carroll Baker wearing a slip, and her constant thumb-sucking was perhaps intended to suggest oral sex, neither director Elia Kazan nor scenarist Tennessee Williams served up anything very explicit in the film itself.

A line of defense that stretched from Budapest to *Baby Doll* could not be maintained for the duration, and indeed the very excesses of so vigilant and inflexible a stance guaranteed a waning of the cardinal's influence. Kennedy's election in 1960 automatically ended Spellman's role as the nation's most powerful Catholic. Before his death in 1968, the papacy was welcoming dialogue with the "godless goons" whom "the American Pope" had made a vocation of denouncing and was urging a negotiated settlement with the Communists in Vietnam. The Church Militant was becoming demobilized.

4

But even during the Cold War, one religious thinker demonstrated the possibility of being deeply Christian without smugly accepting the status quo and proved that theistic belief was compatible with the struggle for social justice. Unlike Spellman, who encouraged self-righteousness and hypocrisy by defining the Cold War as "slavery against democracy, evil against good, might against right, Stalinism against God," Reinhold Niebuhr was attentive to the paradoxes and ironies of the American predicament without becoming an accomplice to overweening pride—and without the escape hatch of otherworldliness. With subtle intelligence, Niebuhr showed how to be a political progressive without shallowness, an anti-Communist moralist without fanaticism, a religious believer without delusion. Though an ornament of the Union Theological Seminary, Niebuhr was no apologist. He knew that religion was "a good thing for honest people but a bad thing for dishonest people," and that "the Gospel gives no special securities or exemptions from the frailties of men and the tragedies of life." Though a liberal founder and chairman of the ADA, he did not yield to exaggerated hopes for reform and modestly defined democracy as "a method for finding proximate solutions for insoluble problems."

His influence was virtually everywhere. Graham claimed to "have read nearly everything Mr. Niebuhr has written, and I feel inadequate before his brilliant mind and learning." When George Kennan became head of the State Department's new Policy Planning Staff in 1947, Niebuhr was appointed chairman of its Advisory Committee, helping to sustain the strategy of containment and offering ideological mobilization against the Soviet threat. Yet as early as 1932, his trenchant *Moral Man and Immoral Society* had proposed civil disobedience as the most effective instrument of black emancipation in the United States. It was piquant that, a generation later, his writings would influence Martin Luther King, Jr., in divinity school. Despite the experience of growing up black in the segregated South, King claimed to have learned from Niebuhr of the "potential for evil," though he "still believed in man's potential for good." For Niebuhr had assaulted the illusions of utopianism in the name of Christian realism and political pragmatism. In insisting upon the inclusiveness of sin, which warps leaders as well as constituents and which corrupts the well-meaning as well as the cynical, he spoke for the Augustinian persuasion. But Niebuhr also spoke *to* the complacent pride of the 1950s in acknowledging that "the Church does not seem to realize how unethical a conventionally respectable life may be."

5

INFORMING:
MANY ARE CALLED

Western society has not allocated a high status to the informer. The central human villain in Christianity is the disciple who betrays Jesus for thirty pieces of silver. Among the Jewish villagers of Eastern Europe, it was traditional to bury counterparts of Judas by placing the corpse on a garbage wagon, which was dragged by a lame horse to the cemetery. Even in prisons, where the most degenerate of our species are confined, the "stoolie" has been considered especially loathsome. In John Ford's indelible 1935 film, *The Informer*, Gypo Nolan (Victor McLaglen) is told by the Irish rebels' court of inquiry that an informer has "got to be wiped out like the first sign of a plague as soon as he's spotted. He's a common enemy." In that same year, the Group Theatre's legendary production of Clifford Odets's *Waiting for Lefty* introduced a young actor named Elia Kazan, who raced on stage to reveal an informer: "The son of a bitch is my own lousy brother!" Even though circumstances might occasionally justify "squealing," even though the presumption against it might be effectively rebutted, this stigma has an ancient and durable lineage.

The culture of the Cold War was distinctive for having punctured the abhorrence of informing, which "in our time . . . is a duty," Chambers's autobiography quotes Soviet defector Walter Krivitsky as proclaiming. Harvey Matusow, a professional informer who eventually fingered 108 Americans as Communists before recanting his testimony, discovered that though he "was on the lowest rung of the ladder of life," his advice was solicited by pillars of respectable society: the president of Queens College, the superintendent of the biggest school system in the country (New York's), and the commissioner of the New York Police Department.

How far the presumption was undercut was revealed in a school text entitled *Exploring American History* (1955), which Yale historian Ralph Henry Gabriel coauthored. After warning vaguely against "false news" and "dangerous propaganda," the text offered its young readers the following advice: "The FBI urges Americans to report directly to its offices any suspicions they may have about Communist activity on the part of their fellow Americans. The FBI is expertly trained to sift out the truth of such reports under the laws of our free nation. When Americans handle their suspicions in this way, rather than by gossip and publicity, they are acting in line with American traditions." While *Exploring American History* seemed to make an oblique criticism of the excesses of congressional investigating committees, the text also failed to separate the categories of military, diplomatic, and industrial secrets—however remote from the purview of high school students—and the general responsibility of surveillance that citizens are supposed to undertake. Exalting young tattlers was a mark of totalitarian societies, but it took the Cold War to include informing among the inventory of "American traditions."

How did one avoid becoming an informer? In 1950, the Supreme Court refused to review the sentences of the Hollywood Ten, a group of scenarists and directors who had taken the First Amendment when HUAC had asked them about their politics during stormy hearings in Washington three years earlier. These "unfriendly" witnesses, all of whom were or had been Communists, had been convicted of contempt of Congress. Once the Supreme Court upheld the validity of HUAC's inquiry into the political activities and beliefs of the targets of its subpoenas, the only apparent recourse available to witnesses was the Fifth Amendment, which provides immunity against compulsory self-incrimination.

The exercise of this constitutional right was highly problematic, however. Professor Hook presumed, for example, that those who invoked it had something to hide. McCarthy shared this view, calling such witnesses "Fifth Amendment Communists." Because of the senator's difficulties in exposing real Communists, he could usually be satisfied with shattering the reputations of such witnesses. Forcing them to take cover behind the Fifth was degrading enough. Its punitive effect was suggested by what happened when his committee got a name confused and subpoenaed the wrong woman. The witness answered the standard question—"Are you or have you ever

been a member of the Communist Party?"—with a simple "No."
Her failure to claim the immunity of the Fifth Amendment produced
shock, her attorney, Leonard Boudin, recalled: "Senator McCarthy
terminated the executive session and we never had a public session. . . . I remember Cohn rushing over to me and saying, 'Leonard,
what a clever trick!'"

Usually, however, the invocation of such a right frustrated and
angered patriots, who otherwise expected the Constitution to be
treated with uncritical reverence. Attorney General Levi Lincoln
had nevertheless taken the Fifth in 1803 when Chief Justice John
Marshall questioned him during the proceedings of *Marbury* v. *Madison.* HUAC's own chairman, J. Parnell Thomas, took the Fifth when
charged with padding the payroll, which resulted in a jail sentence.
Yet resentment against such immunity crops up in the only movie
ever consecrated to the glorification of HUAC, *Big Jim McLain*
(1952), in which the eponymous committee investigator (John
Wayne) is assigned to Hawaii to foil a Communist plot. To his dis-
may, the Reds take shelter behind the right not to incriminate themselves. *Big Jim McLain* implies that only subversives hostile to legitimate authority would hide behind constitutional niceties and
that a democratic society should not misinterpret the Bill of Rights
as a suicide pact.

If a witness before a congressional investigating committee really
was a Communist, taking the Fifth Amendment imposed extralegal
penalties. Though a perjury indictment would be avoided, the witness could expect a pink slip and the blacklist. This was the fate of
teachers in distinguished universities and of reporters with newspapers like the *New York Times* who exercised this constitutional
right. In this era, Communists usually concealed themselves—
either because they would suffer economic or social sanctions for
having promoted so disreputable a cause, or because the Party
wanted such witnesses to come across as martyrs to civil liberties,
or for both reasons. An actual Communist had no constitutional
refuge other than the Fifth Amendment. If the witness was *not* a
Communist, the logic for taking it was far less compelling. But one
justification was the same as for Communists: the fear of getting
caught, even inadvertently, in perjury. Witnesses before congressional committees were denied some protection available to defendants in the criminal courts: the right of cross-examination, the
right to face one's accusers, and the right to rebut evidence. But the
risk of unwittingly committing perjury—when asked about harmless meetings and forgotten petitions of two decades earlier—had

to be weighed against the far more certain obloquy and economic penalties that would result from taking the Fifth Amendment.

Confronted by a committee that insisted upon informing as the test of patriotism, as the price of full citizenship, an ex-Communist or a non-Communist therefore faced three alternatives: (1) to invoke immunity when talking of others but not of oneself, (2) not to invoke immunity at all and to talk of others as well as of oneself, or (3) not to invoke immunity at all and to talk of oneself but not of others. Lillian Hellman chose the first alternative; Elia Kazan, the second; Arthur Miller, the third. Because all three wrestled so publicly with the ethos of informing, they best illustrate this particular imperative of the culture of the Cold War.

1

Though Hellman denied that she had ever been a Communist, and even sweet-talked HUAC with the disclaimer that she was not "a political person" at all, few writers of her fame enlisted more faithfully in the ranks of fellow travelers. The highlight of her political involvement was undoubtedly the pro-Soviet Waldorf Conference, starring Dmitri Shostakovich, that she helped organize in 1949. Her FBI file eventually ran to a thousand pages—much of which was admittedly repetitive, trivial, and goofy, such as an informant's complaint that her play *Another Part of the Forest* (1948) "showed the Communist technique to play up the weak spots of American life. . . . [and] tended to revive the hatred of the North and South in a villainous form." Blacklisted by the film industry, Hellman had not written a scenario since *The Searching Wind* (1946), and though the blacklist was not enforced on Broadway, her later plays had not clicked at the box office. Then, in 1952, a HUAC subpoena converted her into a woman of valor, a legend that may outstrip the impact of the melodramas that made her reputation in the 1930s.

In her actual testimony, Hellman expressed willingness to speak—sometimes—about her own political past, but she refused to discuss her association with others. Unlike the Hollywood Ten, she invoked the immunity of the Fifth Amendment (even though she elsewhere denied Party membership). Unlike them, she was not "unfriendly," did not directly defy the committee, and never spent a second in prison. Indeed, her attorney, Joseph Rauh, later claimed that contrary to the fears of jail expressed in her memoir *Scoundrel Time* (1976), the playwright realized how very unlikely incarceration was, even though the Supreme Court had held in 1951 that witnesses freely testifying about themselves could not decline—on

Fifth Amendment grounds—to testify about others. She trumped the committee only by accident, when a congressman who was not playing with a full deck moved to enter into the record a letter that Hellman had written to HUAC chairman John S. Wood (D-Ga.). With that unexpected opportunity, Rauh rushed up to distribute to the press copies of his client's letter, which infuriated Wood himself.

In it Hellman accepted the civic obligation—in some situations—of becoming an informer: "I do not like subversion or disloyalty in any form, and if I had ever seen any, I would have considered it my duty to have reported it to the proper authorities." But she was "not willing, now or in the future, to bring bad trouble to people who, in my past association with them, were completely innocent of any talk or any action that was disloyal or subversive. . . . I cannot and will not cut my conscience to fit this year's fashions."

No HUAC witness—at least of the playwright's stature—had put the moral case against informing so compactly. But her letter also obscured the unheroic nature of her testimony, which shifted back and forth in invoking immunity. Her recollection in *Scoundrel Time* was that, as she was about to explain to HUAC why she was claiming the right against compulsory *self*-incrimination when testifying about others, a man in the press gallery interrupted her: "Thank God somebody finally had the guts to do it!" Hellman's memoir offers no further explanation of her erratic HUAC testimony on this point, and the vocal support from the gallery was almost certainly a fabrication. No press account ever mentioned the interruption, nor did Rauh, seated next to her, recall having heard it. Moreover, since Hellman was taking the Fifth Amendment anyway, what she majestically "finally had the guts to do" is unclear—either from her testimony itself or from *Scoundrel Time*. But since the design of HUAC was not to gather information related to legislation but rather to inflict (in Emerson's phrase) "pitiless publicity," the committee lost where it counted. The *Times* headline did not proclaim HELLMAN PLEADS THE FIFTH (which she *did* take), but read instead: LILLIAN HELLMAN BALKS HOUSE UNIT. One of her biographers concluded, "Most accounts over the next thirty years would remember little else about Hellman's appearance before the committee except her eloquent and subtly defiant letter."

A beleaguered liberalism required the transformation of so compliant a witness into a rebel against coercive authority. When Hellman stepped on the stage of New York's YM-YWHA Poetry Center soon after her HUAC appearance, the audience that had come for Marc Blitzstein's concert version of her play *The Little Foxes* (1939) gave her a standing ovation. From then on, her *oeuvre* seemed to assume more coherent shape as a critique of the contemporary syndrome of informing. Her 1934 drama, *The Children's Hour*, was restaged seven months after the playwright's congressional testimony; by 1952 its theme of the corrosive effects of false accusations had taken on new political relevance, despite its girls' school setting. The salience of the play could be stretched too far, however. No one defended the propriety of blaming and hurting the innocent, whether they be two teachers accused of lesbianism in such a school or "subversives" hauled before the inquisitors of Capitol Hill. Yet *The Children's Hour* evades the more complex question of what policies would have been sound had the charges been true, just as Hellman herself—a compulsive defender of Stalinist Russia—was reluctant to analyze the unprecedented internal problem of a totalitarian movement that was guided by a democracy's most powerful external enemy. Neither in *The Children's Hour* nor in her own political statements did Hellman do more than condemn the sort of informing that was malicious and irresponsible. This was a harmful consequence of the Cold War—but not the only issue.

After *The Autumn Garden* (1951), no Hellman play was produced on Broadway until 1955, when *The Lark*, her adaptation of Jean Anouilh's *L'alouette*, was mounted. The plight of Joan of Arc might well have triggered some personal and political resonances, since the state forces the female protagonist (Julie Harris) to testify against her will and to compromise her integrity by speaking only what authority wished to hear. For Joan of Arc the consequences were fatal, but for the adapter of her story they were considerably less than the stake. Hellman insisted upon a limousine and driver for the out-of-town tryouts of *The Lark*, and the proceeds of the Broadway production enabled her to buy property on Martha's Vineyard. Her own voices nevertheless continued to dictate pro-Soviet politics. She demanded, for example, that ex-Communist scenarist Budd Schulberg "prove" that some of the greatest Russian writers of the 1930s had been murdered. When Khrushchev denounced some of the crimes of Stalin early in 1956, Hellman was appalled—not by the scale of the "Great Terror" but by the ingratitude of the First Secretary, whose own political career had been given such a boost by the late despot. Indeed, the published text of Khrushchev's "secret speech" is, for all its omissions, far more anti-Stalinist than, say, *Scoundrel Time*. Perhaps his accusations had not been "proven" either, or perhaps charges of perfidy against Stalin could *only* be irresponsible and false. Hellman even blamed Khrushchev for being an informer.

2

By naming names, Elia Kazan epitomized the problem of the ex-Communist subpoenaed to testify before HUAC. While a member of the Group Theatre, Kazan had joined the Party in 1934 and left it in 1936, a year and a half later. By the time of his 1952 summons before the committee, he had probably become the most honored director of his time. But Kazan was suddenly forced to confront the most anguishing political and moral choice of his life. His powerful 1988 autobiography summarizes the questions that he asked himself: "Was I really a leftist? . . . Did I really want to change the social system I was living under? Apparently that was what I'd stood for at one time. But . . . everything I had of value I'd gained under that system. After seventeen years of watching the Soviet Union turn into an imperialist power, was that truly what I wanted here? Hadn't I been clinging to once-held loyalties that were no longer valid? Wasn't what I'd been defending up until now by my silence a conspiracy working for another country?" He wondered, "Why had I taken so long to even consider telling the country—that's what it amounted to—everything I knew? Was it because of the moral injunction against 'informing,' which was respected only depending on which side you were on? . . . If the situation were reversed, wouldn't the 'comrades' protect themselves without hesitation and by any means? Including naming me." At first, when Kazan testified behind closed doors, he refused to name names. For he realized that the congressmen "were conducting . . . a degradation ceremony, in which the acts of informing were more important than the information conveyed. I didn't doubt they knew all the names they were asking for!" But he soon changed his mind and gave them sixteen.

Cooperation with HUAC was more necessary for him than for others, Kazan further rationalized. His friend Arthur Miller could write in jail, but a movie director could not work there. Financing and organization were required to make films. That was the pertinence of Kazan's concluding public statement: "The main pictures I have made and the plays I have chosen to direct represent my convictions. I expect to continue to make the same kind of pictures and to direct the same kind of plays." For had he not cooperated with HUAC, his movie expectations would have been completely dashed. But what made Kazan into the most famous (or notorious) embodiment of the friendly witness was not really his testimony. Others had named far more names (scenarist Martin Berkeley rattled off 161), just as others had put their talents longer and more energetically in the service of a god that failed. But Kazan was soaring at the peak of his career. In one year (1947) he had won both a Tony for directing *A Streetcar Named Desire* on Broadway and an Oscar for directing *Gentleman's Agreement* for Twentieth Century-Fox. His decision thus made the role of informer respectable, and he even paid for an advertisement in the *Times* that advised others to emulate him. Those who knew firsthand about Communism, he urged, should go "either to the public or to the appropriate Government agency."

Kazan's decision was indirectly vindicated with a film that may be the most brilliant American movie of that era and has become a classic. *On the Waterfront* (1954) lacks an explicitly political theme. But because it vividly exemplifies the political ethos of the decade, and because movie making is so collective an enterprise, the history of *On the Waterfront* is as useful an entrée as any into the culture of the Cold War.

"Kickbacks, loan-sharking, petty extortion, theft, and pilferage— and murder" had become "a commonplace of longshore life," labor editor Daniel Bell wrote in *Fortune* in 1951. The New York waterfront consisted of a "rough, racket-ridden frontier domain, ruled by the bull-like figure of the 'shaping boss.' Here brawn and muscle, sustained when necessary by baling hook and knife, enforce discipline. . . . Many of the docks are controlled directly or indirectly by mobsters who dominated the pier union local, parceled out the jobs, and ran the rackets." Where time was crucial, the "industrial racketeer" brought some order and stability to the chaos of the docks, from which trucks had to take the goods quickly to the railroad tracks.

The domination of the mob was obvious not only to Bell and the readers of *Fortune*. Malcolm Johnson's articles on the subject in the *New York Sun* had won a Pulitzer Prize in 1949. Such exposés led to the formation of the Kefauver Commission in 1950 and of a New York State Crime Commission the following spring. The American Federation of Labor was also compelled to intervene. But the International Longshoremen's Association (ILA) and the racketeers soon resumed control, benefiting from connections with Tammany Hall and Democratic party politics and from the connivance of shipping companies. For "in the 'public morality' of American society," Bell concluded, "corruption can be tolerated, if clothed, but naked corruption is unsettling."

Among those who tried to fight the thugs was Peter Panto, a young dock worker who wanted to organize a rank-and-file protest in his local branch of the ILA. He was murdered and his body dumped in the East River. In the Red Hook section of Brooklyn, where "Tough"

Tony Anastasia ruled the waterfront, Arthur Miller had heard Pan-to's story, and in 1951 he completed a screenplay—entitled *The Hook*—based on his short life and sudden death. Miller and Kazan, whose direction of *All My Sons* (1947) and *Death of a Salesman* (1949) had been Broadway sensations, offered the script to Harry Cohn, who disliked *The Hook* but was willing to "green-light" the project in the hope that Kazan would direct a more likely hit for Columbia Pictures. Because the script was devoted to a union, Cohn showed it to Roy Brewer, the most powerful labor leader in Hol-lywood and soon to preside over the Motion Picture Alliance for the Preservation of American Ideals. The chairman of the AFL Film Council liked the screenplay even less than Cohn and called it "a lie." So much criminality, he insisted, could not be entrenched in an AFL union—and especially not the ILA, whose president, Joseph Ryan, was an old friend. (Only later, after the New York State Crime Commission established the union's intimacy with gangsters, would Ryan be forced to resign his presidency. Convicted of grand larceny as well, he was sent to Sing Sing.) No loyal American, Brewer added, could have written such a script, since the movie would gen-erate "turmoil" in the harbor of New York, where military supplies for Korea were being handled.

Indeed, Brewer was so concerned that he and Cohn passed the screenplay on to the Los Angeles office of the FBI, which would be expected to confirm speculation about the disruption that *The Hook* could ignite on the New York docks. Were Brewer himself to veto the screenplay, Cohn had already warned Miller, union projection-ists throughout the United States would refuse to show any movie from Columbia Pictures. But Brewer was a reasonable man, and he suggested a simple revision to America's premier playwright of so-cial consciousness: rewrite *The Hook* "so that instead of racketeers terrorizing the dock workers, it would be the Communists." This story line would have repeated *I Married a Communist*, a 1949 film in which the villain was based on Harry Bridges of the International Longshoremen's and Warehousemen's Union (CIO), the leftist who had actually fought racketeering on the West Coast, after Ryan had pushed him out of the AFL.

The script change was unacceptable. Miller realized that among the New York longshoremen there were Communists. Indeed, he told Brewer, he knew both of them. But to inflate their numbers and their influence, Miller added, would transform the gangsters into patriots. That was not how he thought of Tony Anastasia, whose brother ran Murder, Inc.; so the author withdrew *The Hook* from consideration. From Cohn, who had accepted a decoration from

Mussolini as late as 1933, came a cable that read, "ITS INTERESTING HOW THE MINUTE WE TRY TO MAKE THE SCRIPT PRO-AMERICAN YOU PULL OUT."

Kazan was still intrigued by the subject, however, and in 1952 invited Budd Schulberg to join the project. Schulberg had given HUAC fifteen names the year before and had independently written another movie script drawn from Johnson's articles in the *New York Sun*. His own draft, entitled *Crime on the Waterfront*, focused on Tony Mike de Vincenzo, a former hiring boss on the Hoboken piers. De Vincenzo had resented the domination of the mobsters, found himself denied employment on the docks, and ended up selling newspapers, while still dressed like a hiring boss. Subpoenaed by the Waterfront Crime Commission, he described the injustices and the corruption, named names, and had managed to remain alive by the time Schulberg and then Kazan met him. "I doubt that Budd was as affected personally as I was by the parallel of Tony Mike's story," Kazan recalled. The scenarist's "reaction to the loss of certain friends was not as bitter as my own; he had not experienced their blackballing as frequently and intensely as I had in the neighborhood known as Broadway. I believe Budd regarded our waterfront story with greater objectivity." But, the director added, "I did see Tony Mike's story as my own, and that connection did lend the tone of irrefutable anger."

The theme of informing, which Miller had ignored in *The Hook*, thus became central to Schulberg's script. When Terry Malloy, the young dock worker who has incriminated the gangsters, exults to their boss, "I'm glad what I done—you hear me?—glad what I done!" Kazan understood: "That was me saying, with identical heat, that I was glad I'd testified as I had." And the subsequent scene of the "shape-up," in which Malloy's co-workers ostracize him—"that, too, was my story, now told to all the world." Kazan added: "When critics say that I put my story and my feelings on the screen, to justify my informing, they are right. That transference of emotion from my own experience to the screen is the merit of those scenes," for "in the mysterious way of art, I was preparing a film about myself."

HUAC testimony had earned the director and scenarist of *On the Waterfront* the chance to continue working in Hollywood, but casting decisions were made in the shadow of the blacklist. While doing research for the film, Schulberg had talked to John Garfield about playing the lead. But the actor's past was haunting him, and the pressures that forced him to repent, which included a *Look* apologia entitled "I Was a Sucker for a Left Hook," led to a fatal heart attack.

On the Waterfront was then supposed to star Sinatra, who was actually from Hoboken, where the film was to be shot. But Kazan preferred Marlon Brando, whom he had directed in both the stage and screen versions of A Streetcar Named Desire. Brando had not wanted to work with Kazan again, however, because of his HUAC testimony. Fortunately for the annals of legendary acting, producer Sam Spiegel persuaded Brando to change his mind, and a brilliantly sympathetic portrayal of a stool pigeon was thus created by a star who had resisted working with an informer. Leonard Bernstein composed the score, and then Kazan went back west to show the final cut to Cohn, who had financed it. Before the projection started, Cohn asked the director only one question: "How much did it cost?" When Kazan answered that it was under $900,000, the president of Columbia Pictures nodded, signaled the projectionist to begin, and—about a third of the way through the screening—could be heard snoring. On the Waterfront was indeed a sleeper. For though a film about longshoremen was expected to be a box-office disaster when it opened in the spring of 1954, it became a major hit, winning eight Oscars—including Best Production, Best Direction, Best Screenplay, and Best Actor.

Kazan himself guessed that, despite the preliminary title reassuring audiences that "self-appointed tyrants can be defeated by right-thinking people in a vital democracy," the theme of informing gave the film its special power: "After all, Terry's act of self-redemption breaks the great childhood taboo: Don't snitch on your friends. Don't call for the cop! Our hero is a 'rat,' or for intellectuals, an informer. . . . Schulberg struck a deep human craving there: redemption for a sinner. . . . Something central has been touched." Having set up Joey Doyle to be pushed from the roof, Terry is a sinner who redeems himself through repentance, confessing first to Father Barry and then to the victim's sister, Edie Doyle. But only public confession—testimony before the Waterfront Crime Commission—can really bestow absolution of guilt. It does not detract from the compelling impact of On the Waterfront, however, to recognize how heavily the moral scales are tipped in favor of the protagonist, who eventually decides to violate the code of "deaf and dumb." Since the hoodlums have already slain two other stevedores who had spoken to the Crime Commission, audiences are probably as desperately eager for Terry to snitch as are his blonde girlfriend and the waterfront priest who awaken Terry's conscience. Just as Kazan had written in the Times that "secrecy serves the Communists," so too On the Waterfront makes silence serve the interests of the mob, which can be countered only by those who have known its operations from inside.

However wrenching Kazan's own ethical choice had been in 1952, his protagonist is permitted far less justification for self-doubt. For if Terry's "informing had meant that the loyal and loving Terry would be sending his brother [Rod Steiger] to prison or perhaps the electric chair, then the dilemma posed by the act of informing would have been real," journalist Victor S. Navasky perceptively observed in his book *Naming Names* (1980). "But Kazan-Schulberg have the mob rub Charlie out, thereby giving Terry a socially sanctified personal motive (revenge) for testifying against the mob, as well as a political one (anti-corruption). This denies the audience any opportunity for genuine consideration of the ambivalent and dangerous complexities of the informer issue. 'Squealing' may be relative," Navasky concludes, but *On the Waterfront* makes it "mandatory."

Nor is mob boss Johnny Friendly (Lee J. Cobb) endowed with any redeeming qualities or given any right to exact allegiance (unless one counts Terry's indebtedness for invitations to baseball games as a kid). The odious Friendly never seems to have felt a streak of idealism that turned rancid—which vitiates any effort to find a parallel between the rule of the gangsters and Kazan's own brief attraction to Communism, as he himself recognized upon rereading, late in life, *Waiting for Lefty*. Kazan found himself responding to the play "as I had when I first read it. I was thrilled to the verge of tears. In the passing of that half century of time, I'd turned violently anti-Communist. But the yearning for meaning, for dignity, for security in life, stirred me now as it had then. The Communists got their influence and their power by speaking up for these universal human desires." But no equivalent hint of an appeal, however perverted, is granted the mobsters who run the waterfront local. They are merely despicable, having aborted Terry's promising boxing career by forcing him to take a dive, demoting him from a contender to a bum.

Friendly and his pistoleros are simply murderers, and reporting their transparent criminality to the police is not an act that any citizen is likely on principle to oppose. The names that Kazan and Schulberg (and Cobb himself, another cooperative witness) gave HUAC belonged to colleagues and acquaintances who had committed no crimes whatsoever, much less gangland slayings. By transposing the issue of informing from the politics of entertainment to the underworld of the waterfront, the filmmakers oversimplified the moral conundrum that they themselves faced. Terry's mandatory choice in *On the Waterfront* turns out to be heroic, and a decision for Christ as well. Though the populace may despise the "canary," and his own gang of "Golden Warriors" may repudiate its founder, movie audiences had to respect the guts that this informer exhibits when, badly outnumbered, he tries to secure his "rights" on the waterfront. That climactic shape-up walk resembles Christ's final bearing of the weight of the cross at Calvary and the longshoreman's hook His cross, just as Terry's forehead is bloodied as though from a crown of thorns. Father Barry (Karl Malden) has already called the killing of the second informant, "Kayo" Dugan, "a crucifixion." The jacket that each martyred informer in turn has worn, before it is passed on to Terry, is like the garment of Jesus. (Lloyd C. Douglas's *The Robe* was the bestselling novel of 1953 and was released as a film that same year.) When Terry slams his hand through the window while escaping the mobsters, his wounds are like stigmata. The culture of the Cold War thus managed to convert a Judas figure into a Christ symbol.

3

Other than directing *On the Waterfront*, Kazan kept largely silent for well over three decades on the general question of informing. Even his autobiography skirts the spectrum of ethical and political questions that such testimony raised. His collaborator, Schulberg, was more voluble; though he was never authorized to speak for Kazan too, perhaps no else made a sharper political case for cooperating with HUAC. Schulberg admittedly "expressed doubts" about informing: "It would be inhuman not to. But I truly felt the Communist Party was a menace." For "the idea of a clandestine organization in our democracy" was incompatible with American political values, he explained to Navasky over two decades later; and the domestic version of Stalinism needed exposure as something alien to the liberalism under which it often pretended to march. "I testified," Schulberg added, "because I felt guilty for having contributed unwittingly to intellectual and artistic as well as racial oppression."

In his interview with Navasky, Schulberg offered six justifications for his full compliance with a HUAC subpoena:

1. American Communists and fellow travelers "helped by their silence to create not a blacklist but a death list" in Eastern Europe, and their complicity in Soviet crimes overcame any reluctance that he might have felt about testifying about his nefarious former comrades.

2. Having been a Communist from 1937 until 1940, Schulberg had acquired inside operational knowledge of the Party as "a totalitarian society" even within the United States. Its foreign allegiances demonstrated the hypocrisy of its own commitment to freedom. Had the true believers like John Howard Lawson of the Hollywood Ten and Lillian Hellman "ever got into power," Schulberg speculated, "I think no one would have any freedom." For they were not "civil libertarians" but "thought controllers, as extreme in their way as Joe McCarthy was in his."

3. Schulberg could not imagine doing anything to help the Party that had betrayed the ideals of social justice. He owed his former comrades no loyalty: "They have been toads." Though he also considered himself an opponent of HUAC ("I thought it was a sleazy Committee and I denounced it"), he could not imagine how its inquiry would "incriminate" him. That foreclosed the use of the Fifth Amendment, giving an anti-Communist no real alternative to informing.

4. He gave the committee names that it already had: "There wasn't much new I could add."

5. The retrospective judgment that such committees vastly exaggerated the danger of domestic Communism is unsound, Schulberg asserted: "It's easy to say that the Communist Party here was weak—but it was a splinter in the heart of the United States. What's overlooked is the mind control they were able to exert."

6. Nor was he disturbed—even in the 1970s—by the wrecked careers and wasted talents that the Red Scare wrought: "These people, if they had it in them, could have written books and plays. There was not a blacklist in publishing. There was not a blacklist in the theater." He concluded, "My guilt is what we did to the Czechs, not to Ring Lardner" of the Hollywood Ten.

Schulberg and Kazan were correct in their assessment of the moral squalor of American Communism. As the democratic socialist Irving Howe asserted, "Those who supported Stalinism and its political enterprises, either here or abroad, helped befoul the cultural atmosphere, helped bring totalitarian methods into trade unions, helped perpetrate one of the great lies of the century, helped destroy whatever possibilities there might have been for a resurgence of serious radicalism in America." The democratic imperative of anti-Communism, however, did not constitute a blank check for every action taken in its name, and the principled commitment to an open society did not legitimate every means proposed to reinforce it. That is why the option that Kazan and Schulberg exercised was, of the three choices with which HUAC presented non-Communists, the only course to have generated moral controversy. Kazan and Schulberg did not explicitly condemn other non-Communists for refusing to name names, and therefore the rationale that Schulberg himself offered merits scrutiny.

1. The American Communists and their sympathizers committed many sins of falsification, evasion, distortion, and omission. But it is bizarre to hold them historically accountable for not having prevented or stopped totalitarian terror in Eastern and Central Europe. The Hollywood Communists and fellow travelers had no more power to affect the destiny of Eastern Europe, since totalitarianism is by definition impervious to public opinion, than did the fervent anti-Communists who managed American foreign policy, since any military effort to end Soviet domination might well have devastated the very countries subjected to such tyranny.

2. Membership in the Party produced far more ex-Communists than Communists, largely because it was indeed a totalitarian movement. But however obnoxious their politics, Communists in the entertainment industry did not violate the criminal law. Because the Party engaged in thought control, because its members and sympathizers were not civil libertarians—Schulberg seemed to be telling Navasky—it was unnecessary for anti-Communists to consider the First Amendment applicable. But that is obviously to adopt the values of one's adversaries, not to have a principled democratic position of one's own.

3. If the American Stalinists were such toads and the movement that they promoted in such need of exposure, why wait for a congressional subpoena to combat it in public? The anti-Communism of Kazan and Schulberg was genuine, but it was hardly disinterested. Revulsion coincided with the realization that uncooperative witnesses could not work in Hollywood.

4. In throwing the committee stale morsels rather than raw meat, Schulberg did not realize that the reiteration of certain names might have worsened opportunities that they might have taken to rehabilitate themselves. Schulberg seemed to be assuring Navasky that he inflicted no additional harm upon anyone. But if Communism was so repellent, why *not* wish to harm its proponents? Rationale (3) seems to collide with (1) and (2).

5. The mind control that the Party exerted was over its own members but not over the mass audience, which rarely got any messages at all in its movies—much less Marxism, since the work of writers and directors was subject to the decisions of studios. Not even

HUAC could find much of an ideological virus infecting American films. By 1951, when Schulberg testified, the full force of the Red Scare had effectively inoculated the system against Communism.

6. It is necessary to record the horrible injustice meted out to the Czechs and to other peoples of Eastern and Central Europe. Yet even after acknowledging the systematic terror of Stalinism there, why deny that Ring Lardner, Jr., was penalized for beliefs that were freely—and obtusely—chosen? After vainly invoking the First Amendment, the scenarist went to jail. He lost his livelihood, his opportunities to publish his writing, his reputation in the community. Though no blacklist pervaded the book industry, Lardner's novel *The Ecstasy of Owen Muir* had to be published in England. When it finally appeared here, a decade after the author's prison sentence, the New American Library included it in a series designated as "classics."

Many of the victims were not writers but actors and actresses, who were shut out of television as well as film. Zero Mostel, for example, called himself "a man of a thousand faces, all of them blacklisted." So he became a painter. Bouncing back early in the following decade, especially in the "theater of the absurd," Mostel won two Tony Awards and one Obie within four years for his comic and musical performances. But his was an outsized talent. He had already confronted the politics of the absurd in 1955, when HUAC disapproved of his "imitation of a butterfly at rest," performed under the auspices of *Mainstream* magazine. "There is no crime in making anybody laugh," Mostel argued, "I don't care if you laugh at me." One congressman explained, "If your interpretation of a butterfly at rest brought any money into the coffers of the Communist Party, you contributed directly to the propaganda effort of the Communist Party." "Suppose I had the urge to do the butterfly at rest somewhere?" Mostel inquired. Another congressman advised: "When you have the urge, don't have such an urge to put the butterfly at rest by putting some money in the Communist Party coffers as a result of that urge to put the butterfly to rest. Put the bug to rest somewhere else next time."

Schulberg's argument for career alternatives cut both ways. If Miller could always write behind bars but Kazan and Schulberg could not make movies from there, it was also true that Kazan could have continued directing on Broadway. Schulberg was a successful novelist (*What Makes Sammy Run?*, *The Harder They Fall*, *The Disenchanted*) before winning an Oscar for *On the Waterfront*, and he could have written fiction anywhere that Miller could compose plays. Schulberg himself published a novel entitled *Waterfront*—an enlargement and revision of his screenplay—a year after the film was released, and Kazan eventually abandoned movies to become a successful novelist.

HUAC and the peculiar rules that it established had put a premium on repentance; by overcoming the traditional repugnance against informing, the ex-Communist could win not only absolution but also a job. The indifference of the scalp hunters to the *content* of films, and the niche for social criticism that could still be carved out of mass culture, were illustrated in *A Face in the Crowd* (1957). Directed by Kazan and scripted by Schulberg, this Warner Brothers film assaulted the ease with which the mass media—especially television—could be manipulated. Neither subtle nor oblique, *A Face in the Crowd* slashed melodramatically at national values and contemporary politics in a way that was rare for the 1950s. The patriots looked the other way. Schulberg claimed that the film was intended to suggest McCarthy, who had "used television to destroy others until it helped to destroy him."

Yet television had little to do with the senator's rise—only with his fall, when his coarse personality and methods were exposed for the first time. The daily press deserved far more blame for letting McCarthy manipulate it. The protagonist of *A Face in the Crowd* is a shameless political huckster, an icily ambitious opportunist, a hypocritical scoundrel named "Lonesome" Rhodes (Andy Griffith). A hillbilly singer who wields political power, he has virtually nothing in common with McCarthy, who was a lawyer, a judge, and a U.S. Marine before seeking elective office. Rhodes is closer to provincial good ol' boys like Louisiana governor Jimmy Davis and Texas governor W. Lee "Pappy" O'Daniel, or perhaps even to Ronald Reagan—which suggests how prophetic the movie was. Reviewing *A Face in the Crowd* for a French film magazine, the future director François Truffaut generalized that, "in America, politics always overlaps [with] show business," a comment that was applicable to HUAC itself.

4

Arthur Miller, for example, might well have wryly pondered the overlap. Though he had signed sheaves of leftist petitions, he was not subpoenaed until 1956, after the announcement of the social event that one newspaper headlined as "Pinko Playwright Weds Sex Goddess." Even then, HUAC chairman Francis E. Walter (D-Pa.) privately offered to cancel the hearings into Miller's subversive career for a small fee: the congressman wished to be photographed shaking hands with Marilyn Monroe.

Unlike Kazan, Miller had no Communist past to disown, but the wrath of right-wing patriots was aroused anyway. He had been attached to a host of progressive causes and had been willing to allow Party fronts like the Civil Rights Congress to exploit his name. When Miller's opposition to HUAC became public, the American Legion exerted enough muscle in a couple of towns to close down road company productions of *Death of a Salesman*. The American Legion picketers considered the play "a time bomb under American business." Indeed, "I hoped it was," Miller acknowledged in his 1987 autobiography, wishing that his play might have exploded "this pseudo life that thought to touch the clouds by standing on top of a refrigerator, waving a paid-up mortgage at the moon, victorious at last." Kazan's HUAC testimony had been disingenuous, claiming that this classic anatomy of the drive for success (at the cost of despair, family disintegration, and suicide) "shows the frustrations of the life of a salesman and contains an implicit criticism of his materialistic standards."

After Miller read Marion Starkey's historical account of *The Devil in Massachusetts* (1949), the playwright excitedly told Elia and Molly Kazan that "it's all here—every scene." But though there have never been witches, she demurred, there *are* Communists. Kazan shared his wife's skepticism: "I thought Art's bright idea questionable, and his claim later that his play should not be read for 'contemporary significance' seemed dishonest to me"—since the dramatist was to deny at first that *The Crucible* was as much about 1952 as 1692. For Miller, the parallel had more to do with a general atmosphere of spurious charges, fake "confessions," and betrayal— the phenomenon of mass hysteria—that linked the two epochs. The HUAC hearings, he was to argue, had the same aim as the trials in Salem: the accused were required to confess in public, to denounce their confederates, to show contrition for a repugnant past, and thus cleansed could rejoin decent society. In the mid-twentieth century, "the rituals of guilt and confession followed all the forms of a religious inquisition," Miller later claimed, "except, of course, that the offended parties were not God and his ministers but a congressional committee."

Indeed, he had been on his way to Salem for his first examination of the court records when he visited Kazan, who disclosed that, after initially refusing to cooperate with HUAC, he was going to name names. Miller, who had wanted his close friend to direct the play he was writing, recognized "a certain gloomy logic in what he was saying: unless he came clean he could never hope, at the height of his creative powers, to make another film in America, and he would probably not be given a passport to work abroad either." To be expelled from his world "would be for him like a nightmarish overturning of the earth itself," Miller recalled Kazan saying. The playwright "felt my sympathies going toward him and at the same time I was afraid of him. Had I been of his generation, he would have had to sacrifice me as well. And finally that was all I could think of." Had Arthur Miller spoken at one of those radical meetings in the mid-1930s, Elia Kazan might well have been forced to accuse him too. The writer continued his drive up to Salem, began research at the Historical Society on what became *The Crucible,* and, as he was driving away, heard on the radio the announcement of Kazan's testimony. Though Miller made no explicit public statement about it, his autobiography acknowledges feelings akin to "embarrassment" for Kazan. "It was not his duty to be stronger than he was," Miller reflected. "Who or what was now safer because this man in his human weakness had been forced to humiliate himself? What truth had been enhanced by all this anguish?" And for the first time, the playwright felt embittered toward a nation that was stupidly "throwing away . . . its freedom."

Beatrice Straight and E. G. Marshall discovered that artistic association with the playwright inflicted penalties. After they appeared in *The Crucible* on Broadway in 1953, the roles that they had been offered in television productions were mysteriously withdrawn. Neither actor was politically active, and no reason was given—though the real cause was the threat of a boycott that grocer Laurence Johnson might orchestrate from upstate New York. His Aware, Inc., was willing to penalize actors for nothing other than appearing in an Arthur Miller play. Several months after this realization struck her, Beatrice Straight was telephoned by a priest who taught in a Catholic university.

"I understand that you are on the blacklist," he said.

She told him of her failure to be cast in any new television roles.

"Are you prepared," the priest then asked, "to sign a sworn statement affirming that you are not now and never have been a member of the Communist Party or of any other organization designated by the Attorney General as subversive?"

"I suppose so," the actress replied.

"Are you further prepared to affirm in writing your unswerving loyalty to the Constitution of the United States?"

"Of course."

"Very good," the priest concluded. "In that case, for a fee of $500,

I can have you removed from the blacklist." Thus, the anti-Communism that had begun as a principle (Niebuhr) was transformed into a crusade (Spellman, Graham) before degenerating into a racket.

In 1953 the Belgian-American Association, a business group, invited Miller to attend the Brussels premiere of *The Crucible*. But Ruth Shipley, who headed the Passport Office, decided that it would not be "in the national interest" for the playwright to travel abroad. Miller withdrew his acceptance of the invitation; when the curtain went down on the performance, it was the American ambassador to Belgium who had to stand up in a front row to bask in the prolonged applause. "It didn't harm me, it harmed the country," Miller later commented. "I didn't need any foreign relations."

Miller's next play, *A View from the Bridge*, reached Broadway in 1955. Though it was produced a year after the release of *On the Waterfront*, Miller's drama was not a direct rebuttal to the film, since it was based on a story that he had heard in Red Hook in 1949: a longshoreman informs American immigration authorities that two of his wife's relatives had illegally sneaked in from Italy. Though he is not villainous, his life is destroyed—as Miller later explained—by "the built-in conscience of the community whose existence he had menaced by betraying it." The playwright told critic Nora Sayre that *A View from the Bridge* sought "to throw a different light on the whole informing theme." Though he was admittedly "very upset" that friendly witnesses named names, he was far more troubled by the power that HUAC was allowed to exercise: "I have never ceased to blame the Committee first and foremost."

In the same year as the Broadway production of *A View from the Bridge*, Miller attempted to make a film about teenage gangs in New York, for which he needed the cooperation of the New York City Youth Board. The project was never completed because most of the city commissioners or their deputies voted against it—since the instigator was Miller, who had declined to discuss his politics when presenting his credentials. "I'm not calling him a Communist," one of the officials explained. "My objection is [that] he refuses to repent." What exactly Miller was supposed to feel guilty about—and before which tribunal he was expected to confess—was left unspecified. But so vague a criterion of civic virtue had become pivotal to the culture of the Cold War. "What you repented *of* was of minor importance," Professor Eric Bentley inferred from the episode, "just so long as you repented of it, and it was at least pink."

The incident drew the interest of HUAC, which in the guise of investigating passport abuse summoned Miller a year later. Since the State Department's denial of his trip to Belgium, he had lacked a valid passport. HUAC was blocking the way to London, where he wanted to honeymoon with Miss Monroe and to assist in the British production of *A View from the Bridge*. Though Miller had never even joined any organization on the attorney general's list, though no one had accused him of having broken any law, and though he realized that what was demanded was a ritual of contrition, the playwright did not challenge the congressional prerogative to sniff into his politics. Perhaps because his own situation was so privileged, he never tried to present himself as a martyr to the inquisitorial methods of the committee.

But Miller had signed Civil Rights Congress statements against HUAC itself. In 1947 he had also lent his name to a petition against the prosecution of Gerhart Eisler, the Communist agent who had been arrested two days before his own scheduled HUAC testimony, Attorney General Tom Clark had explained, because of "speeches around the country that were derogatory to our way of life." Though the American Committee for Cultural Freedom criticized him that year for harboring insufficient hostility toward the Soviet Union, Miller was completely independent of the orbit of the Party. He must have been vexed that the Communist novelist Howard Fast, whose rights Miller had also defended, had interpreted *The Crucible* as an assault on the Rosenberg prosecution. When asked about his relationship with the most famous of the friendly witnesses, Miller replied that he had "never attacked" Elia Kazan. HUAC also asked Miller his opinion of Ezra Pound, who was described as an "anti-Communist writer." The interrogation clearly had little if anything to do with passport abuse, or with pending or potential legislation. But in general Miller was a firm and effective witness.

His testimony offered only one novelty item, which was an assertion of the right to find his own ethical marker. Willing to talk about himself, he did not invoke the Fifth Amendment. But when asked whether a certain writer was present at a meeting, Miller refused to jog his memory publicly. For naming names would violate his sense of himself: "My conscience will not permit me to use the name of another person." Betraying others would betray himself. By then no one had wrestled more fully with the moral and political problem of informing, which may be why HUAC wanted Miller to help make this new loyalty test acceptable to his own sizable liberal constituency. But since Miller had committed no crime and was not even an ex-Communist, he saw no reason to feel guilty. Since the other writer he was asked about had already been denounced, Miller saw no point in squirting more oil on the pyre. In refusing to accept betrayal as a civic duty, he relied solely on his conscience.

The refusal to invoke a constitutional right (as Hellman had done) provoked HUAC to ask Congress to issue a contempt citation against him in the summer of 1956. Some legislators balked at punishing so eminent a representative of American letters for the effrontery of not answering a couple of questions. One congressman correctly noted that the playwright had been responsive and respectful and warned that citing the renowned playwright would do America no good abroad. Another New York Democrat inserted into the record a study that Miller's attorney, Joseph Rauh, had submitted to Chairman Walter, a document showing that other witnesses had refused to give names to a committee of Congress and yet had escaped citation. Another congressman asked a member of HUAC, "What legislation has been interfered with because you do not know the names of certain persons associated with this man?" The question struck too close to the *modus operandi* of the committee and elicited no reply. But by a vote of 373 to 9, Miller was cited for contempt of Congress.

The playwright was fined five hundred dollars and given a suspended thirty-day jail sentence, which Rauh appealed. The attorney asked the court: "What could have a more restraining effect on a man's future writing than forcing him publicly to perform an act openly condemned by his current writing?" The question was a peculiar one, since it opened up the implication that a murderer might escape punishment if his novels had glorified homicide. Yet Rauh's query suggested how deeply Miller felt about naming names. Again, like Rauh's other client from the theater, Lillian Hellman, Miller was not against informing in all circumstances. (*All My Sons*, for example, had been triggered by a news report that a young Ohio woman had turned in her father to the FBI for having knowingly manufactured faulty airplane parts for the army.) The dramatist had no reason to believe, however, that anyone who attended the same meetings as he had a decade or two earlier had committed any crimes. Unlike Hellman, he made it plain that he would go to jail rather than name names—a fate that he was spared when the Circuit Court of Appeals unanimously acquitted him in 1958.

The former friends were reunited—at least for artistic purposes— in 1964, when Kazan directed Miller's *After the Fall*, a play in which one character is an ex-Communist who turns informer. It must have been sticky for Kazan to bring out the passion of a scene in which an attorney named Mickey decides to name Party members before the committee. They include his own partner Lou, who turns on Mickey: "You are selling me for your own prosperity. . . . You will ruin me. You will destroy my career. If everyone broke faith there would be no civilization! . . . And it astounds me that you can speak of truth and justice in relation to that gang of cheap publicity hounds. . . . You are terrified! They have bought your soul!"

5

But by then HUAC itself had become too decrepit to enforce such Faustian pacts, having picked its archives clean of the controversial names that would enhance its publicity and provide steady work. After the perjurer Alger Hiss in 1948, the committee never found another traitor. Its power to frighten movie stars and to wreck the careers of scenarists and directors was eroding—a sign that the orthodoxies of the Cold War were easing their grip on public consciousness. By 1959, HUAC was reduced to monitoring contemporary painting, though the unfamiliar subject of abstract expressionism was hardly the stuff of headlines or of popular fascination. In July, Chairman Walter charged that artists contributing to the American National Exhibition in Moscow had "significant" records tainted with Communist causes and fronts. Wheeler Williams, who had sculpted a statue of Senator Robert A. Taft (R-Ohio) in Washington, complained to HUAC that the exhibition had contributed "next to nothing to show the wondrous natural beauty with which God had endowed our beloved land, to portray its glorious history, its heroes or its valiant people of various races, and nothing to picture the wondrous architecture of our cities or charm and beauty of our villages and towns." Such a belief in the uplifting purpose of art sounded oddly like the official aesthetic doctrine of the Soviet Union, and indeed Wheeler admired socialist realism. The president was soon asked about HUAC's venture into art criticism. Whatever else could be decoded from Eisenhower's response, the committee hardly received a ringing endorsement: "Now I think I might have something to say, if we have another exhibition anywhere, to the responsible officials of the methods they produce, or get the juries, and possibly there ought to be one or two people like that, like most of us here say, we are not too certain exactly what art is but we know what we like and what America likes—whatever America likes is after all some of the things that ought to be shown."

A less delphic Supreme Court also became firmer in restricting the scope of congressional inquiry. After *Watkins* v. *U.S.* (1957), committees were prohibited from asking witnesses questions unless the answers would be demonstrably relevant to legislation that such committees were actively considering for submission to Congress. Asserting that "there is no congressional power to expose for the sake of exposure," Chief Justice Warren scolded HUAC for its vagueness in defining which activities were "un-American" and condemned its intrusions into the lives of private citizens—one of whom, in May 1958, made a direct hit at the ethos of surveillance and contrition. Cyrus Eaton could hardly be accused of class *ressentiment*, having made millions of dollars in coal, iron, and steel. He nevertheless became the first person on television to criticize the FBI. For its unsavory role "in investigating, in snooping, in informing, in creeping up on people," the chairman of the board of the Chesapeake & Ohio Railroad compared the bureau to the Gestapo. Eaton denied that there were significant numbers of U.S. Communists, "except in the mind of those on the payroll of the FBI." So explicit a challenge to the bureau's estimation of the Red Menace meant a HUAC subpoena. But protests against the committee were so vocal that the subpoena was never served on the maverick capitalist. "No useful purpose can be served," Congressman Walter averred, "by permitting Mr. Eaton to repeat the groundless accusations that Iron Curtain countries have used for propaganda purposes." Eaton remarked soon thereafter that some members of HUAC were "not noted for their intellectual depth or high ethical standards."

Then in April 1959 a former president of the United States, Harry Truman, labeled HUAC the "most un-American thing in the country today." The son of another president, Representative James Roosevelt (D-Cal.), soon called for its abolition. HUAC became so weakened that Hoover gave the committee his most precious treasure—the list of the FBI's own Party informants, whom he normally saved for use as surprise witnesses in Smith Act and sedition trials. When HUAC held hearings in San Francisco in 1960, student protests were so vigorous that the police used violence to quell them. Hoover called these demonstrations the biggest "communist coup" in twenty-five years—thus inadvertently revealing the impotence of the enemy during the span of the Cold War. "It *can* happen here," he warned.

The first lines of defense against domestic Communism had collapsed. When HUAC was reduced to investigating an organization called Women Strike for Peace in 1962, Herblock lampooned a congressman arriving late and wondering, "Which was it that was un-American—women or peace?" The FBI had placed the group under surveillance since its birth in 1961, when an estimated fifty thousand women (virtually all white and middle class) engaged in peaceful demonstrations against the threat of nuclear war. When a member of HUAC asked the leader of the group "whether you would

knowingly permit or encourage a Communist Party member to oc-
cupy a leadership position in Women Strike for Peace," Dagmar
Wilson of Washington, D.C., responded: "Well, my dear sir, I have
absolutely no way of controlling, do not desire to control, who
wishes to join in the demonstrations and the efforts that the women
strikers have made for peace. In fact I would like to go even further.
I would like to say that unless everybody in the whole world joins
us in this fight, then God help us." Asked about whether she planned
to expel Communists from the leadership of the organization, Mrs.
Wilson replied, "Certainly not." Though a few earlier "progressive"
witnesses had been truculent in their HUAC testimony, a non-Communist had now openly surmounted the committee's limits of legitimate political behavior and association.

Then came ridicule. Mort Sahl satirized the countersubversive
imagination by remarking that whenever the Soviets threw someone
in jail, HUAC retaliated—"by throwing an American in jail." In
1966 Jerry Rubin responded to his HUAC summons by arriving in
the uniform of a Revolutionary War soldier, cheerfully blowing soap
bubbles. Then Abbie Hoffman showed up wearing the star-spangled
banner as a shirt, which so outraged Capitol guards that they ripped
it off, only to expose the Cuban flag painted on Hoffman's bare back.
The future founders of the Youth International Party (Yippies)
trounced the committee by spinning publicity in their favor, turning
a yoke into a joke. A HUAC subpoena had become an invitation to
send in the clowns—and an occasion for political counterattack.
Other witnesses eagerly testified about their revolutionary intentions, feeling none of the shame that had once been the whole point
of the exercise. Instead, a new generation relished the chance to
come under the Capitol Hill klieg lights and proclaim their radicalism—just as the authors of *The Communist Manifesto* had defined appropriate revolutionary conduct little more than a century
earlier: "The Communists disdain to conceal their views and aims.
They openly declare that their ends can be attained by the forcible
overthrow of all existing social conditions."

One of the most decisive blows to the culture of the Cold War
was struck by a former aide to Senator McCarthy himself, Attorney
General Robert Kennedy, who later explained to an interviewer that,
early in the 1950s, he "thought there was a serious internal security
threat to the United States; I felt at that time that Joe McCarthy
seemed to be the only one who was doing anything about it. I was
wrong." One of the injustices of that era that Kennedy later had the
power to rectify involved Junius Scales, the only person ever to be
incarcerated for the federal crime of *membership* in the Communist

party. The situation was freakish. Scales had never been accused of espionage or of any criminal act. He had not attempted to overthrow the government by force and violence, nor had he *advocated* its overthrow, nor had he *conspired* to advocate its overthrow. He was jailed for joining a party whose *leaders* had been convicted of conspiring to advocate its overthrow. Yet he was sentenced to a longer prison term than the leading Communists who were convicted under other sections of the Smith Act. After Soviet tanks rumbled into Hungary in 1956, Scales got so disillusioned that he had become an ex-Communist by the time he began to serve his seven-year sentence in October 1961.

Soon liberal and socialist anti-Communists, such as Rauh and Norman Thomas, were urging Kennedy to pardon Scales. There was only one impediment to a gesture of mercy. Even though the prisoner had broken with the Party, he refused on principle to finger his former comrades. Loyalty to this code infuriated Hoover, who told the attorney general that Scales's release would make it impossible for the bureau to require other Communists and ex-Communists to name names. Over the director's protests, Scales was sprung loose and was reunited with his family on Christmas Eve 1962. Hoover, though an active churchman, had put Cold War dogmas ahead of charity—unlike Kennedy, who had not yet been born when Hoover had taken charge of the FBI. That was the historic significance of the decision to overrule Hoover. "The act of granting clemency to Scales without his 'cooperation' by 'naming names' is a repudiation of the loyalty test long used by the FBI and these Congressional investigating committees," Rauh concluded. Finally, "an Attorney General has refused to treat a man's unwillingness to inform on others as a ground for withholding favorable government action in his case."

6

REELING:

THE POLITICS OF FILM

The movie industry was conscripted into the Cold War in 1947 when HUAC was invited to Los Angeles. The committee's host was the Motion Picture Alliance for the Preservation of American Ideals, an organization that struck a typical postwar stance in asserting that "co-existence is a myth and neutrality is impossible . . . anyone who is not FIGHTING Communism is HELPING Communism." About fifteen hundred members of the film community had founded the alliance three years earlier; they included John Wayne, Gary Cooper, Walt Disney, Adolphe Menjou, and Cecil B. De Mille. Its first president was director Sam Wood, who felt so strongly about the subject that his will imposed as a condition of inheritance that his relatives (other than his wife) file affidavits in court that they "are not now, nor have they ever been, Communists."

When the alliance was established, Hollywood was tentatively helping Communism rather than fighting it, because in 1944 the Red Army was fighting against the Third Reich. The American cinema was never saturated with Red propaganda, but it did go through a rose period when three pro-Russian movies were released. The most political of these films was Michael Curtiz's *Mission to Moscow* (1943), which was based on the memoirs of Joseph E. Davies, Roosevelt's ambassador to the Soviet Union (1936–41). Davies had been so diplomatic about Stalinist tyranny that the film version was nicknamed *Submission to Moscow.* The ambassador (Walter Huston) is shown justifying the purge trials, the Nazi-Soviet pact, and the Red Army invasion of Finland. Warner Brothers, a New Dealish studio, produced this apologia under the impression that Roosevelt would be pleased. Stalin certainly was. After Davies took prints of the film to Moscow, the dictator personally endorsed the film for distribution throughout the Motherland.

Though Hellman later scoffed at the idea that there had ever "been a single line or word of Communism in any American picture at any time," her own script for *The North Star* (1943) managed to promote pro-Russian sentiments without the ideological clumsiness of *Mission to Moscow*. Indeed, this RKO film about a village collective resisting German invaders exuded Hollywood production values. Produced by Sam Goldwyn, directed by Lewis Milestone, scored by Aaron Copland (with lyrics by Ira Gershwin), *The North Star* boasted an all-star cast that included Dana Andrews, Anne Baxter, Walter Huston, Farley Granger, Erich von Stroheim, Ann Harding, and Walter Brennan. Though Hellman was sufficiently proud of her screenplay to have it published, its depiction of the selfless nobility of the Russian peasants is hardly fraught with the complexity of dramatic interest. Communism is neither depicted nor mentioned in this coy film, which even neglects to indicate that the setting is Russia—a locale that can be inferred only from the lovely costumes and sets. Mary McCarthy's review of *The North Star* complained that the collective seemed so autonomous that the characters were like "feudal Serbian mountaineers, or Norwegian fishermen, acting naively on their own initiative."

M-G-M's *Song of Russia* (1944) was the third movie that put America's morally problematic ally in a favorable light. Devoid of any serious ideas (including political ideas), it starred Robert Taylor as an American conductor who tours the USSR prior to the German invasion and falls in love with a peasant (Susan Peters). After visiting her at her parents' farm (which is not revealed as a collective), they get married. The dance number described as "a traditional Russian wedding dance" looks suspiciously like the Charleston. This musical implies that Hitler's Operation Barbarossa is evil largely because it separates the newlyweds: she goes off to make Molotov cocktails while her countrymen burn their own villages before the Nazis arrive. The wartime message is conveyed when Taylor returns home to tell *his* countrymen that "we are soldiers side by side—in the fight for all humanity."

As the political climate changed again after World War II, such films began to look more sinister than silly—especially to HUAC, which sensed a marvelous opportunity for publicity and accepted the alliance's invitation to expose cinematic Communism. The most anti-Semitic member of Congress, HUAC's John Rankin (D-Miss.), was especially keen on an investigation. He charged that conspirators seeking to "overthrow the government" had their "headquarters in Hollywood," which he called "the greatest hotbed of subversive activities in the United States." But though Rankin put on the record the peculiar, alien names with which some movie stars had been born, the hearings were not a striking success for the committee. In 1947, a case could be made that Communists in government service might endanger the nation's security, but the peril that scenarists and directors posed was far less obvious. Major newspapers like the *New York Times*, the *New York Herald Tribune*, the *Washington Post*, and the *Detroit Free Press* not only failed to echo the Hearst chain's demand for federal censorship of movies but editorially denounced the unfairness of procedures that enabled HUAC to act as prosecutor, judge, and jury. A Gallup poll showed that 36 percent of Americans queried were against the film industry investigations, and 37 percent were for them. Even the Hollywood Ten—the Communist writers and directors who had invoked the First Amendment when queried about their politics—initially galvanized support from some top directors and stars and were confident that the Supreme Court would eventually overturn their contempt of Congress citations.

But one of the friendly witnesses spearheaded the drive to rewrite the messages that Hollywood had transmitted during World War II into anti-Communist ones. In this instance, the alteration of her Russian Jewish name did not seem to bother Congressman Rankin. *Née* Alissa Rosenbaum in St. Petersburg, Ayn Rand had been an extra in De Mille's *King of Kings* (1926) before becoming a screenwriter for Universal, Paramount, and M-G-M in the 1930s. She also became a scourge of collectivism (which included the New Deal), had campaigned for Wendell Willkie in 1940, and three years later published her novel *The Fountainhead*. By 1952, an astonishing two million copies had been sold, though her adaptation for the 1949 Warner Brothers film was not a hit.

By then, however, Rand had taken on another role. Insofar as HUAC showed any particular concern with the ideological orientation of the American cinema, the impetus came as much from her as from anyone else. Thus, Rand contributed to the starboard drift of the culture of the Cold War. She was especially angered by *Song of Russia*, and her testimony challenging its presentation of Soviet life led Congressman John McDowell (R-Pa.) to remark: "You paint a very dismal picture of Russia. . . . Doesn't anybody smile in Russia any more?" Not even Rand's closest associates ever claimed that she had much of a sense of humor, and she replied, "Well, if you ask me literally, pretty much no." A skeptical McDowell pressed her: "They don't smile?" Rand elaborated upon her earlier answer: "Not quite that way, no. If they do, it is privately and accidentally. Certainly, it is not social. They don't smile in approval of their system." Rand's stern response became famous, but less noticed at the time was her denunciation of the hugely successful *The Best Years of Our Lives* (1946), which happened to show a banker's reluctance to give a war veteran a G.I. loan. William Wyler's film thus amplified "the party line of making the returned soldier fear that the world is against him" and "that business is against him," she charged. Rand added that "it was much more important to show the really serious propaganda show going on right now, and about America" than to pillory the obvious disinformation that wartime movies like *Song of Russia* projected.

Her ambition to unmask the insidious content of films was not widely shared, even by other friendly witnesses. "I do not believe the Communists have ever at any time been able to use the motion-picture screen as a sounding board for their philosophy or their ideology," Ronald Reagan told HUAC. Scenarist Rupert Hughes, a founder of the Motion Picture Alliance for the Preservation of American Ideals, argued that no open Communist propaganda could be found on the screen. But Hughes also told HUAC that "where you see a little drop of cyanide in the picture, a small grain of arsenic, something that makes every Senator, every businessman, every employer a crook and which destroys our beliefs in American free enterprise and free institutions, that is communistic." Robert Taylor could not cite any specific examples of Communist propaganda in films (not even the one in which he had starred). Nor could Menjou, though he conjectured that propaganda might be done with merely a glance or an inflection. This was not helpful.

Rand therefore filled this vacuum with her pamphlet *Screen Guide for Americans* (1950), which provided instructions for scenarists, directors, and producers. "The purpose of the Communists in Hollywood is *not* the production of political movies openly advocating Communism," she announced. "Their purpose is *to corrupt our moral premises by corrupting non-political movies . . . making people absorb the basic principles of Collectivism by indirection and implication.*" Since Rand associated the New Deal itself with collectivism, her definition of Communism was rather expansive, apparently embracing Roosevelt's effort to regulate and restrain the excesses of capitalism. "Don't Smear Industrialists . . . don't smear the Free Enterprise System. . . . Don't Smear Success," she warned filmmakers. "Don't give your character—as a sign of villainy, as a damning characteristic—a desire to make money. . . . Don't ever use any lines about 'the common man' or 'the little people.' It is not the American idea to be either 'common' or 'little.'. . . It is the moral duty of every decent man in the motion picture industry to throw into the ash can, where it belongs, every story that smears industrialists as such." Rand herself defiantly wore a gold brooch in the form of the dollar sign and lamented that the most grievous American fault was too much altruism. Her own favorite contemporary novelist, she said, was Mickey Spillane ("a true moralist").

Screen Guide for Americans was distributed by the Motion Picture Alliance and was reprinted on the front page of the entertainment section of the *New York Times*. Several other newspapers reprinted the pamphlet as well. And even though she was privately contemptuous of the committee members (apart from Nixon), who were "intellectually out of their depth, and motivated by a desire for headlines," her influence could be deduced from HUAC's 1951 report. "We are less interested in a film that has [a] Communist context, where a few hundred people will come and see it," HUAC announced. "We are more interested in an ordinary John-and-Mary picture where there is only a drop of progressive thought in it." Rand gave herself credit, which was partly correct, for the disappearance from the screen of certain sorts of businessmen, who ceased to be "crooks" and "chiselers," the occasional felons of movies in the 1930s and 1940s. But depictions of "the chromium jungle" in *Executive Suite* (1954), *The Man in the Gray Flannel Suit* (1956), and *Patterns* (1956) hardly showed the absence of tension and conflict. In these movies unsympathetic bosses remain, intense competition causes coronaries, and domestic harmony can be strained. Left unquestioned, however, is the legitimacy of the corporate system itself. Rand's own later books were so eccentric and pretentious that they met a hostile reception even on the right, where—in the *National Review*, for instance—Chambers blasted the "mischief" of the "materialist ideas" in her novel *Atlas Shrugged*. But that 1957 saga of selfishness still found 125,000 buyers upon publication, and eventually over two million copies were sold. And Hollywood would very carefully monitor the political and economic signals that it would send to its audiences after her *Screen Guide for Americans*.

1

It was safer to produce films without any political or economic themes or implications at all. Although *Broken Arrow* (1950) had presented Cochise sympathetically as a peace-loving Apache, Monogram Studios abandoned its plans for a movie on Hiawatha, whose efforts to achieve peace among the Iroquois nations might be interpreted as a boost to Communist peace propaganda. Because novelist Theodore Dreiser had formally converted to Communism shortly before his death in 1945, Paramount got the jitters in adapting his classic of a generation earlier, *An American Tragedy*. So director George Stevens toned down the social analysis and highlighted the romance in *A Place in the Sun* (1951). Stevens's protagonist (Montgomery Clift) is no longer a victim of certain class relationships that Dreiser had shown motivating Clyde Griffiths toward homicide. Then even the inflated love story posed a problem when supporting actress Anne Revere took the Fifth Amendment, so Paramount cut out most of her major scenes. In the new climate, Wyler doubted whether he would have been able to make *The Best Years of Our Lives*, or whether John Ford could have directed *The Grapes of Wrath* (1940).

Certainly, *The North Star* would have been inconceivable. When shown on television in 1957, it was renamed *Armored Attack*, and it had been edited in a video equivalent of Orwell's Ministry of Truth, turning the politics of the film upside down. Comments are inserted throughout *Armored Attack* to repudiate the sentiments that had animated *The North Star*. A new ending was added as well—documentary footage showing Russian tanks suppressing the Hungarian Revolution of the previous year. Just in case the audience still did not get the point, a narrator announces that the valor of the peasants depicted in *Armored Attack* should not obscure the brutality of the Soviet leadership, which was equated with the German invaders who are repelled in the film. A voice-over prologue nevertheless apologizes for any pro-Soviet impressions that might have inadvertently remained.

But normally it was prudent to avoid overtly political films. Consider, for instance, the fate of Universal's *The Senator Was Indiscreet* (1947), a satire about a bumbling Senator (William Powell) who does not realize that a new income tax bill applies to him as well. He runs for the presidency on a platform that includes adding his relatives to the payroll and giving every citizen the right to attend Harvard. The movie also dares to suggest that White House aspirants can be packaged with images that can maximize their appeal to the electorate. *The Senator Was Indiscreet* was written by Charles MacArthur, was rewritten and produced by Nunnally Johnson, and was the only movie that George S. Kaufman ever directed. None of the three was a political activist. All were renowned for their wit, which was lost on Congresswoman Clare Boothe Luce (R-Conn.) when it was screened for her. "Was this picture made by an American?" she demanded to know. *Life,* which her husband published, retracted its own favorable review of the film in a column called "On Second Thought." Editorials in other forums, plus the American Legion, also attacked the un-American propaganda of *The Senator Was Indiscreet.* Having approved the script, the Motion Picture Association of America had somehow missed its incendiary implications, leaving the trade organization with only the option of prohibiting the showing of *The Senator Was Indiscreet* overseas, which it did.

Partly as a result, the few dozen political films that were released in the postwar era bristled with titles like *The Iron Curtain* (1948), *The Red Menace* (1949), *The Red Danube* (1949), *Red Snow* (1952), and *The Steel Fist* (1952). The election year of 1952 was the peak, when twelve explicitly anti-Communist films were produced. Though Elizabeth Taylor and Robert Taylor were featured in *Conspirator* (1950) and John Wayne glamorized HUAC in *Big Jim McLain,* very few of these movies had large budgets or major stars. They were shot on the cheap and usually ended up as the second features on double bills. Because strongly ideological films were considered unlikely to attract the masses anyway, the studios apparently reasoned that anti-Communist pictures might mollify the American Legion and right-wingers in Congress without losing too much money. And although Menjou had predicted to HUAC that such movies "would be an incredible success," the studios' apprehensions proved correct: most of them bombed at the box office.

How was domestic Communism depicted in the films of the Cold War? Its adherents show no respect for national sanctums and symbols, which Party members traduce. They treat the Stars and Stripes with contempt. They conspire to meet one another by carrying an edition of *Reader's Digest* or a TWA flight bag and by picking such agreeable settings as the Boston Public Garden amid the swan boats. Communists are rude, humorless, and "cruel to animals," Nora Sayre noticed. "But we don't know how they treat children, since they never have any." Women in the Party are either disturbingly unfeminine, downright unattractive, or nearly nymphomaniacs. Bereft of the experience of "normal" love, they use sex for political seduction. A Party target in Republic Pictures' *The Red Menace* tells a blonde *femme fatale:* "I always thought the Commies peddled bunk. I didn't know they came as cute as you." After the comely comrade lets the dupe kiss her, she teasingly withdraws, then gives him a copy of *Das Kapital.*

But "idealism" is even more effective bait. In *I Was a Communist for the FBI*, Matt Cvetic (Frank Lovejoy) is shocked when he attends his first Party convention. His comrades, who have gathered to honor Gerhart Eisler, reveal their actual disdain for the modesty and simplicity of the poor by throwing a lavish banquet in a luxury hotel. Gorging themselves with caviar and guzzling bottles of costly wine, the Communists revel in a corruption that mocks the dedicated idealism that presumably drew Cvetic into the Party. Unfazed, one of its leaders sneers, "This is the way we're *all* gonna live after we take over the country!" The protagonist is depicted as an ordinary Pittsburgh steel worker, which makes him far less susceptible to the Party's sucker tactics than intellectuals, liberals, blacks, and nougat-soft teachers like Eve Merrick (Dorothy Hart). Far from trying to live up to the ideal of equality, the Party scorns the aspirations of ethnic and racial minorities; underdogs are good for kicking.

I Was a Communist for the FBI was typical of these formulaic movies. It purported to be "based on the story of" Cvetic, who told it to a ghost writer for the *Saturday Evening Post*. Hoover had recruited Cvetic for undercover work in the Party, which is shown exploiting liberal sentiments rather than deserving them. The film promotes distrust of the Bill of Rights, suggesting that a desire to strengthen it emanates from the Kremlin, which is campaigning to torpedo the authority of HUAC. As for non-Communist "suckers," a Party organizer grins: "Let them howl their heads off about the rape of the First Amendment. We need some pinko chumps."

Blacks, who overestimate the scale of the bigotry directed against them, and union members, who might sometimes favor strikes, are especially soft touches for Communist propaganda. The film implies that *any* opposition to the conservative drift of the American government may well be orchestrated from Moscow. These are the lessons that the cinematic Cvetic picks up in the underground, from which he surfaces to warn loyal Americans about the cunning of his erstwhile comrades. Though he achieves the catharsis of beating up a Party functionary, *I Was a Communist for the FBI* has an even more rousing finale. As "The Battle Hymn of the Republic" booms on the soundtrack, director Gordon Douglas's camera executes its last shot: a close-up of a tiny bust of Abraham Lincoln. Though mostly fictional, the movie seemed so plausible an account of Communist activities and intentions ("to deliver America to Russia as a slave," Cvetic testifies) that it was nominated for an Oscar as best feature-length documentary of 1951.

I Was a Communist for the FBI became a 1952 radio series as well, with Dana Andrews as the protagonist. Each week he had to work effectively enough as an undercover agent to defeat evil, but not enough to blow the rest of the series. As though to heighten the contrast between "the American way of life" and its Stalinist adversaries, Andrews's voice operated in two different ranges. Playing Matt Cvetic, FBI informant, he spoke with the resonance of star-spangled radio heroes. But in his "Communist" persona, historian Richard Gid Powers noticed, Andrews seemed slower and dumber, as though adapting to the cumbersome mental habits of his comrades, who "sounded like Peter Lorre and referred to guns as 're-wolwers.'"

Such media attention catapulted Cvetic himself onto the lecture circuit. As an "expert" on Communism, he made sixty-three appearances before various official committees and named about three hundred persons as Communists. Among them, however, were several congressmen, since Communists were alleged to have infiltrated both the Republican and Democratic parties. Soon his testimony became discredited. Defense attorneys for plaintiffs who lost their jobs in Pennsylvania because of his accusations sometimes challenged his reliability, since Cvetic had been hospitalized both for mental illness and for chronic alcoholism. He eventually joined the John Birch Society. Attributing his drinking problems to the "constant harassments and smears by Communists," Cvetic suffered a fatal heart attack only eleven years after *I Was a Communist for the FBI* made him something of a national hero.

The most striking characteristic of celluloid Communism, however, is not the Party's contempt for liberals or its hypocrisy but its hardened criminality, its proclivity for the raw violence that also pervaded gangster pictures. Indeed, in *Pickup on South Street* (1953), the "Commies" are *more* dangerous and *more* brutal than ordinary criminals, who at least adhere to their own code of honor. The plot of this Samuel Fuller film, featuring Richard Widmark and Jean Peters, revolves around the theft of microfilm intended to provide atomic secrets for the Soviet Union. (When *Pickup on South Street* was dubbed into French, heroin was substituted for the microfilm, without apparently making the movie any less comprehensible.)

Earlier gangster pictures had conveyed a measure of empathy for their desperate protagonists as creatures of nasty social conditions. But the Cold War movies shifted audience sympathy toward the representatives of justice and authority—especially the FBI. Occasionally Communists are given at least superficial motives for joining the Party—"idealism," anti-Fascism, even poverty. But the sentiments of the "bleeding hearts" are inevitably betrayed, the

Russians show themselves to be as vicious as Fascists, and the corrupt Party functionaries reveal that their identification with the working class is a sham. Defection and redemption can, however, provide a happy ending—unless the Communists, racing through the streets in their sleek limousines, use their tommy guns to rub out the renegades before the "stool pigeons" reach the haven of an FBI office.

2

The film that most feverishly reflected the political traumas of the Cold War was *My Son John* (1952). Indeed, if it did not exist, students of Red Scare movies would have been compelled to invent it. When HUAC had conducted its 1947 hearings in Hollywood, Chairman Parnell Thomas had asked Leo McCarey, whose credits included Oscars for directing *The Awful Truth* (1937) and *Going My Way* (1944), if he thought anti-Communist movies would enlighten Americans about the crisis. McCarey himself was a friendly witness who would join De Mille three years later in urging members of the Screen Directors Guild to take a loyalty oath, and he stumbled through a reply. He did tell HUAC, however, that his *Going My Way* and *The Bells of St. Mary's* (1945) had not generated any income from the Soviet Union because "I have a character in there that they do not like." When his interrogator guessed Bing Crosby, the director corrected him: "No, God." Five years after his HUAC testimony, Paramount contributed to public education about atheistic Communism with a film that McCarey produced as well as directed. The script, which he coauthored with Myles Connolly, was nominated for an Oscar, though not necessarily because of its virtues, which very few reviewers detected. The nomination of *My Son John* was a cue to HUAC that Hollywood was vigilant.

Since the movies of the era were not permitted to locate the motivations for turning toward Communism in economic or social conditions, since themes of class and race, injustice, and impoverishment contradicted the complacent ideology of the 1950s, *My Son John* pursued the logical consequences of the only dramatically plausible alternative. For McCarey defined the family not only as the refuge of security and comfort against the pressures of the public realm, and not only as the traditional institution that best justified the remorseless struggle against Communism. The family could also be seen as the source of the problem. The dynamics of parenting were as much a source of danger as the impersonal historical forces that lurked outside (but that could no longer be depicted cinematically).

To play John Jefferson's mother, Lucille, Helen Hayes returned to the screen for her first starring role in seventeen years. Her two other sons, Ben and Chuck, are two clean-cut football players who have eagerly enlisted for the Korean War, "fighting on God's side." But when John (Robert Walker), whom she adores even more than her "fighting halfbacks," fails to come home from Washington for the farewell party, Lucille suspects that something is wrong. When John later comes back to visit, he shocks his mother by making fun of the forthright loyalty that his father, Dan (Dean Jagger), displays toward the American Legion and by arguing that perhaps the books of the Bible should be understood symbolically rather than literally. For Lucille, this is blasphemy. Unable to control herself, she forces her son to swear on the Bible that he is not and never was a Communist. John seems to have no compunction about taking such an oath, and his mother is reassured. After all, she concludes, John is "just a liberal. Saint Paul was a liberal."

But after John returns to his mysterious job in the capital, Lucille hears that the FBI is investigating him as a possible security leak. She interprets the mere fact of an investigation as though her own suspicions about her son have been corroborated. And when she discovers that he has been dating a woman (Irene Winston) who is also suspected of espionage, Lucille becomes even more certain. The full vindication of such suspicions, however, depends upon a twist in the plot. John has mistakenly left his key to his girlfriend's apartment in a pair of torn pants that he gave to his mother to donate for charity. With the key in her possession, Lucille flies to Washington and discovers that she can get into the apartment of the spy, the woman for whom John has in effect betrayed his own mother. Fearing that Lucille is hiding the key that he cannot find, he even twists her wrist as he asserts, "There are millions on our side." But when her clenched hand opens to reveal not a key but a rosary, she responds, "There are millions on *my* side."

Because of her son's hostility to the hyper-patriotism and fundamentalism that were inculcated at home, Lucille has begun to question his loyalty. Realizing that John is a Red, she also deduces that he must be a spy—a logic that the film fully endorses. She therefore turns her son over to the FBI, making a forceful and lengthy speech in front of one of its agents, a steady man named Stedman (Van Heflin), to whom she wants John to confess. But he refuses to admit his perfidy, which leaves a good citizen no choice. Collapsing on a sofa, Lucille shouts to the G-man: "Take him away! He has to be punished!" Eventually her son agrees to confess and phones the FBI office to announce his decision, realizing that he had sunk into moral corruption so deep that repentance is required. But as he rushes to cleanse himself, his Party comrades dispose of him with a slaying (gangland-style) on the steps of the Lincoln Memorial. Fortunately, John had taped a speech that he had expected to deliver at the commencement ceremonies of his alma mater. The recorded voice addresses the stunned graduates, who are warned that "even now, the eyes of Soviet agents are on some of you. . . . I am a living lie." John posthumously concludes, "I am a traitor, I am a native. American. Communist. Spy. And may God have mercy on my soul."

How could John have gone wrong? Since the appeal of Communism could not be attributed to larger social conditions, it had to be psychologized. Since the sources of this plague could not traced to bosses or bankers or bigots or cops, *My Son John* inexorably targeted parents instead. Ironically, the film converted into a question the very institution—the family—that was supposed to provide an answer. The haven that domesticity and privacy represented need not offer protection against the evil of politics; it could also stimulate the politics of evil. Hence the unpleasant characterization of actor Robert Walker, who died so suddenly during the production that *My Son John* had to be padded with scenes inserted from Alfred Hitchcock's *Strangers on a Train* (1951). "In a period when sexual or political 'deviation' were considered equally disgusting," Nora Sayre observed, "he's sly, furtive, flirtatious with his mother and simmering with snide hostility toward his father. . . . His overconfident smile hardly ever falls out of his face, even after he camps up an ultra-patriotic song as his father clenches his fists in fury." The syndrome was unmistakable. The father is emotionally remote and insensitive, and he truculently roars that, if John should ever turn out to be a Communist, "I'd take you out in the backyard and give it to you with both barrels!" Lucille is overprotective and possessive, flighty, and even somewhat hysterical. She is a textbook Mom to be blamed for what the feminist Betty Friedan would later call the "murky smog" of male homosexuality that was "spreading" across America. Audiences watching *My Son John* had little choice except to infer that such parents bore responsibility for Communism too.

John's own diagnosis differed, however. "I was going to help to make a better world," his taped legacy explains to the graduates. "I was flattered when I was immediately recognized as an intellect. I was invited to homes where only superior minds communed. It excited my freshman fancy to hear daring thoughts." Since Lucille remarks that John has always been studious ("he has more degrees than a thermometer"), since the father—an elementary school principal—insists that he himself is "not bright" (perhaps to trump his supercilious son), and since John feels closer to his professor than to his own uneducated parents, the movie warns that intellectual vitality ("daring thoughts") is the first temptation on the slippery slope toward espionage. Not only John's personality but also his mind has been perverted.

My Son John also tipped audiences off to another telltale sign of Communism. "We take care of you in this world, father," John snickers at a parish priest who is collecting for charity, "and you *promise* to take care of us in the next." In this and other films of the 1950s, Communism is so incompatible with Christianity that Party members even look uncomfortable when someone realizes, "It's time for mass." Christianity can be a fighting faith, as when the father slams the family Bible on John's head and then hurls his antireligious son to his knees. The movie opens with all the Jeffersons—except the absent John—going to church, and it concludes with the grieving parents entering a chapel to pray for the soul of their wayward son.

Though such conflicts cannot be resolved within so shattered a family, *My Son John* makes it clear that not even the church can salvage a family that has produced a Communist, nor can it absolve these parents of their guilt. It is not a priest who counsels anguished souls, who hears the confessions of the contrite, who delivers what amounts to a eulogy, and who heals the wounded. It is Stedman, the FBI agent, who offers the reasonable and legitimate alternative to the father's solution ("both barrels") and thus discredits and displaces the authority of the father. But by vindicating Lucille's suspicions and requiring her to become an informer, *My Son John* also undercuts the function of the mother. By making her choose love of her country over love for her son, the film violates the sanctity of the home that maternal care was supposed to ensure. By surrendering her own flesh and blood to the state, she has elevated the FBI above even so primary an institution as the family and has correspondingly devalued the emotional loyalties that patriotic vigilance was supposed to protect. *My Son John* thus unintentionally springs a trap on the sort of anti-Communism that made informing into a civic obligation and even a noble act.

Though Gary Cooper had told HUAC in 1947 that he could sniff out Communism because "it isn't on the level," these films inadvertently reveal that Moscow had no monopoly on duplicity. In *Big Jim McLain*, Wayne and a HUAC colleague check out the effectiveness of their surveillance equipment by eavesdropping on their honeymooning neighbors in a Hawaiian bungalow. In *My Son John*, Stedman uses an automobile accident to gain entrance to the Jefferson house. Without disclosing his identity as an FBI agent, he shows enough interest in Lucille's sons to win her trust and extract information from her. The bureau trails her to the apartment of John's girlfriend in Washington, then films the humiliating confirmation of Lucille's hunch that her son is a Communist spy. By endorsing official snooping, which the Fourth Amendment is generally supposed to prevent, the film further sabotaged the sacrosanct character of the family and strained the ideology of the Cold War past the breaking point. Critic Robert Warshow pointed out that *My Son John* represented "a wrong way, a dangerous way, to be anti-Communist"; for "what is being upheld is, precisely, stupidity." McCarey never quite recovered his equilibrium after the critical barbecuing that he received, even from Catholic journals like *America* and *Commonweal*; and a superlative directing career that had skyrocketed with *Duck Soup* (1933) was stalled. Perhaps the difficulties of making the transition from Groucho to Karl Marx also signified that, even at the nadir of the Red Scare, counterforces were strong enough to resist the right-wing definition of American values.

The merger of the underground and the underworld in such films, which equated conspiratorial Communism with organized crime, also turned out to be doubly ironic. Historical evidence in the form of memoirs, oral history, and documentation overwhelmingly repudiates the image of the Party's violence-prone thuggery. Consisting mostly of meetings, the life of the Party was in fact rather dull; and the typical Communist was far more familiar with the mimeograph machine than the machine gun. Even Cvetic, who had once testified that the Communists planned assassinations, was forced to concede that during his seven years as an undercover agent, he never saw any of his comrades kill anybody.

The FBI nevertheless tracked Communists so obsessively that little energy or interest was left over for the pursuit of actual criminals. Even as the bureau was fighting Communists on the screen as though they were gangsters, the real gangsters were ignored. Ever since 1933, Hoover had denied that an entity such as organized crime even existed, and two decades later he was still calling the idea of a national crime syndicate "baloney." But late in 1957, a New York state police sergeant stumbled across a conference of six dozen Mafia dons in the upstate town of Apalachin, making the FBI director's earlier statements suddenly inoperative. William P. Rogers, who served as attorney general under Eisenhower, acknowledged that Hoover had to be pushed "kicking and screaming" into investigating the machinations of the underworld, which flourished while the bureau's attention was diverted elsewhere. In 1959, a year before the top G-man first publicly conceded that maybe something like a syndicate existed, the FBI's New York office had assigned only four of its agents to investigating organized crime. Four hundred agents— or a hundred times that number—were then monitoring the activities of Communists.

3

Willingness to make these lurid and simplistic movies was not only a loyalty test for Hollywood, participation in these projects also became such a test *in* Hollywood. Actors, writers, and directors would be asked to work on a film like *The Red Menace*, and their refusal to do so encouraged the inference of Party membership or sympathies. After Joseph Losey declined RKO's offer to direct *I Married a Communist*, he was blacklisted, and by 1951 he had gone into exile in England. (When the film was released, *Time* hailed it as "a celluloid bullet aimed at the U.S.S.R.") Even Kazan, perhaps the hottest director of the era, was invited to film Philbrick's *I Led Three Lives* because the president of Twentieth Century-Fox doubted that the director's *Viva Zapata!* (1952) was "something definitely anti-Communist."

Kazan refused and got away with it. But for others the consequences were serious. The studios suspended the Hollywood Ten, who were not rehired when their appeal to the Supreme Court failed. Offering anti-Communist message pictures to "controversial" members of the film community was inadequate, especially since the conventional wisdom of the studios was that messages were for Western Union. The Waldorf statement that the producers had signed in 1947 saluted the "30,000 Americans employed in Hollywood who have given our Government invaluable aid in war and peace" and assured HUAC that no one would be employed whose political allegiance was in doubt. By 1951, when the committee conducted further hearings into the movie industry, the blacklist was institutionalized. To determine political purity, employers turned elsewhere for expertise, shuffling through American Legion dossiers, for example. Others who determined the hiring and firing policies of the studios, at least by 1952, included Roy Brewer, a Democrat who chaired the Motion Picture Alliance for the Preservation of American Ideals, and another alliance member, gossip columnist Hedda Hopper, plus such right-wing columnists as George Sokolsky and Victor Riesel.

The Screen Actors Guild also fully supported the blacklist. Reagan, who served as guild president from 1947 to 1952 and who was also briefly president of the Motion Picture Industry Council, was more moderate than some other anti-Communists in Hollywood. He nevertheless ensured that the blacklist was fully enforced against his fellow actors. He not only favored a provision in the union's constitution denying membership to Communists but also identified for the FBI actors and actresses who "follow the Communist Party line." The guild president was a frequent enough FBI source to have a code name, Confidential Informant T-10. He told the bureau in 1947 of his hope that Congress would declare the Communist movement "a foreign-inspired conspiracy" rather than "a legal party." Such branding would then make it easier, T-10 argued, for Hollywood to construe Party membership "as an indication of disloyalty" in the effort at "cleansing of their own household," an FBI memorandum stated. As though living out Hollywood's confusion of Communism with organized crime, T-10 packed a gun as the blacklist was imposed, though the Red reprisals that he feared never materialized. But whether or not his activism ever endangered his life, it did provide him with a second wife. Reagan met Nancy Davis by clearing her from a list of Communist sympathizers that mistakenly included the starlet. The president of the Screen Actors Guild soon appointed and reappointed her to its board. Such was the romance of American anti-Communism.

Other actresses were less lucky. Though Kim Hunter had won an Oscar for *A Streetcar Named Desire* (1951), she was offered no movie roles for the next three years, and her once-frequent television engagements virtually stopped. Hunter had made the mistake of attending a meeting for the Hollywood Ten, of signing the appeal for the Waldorf peace conference in 1949, and of allowing her name to appear on a Civil Rights Congress telegram asking the Supreme Court for a new trial for Willie McGee, a Mississippi black falsely accused of raping a white woman. In 1951 Hunter had played Arlova, the victim of Soviet cruelty in the Broadway version of Arthur Koestler's novel *Darkness at Noon*. But even such resolutely anti-Communist auspices did not appease her own real-life examining magistrate, an ex-Naval Intelligence officer named Vincent Hartnett. His Aware, Inc., was set up to ascertain the politics of potential employees in entertainment. Hunter could work again only after clearing herself with him, which she did in 1955 for two hundred dollars, though she later testified feeling no regret about that petition for Willie McGee, who was executed anyway.

According to the leaflets of the Catholic War Veterans, Judy Holliday was "the darling of *The Daily Worker*," and the organization picketed her movies, like *Born Yesterday* (1950), for which she nevertheless won an Oscar, and *The Marrying Kind* (1952). Having supported the presidential campaign of Henry Wallace in 1948, she was called to testify before the Senate Internal Security Subcommittee four years later. She had learned her lesson, Holliday assured her interrogators: "I don't say 'yes' to anything now except cancer, polio, and cerebral palsy, things like that." Left-wing causes had not seriously harmed Holliday's career. But they had become the equivalent of the most dreaded diseases, which were far safer to oppose than social and political injustice.

The Cold War also touched the screen's leading enchantress. Adlai Stevenson once defined an egghead as anyone "who called Marilyn Monroe Mrs. Arthur Miller," and she brushed aside warnings that the playwright's leftism might hurt her own career—which was in fact unimpeded. Monroe stood by her husband and contributed to his legal fees after his conviction for contempt of Congress, perhaps because she was already familiar with the timorousness that paralyzed postwar Hollywood. Trying to remedy her limited education, she had come across the "bitter but strong" *Autobiography of Lincoln Steffens* (1931). Its author "knew all about poor people and about injustice," Monroe recalled. "He knew about the lies people used to get ahead, and how smug rich people sometimes were. It was almost as if he'd lived the hard way I'd lived. I loved his book." But then Joseph L. Mankiewicz, who directed her in *All About Eve* (1950), privately warned the starlet: "I wouldn't go around raving about Lincoln Steffens," he advised. "It's certain to get you into trouble. People will begin to talk of you as a radical." Barely fathoming what the term meant, Monroe concluded that his comments represented "a very personal attitude on Mr. Mankiewicz's part and that, genius though he was, of a sort, he was badly frightened by the Front Office or something. I couldn't imagine anybody picking on me because I admired Lincoln Steffens." So she put the journalist's name at the top of her list of the world's ten greatest men that the Twentieth Century-Fox publicity department asked her, as a gimmick, to devise. The name was erased. "We'll have to omit that one," a flack explained. "We don't want anyone investigating our Marilyn." After that she decided to read the second volume of Steffens's autobiography secretly, stashing both volumes under her bed.

Or consider the worse fate of scenarist Howard Koch, who had never been a Communist but had drawn the assignment of adapting *Mission to Moscow* in 1943. When the political climate got chillier, no studio boss was more eager to discover hidden Communists than

Jack Warner, who blamed the late President Roosevelt for pressuring the studio to make *Mission to Moscow*. The *Reader's Digest*, which had serialized Davies' memoir during World War II, suffered no penalties whatsoever for its global dissemination of excerpts from this egregiously pro-Stalin book. But Koch was blacklisted. The careers even of those who repudiated the Communism of their youth, like the promising actor Larry Parks, were also destroyed. To avoid his fate, circumspection was required. Under such circumstances, Rosalind Russell could write in *Look* in 1951 that Hollywood had become as "normal" as any other American community. The lives of its inhabitants, the actress claimed, were unexceptionable. Movie folks went to bed early and to church on Sundays, and they enjoyed nothing more than to spend time with their children. The notorious sinners of the past had disappeared, and so had the "Commies."

4

When one independent, left-wing film was produced in 1954, it was unclear what was more impressive—the fact that in so politically parched an atmosphere *Salt of the Earth* could be made at all, or the fact that it faced so many barriers imposed by those who believed that liberty was an ornament of American life.

The movie was based on a 1951–52 strike by Mexican-American zinc miners, who demanded better safety regulations as well as equal treatment with Anglo employees. The strike was conducted by the International Union of Mine, Mill, and Smelter Workers, which the CIO had expelled in 1950 because it was Communist-controlled. Since no Hollywood studio would have touched such a subject in the 1950s, *Salt of the Earth* was a venture of the blacklisted. Director Herbert Biberman was a member of the Hollywood Ten, scenarist Michael Wilson took the Fifth Amendment before HUAC in 1951, and producer Paul Jarrico had co-written *Song of Russia*. The circumstances under which they operated were not propitious. *Salt of the Earth* was highly sympathetic to the plight of workers in an era bereft of labor militancy. Indeed, George Meany boasted that he "never went on strike in my life, never ran a strike, never ordered anyone else to run a strike and never had anything to do with a picket line." Because the makers of *Salt of the Earth* excluded themselves from the Cold War consensus that Meany was helping to forge, representatives of organized labor aggravated the difficulties of Biberman's Independent Productions Corporation. Members of Brewer's International Alliance of Theatrical Stage Employees were not allowed to participate in the film, which was made in Silver

City, New Mexico. Vigilantes also shot at the automobiles of the filmmakers, beat some of them up, and disrupted the production. Victor Riesel, a Hearst columnist who would be blinded by labor hoodlums in 1956, found it ominous that Communists were making a movie so close to the atomic testing site of Los Alamos.

Riesel's warning was repeated by HUAC's Donald Jackson, who reinforced the right-wing speculation that, since the Korean War was still raging, a subversive conspiracy might instigate a copper miners' strike to block weapons production. Nor was HUAC the only unit of the government to take an interest in *Salt of the Earth*. Its female lead, Rosaura Revultas, could not complete the picture because the Immigration and Naturalization Service (INS) deported her to Mexico as an illegal alien. Though the picture somehow was finished without her, technicians and laboratories then refused to participate in the postproduction work on the sound and film developing. Brewer had promised Congressman Jackson that the Hollywood AFL Film Council would try to stop the exhibition of *Salt of the Earth*, which projectionists and staffers who belonged to Brewer's union indeed refused to show. Other theater owners were intimidated by the American Legion. Miraculously, the movie was briefly shown in ten cities. But so many distributors declined to show it that Biberman's Independent Productions Corporation brought suit against Loew's Incorporated and sixty-seven other defendants, charging them with violating the antitrust laws in hindering the distribution of *Salt of the Earth*. The lawsuit dragged on for a decade before Biberman gave up.

After the harassments, the boycotts, and the violence that punctuated the making of this film, there was something macabre about the hostile review that it received in *Films in Review*, which claimed that *Salt of the Earth* would be "unbelievable to all except those, here and abroad, who resent the measure of individual freedom that Americans possess." The "basic situations" that the film pretended to depict were "untrue in terms of American life"—where the exploitation of workers, women, and ethnic minorities was unknown, and where corporate indifference to the health and safety of employees was implausible. Anyone who disagreed with such smug patriotism was possibly disloyal, therefore unworthy of those freedoms that other Americans enjoyed. This obtuse intolerance not only ensured that the only tenacious dissidents might well be Communists and their allies. It also narrowed the range of available cultural options, thus rendering the nation more like the monolith that it found so repugnant. The fate of *Salt of the Earth* revealed that the phenomenon of repression had double features.

Another sign of the fragility of civil liberties was that the Anti-Defamation League of B'nai B'rith chose to celebrate its fortieth anniversary in 1953 by giving a Democratic Legacy Award to President Eisenhower—not because he had done so much to enlarge the definition of an open society, but because he had done so little. Bestowing such an award, the donors hoped, might quicken the president's interest in civil rights and liberties. He agreed to accept on national television and then, with all three networks covering the presentation, was suddenly inspired enough to ad lib some objections to McCarthyism. The president mentioned his own origins in Abilene, Kansas, where "Wild Bill" Hickok had served as marshal. "Now that town had a code," Ike reminisced, "and I was raised as a boy to prize that code. It was—meet anyone face to face with whom you disagree. You could not sneak up on him from behind—do any damage to him—without suffering the penalty of an outraged citizenry. If you met him face to face and took the same risks he did, you could get away with almost anything, as long as the bullet was in the front." The frontier moral that Eisenhower applied was that "in this country, if someone dislikes you or accuses you, he must come up in front. He cannot hide behind the shadow. He cannot assassinate you or your character from behind, without suffering the penalties of an outraged citizenry."

The president's point might have been a little too oblique. His own administration continued to sanction the faceless and nameless accusations that he deplored, and the right not to be shot in the back—but only in front—had been omitted from the first ten amendments to the Constitution. But the lesson of forthright courage that the president drew from Abilene was also the message of the Western that, better than any other film of the 1950s, exemplified political criticism in the shadow of the blacklist: *High Noon*.

Perhaps because its director, Fred Zinnemann, was born in Vienna (where chuck wagon grits are not part of the cuisine) and was never to direct another Western, scenarist Carl Foreman has usually been credited with primary responsibility for this 1952 movie. In later interviews, Foreman did not disavow the political intentions that animated his screenplay. He insisted that *High Noon*, though set in a frontier hamlet called Hadleyville, is really about a town farther west called Hollywood—and about "no other place but Hollywood." With Stanley Kramer, who produced *High Noon*, Foreman had created a large independent company in 1947 and had brought out "liberal" films like *Home of the Brave* (1949) before the full force of the Red Scare struck. Though Foreman had quit the Communist party as far back as 1942, he feared for the timidity of the movie industry in the face of hyper-patriotic attacks, and he deliberately made the threat posed by a gang of desperadoes into a parable of what HUAC was doing to Hollywood. The committee subpoenaed the scenarist in 1951 while *High Noon* was already in production. Expecting the movie to be the last that he would ever make in the United States, Foreman worked with a sense of imminent closure that haunts the film with its ominous, clock-ticking tension.

It was a deft touch to have cast Gary Cooper as the lone marshal— and not only for the obvious reason that the role was quintessential, enabling him to win his second Oscar as Best Actor. The very conservative Cooper had also been a founder of the Motion Picture Alliance that had first invited HUAC—Foreman's outlaws in *High Noon*—to Hollywood. He had also played the visionary architect Howard Roark in Ayn Rand's own paean to pelf and self, *The Fountainhead*. As an added gesture of protective coloration, the filmmakers of *High Noon* did not have Cooper portray a rebel, an outcast, or a misfit but made the protagonist a figure of authority instead, with a tin star on his chest.

Though Foreman later mentioned having felt "morosely pleased" that his political message had been widely comprehended at the time, the star of *High Noon* may not have grasped the larger import of the film, or its provenance. As a friendly witness in 1947, Cooper had boasted to HUAC of having "turned down quite a few scripts because I thought they were tinged with Communist ideas." When a committee investigator asked him to cite some of the rejected screenplays, Cooper retreated: "I don't think I could, because most of the scripts I read at night." Maybe he had given the scenario for *High Noon* a nocturnal perusal too; after all, HUAC itself also experienced difficulty uncovering any Communist influence in American movies. Or perhaps Cooper realized that *High Noon* fit well within the decent bounds of social criticism.

In fact, no film could be more remote from the cultural sensibility of the Party than this Western, which repudiated the populism integral to the Communist faith in the "masses." Whether during the Popular Front period (when Foreman had joined the Party), or the Second Front period of the war (when Foreman quit the Party), or the sentimentality of "progressivism" that persisted thereafter, Communism asserted that it alone truly represented those who were worthy of inheriting the earth. But no film was more disenchanted with "the people" than *High Noon*, or examined more unsparingly the frailties of those whom Marxism exalted as the agents of historical progress. Nor does *High Noon* portray Hadleyville as a "microcosm of the evils of capitalist society," as critic Pauline Kael wrongly claimed. The only businessman in the movie is a decent and fair silent partner of Helen Ramirez (Katy Jurado), who is a victim of racial prejudice—not economic exploitation. The villains are not capitalists but outlaws, and the cowards include a judge but no bosses. Even though the marshal's bride (Grace Kelly) picks up a gun at the end, the one unrebutted speech that she is permitted to deliver is not against the immorality of social arrangements but against the wastefulness of violence and mayhem. In Mark Twain's "The Man That Corrupted Hadleyburg," the sin is greed; but in Hadleyville, the problem is fear.

This Western film is far more intelligible when fixed within a certain critical tradition that began with Tocqueville over a century earlier and was invigorated in the 1950s: the exploration of the pressures of conformity. The reference points in social thought include Riesman's *The Lonely Crowd*, Whyte's *The Organization Man*, and Irving Howe's *Partisan Review* essay "This Age of Conformity" (1954), as well as Solomon Asch's celebrated experiments in social psychology and Erving Goffman's *Asylums* (1959). *High Noon* raised the question of how strongly the private sense of right and wrong—and of personal honor—can resist "the tyranny of the majority." Everyone in Hadleyville but Marshal Will Kane seems to agree that the town will be more secure if he leaves, yet his arguments for remaining are as principled as they are practical. Though fearing for his life, he holds one truth to be self-evident—that dangerous evil must be faced and routed rather than evaded or denied.

In making the case for personal honor, *High Noon* challenged the semiofficial ethos of the era, which film director Robert Rossen put most succinctly. "I don't think," he told HUAC in 1953, "that any one individual can indulge himself in the luxury of individual morality or pit it against what I feel today very strongly is the security and safety of this nation." But "individual morality" is precisely what Kane pits against the townspeople, who fear for their "safety and security" should the lawman remain among them.

John Wayne, a member of the Hollywood Committee for the Reelection of Joe McCarthy, found Reds about as endearing as rustlers, and he strongly objected to the antimajoritarian message of *High Noon*. The three-term president of the Motion Picture Alliance deeply "resented that scene where the marshal ripped off his badge and threw it on the ground. That was like belittling a Medal of Honor." The portrayal of a community of cowards was simply unpatriotic, Wayne argued; for in *High Noon* "four guys come in to gun down the sheriff. He goes to the church and asks for help and the guys go, 'Oh well, oh gee.' And the women stand up and say,

'You're rats. . . . ' So Cooper goes out alone. It's the most un-American thing I've ever seen in my whole life. The last thing in the picture is old Coop putting the United States marshal's badge under his foot and stepping on it." Worried that his close friend Coop would be politically tainted, Wayne even telephoned Foreman to ask him to allow the screenplay to be uncredited.

In a later Western, *The Undefeated* (1969), Wayne and sidekick Rock Hudson encounter some unsympathetic Mexican bandits, whose leader, after some fumbled efforts at communication, Wayne shoots. When the pair return to the wagon train that has been dependent on their guidance below the Rio Grande, Wayne's report appalls an American widow, who exclaims: "You went out there to talk. Why did you have to kill him?" Shrugging and squinting, the durable "shooting star" explains, "Guess the conversation just kinda . . . dried up, ma'am." Wayne's earlier offscreen attempt to parley with Foreman seems to have dried up too. "I'll never regret having helped run Foreman out of this country," he bragged in a 1971 interview, a claim that was quickly, partially retracted, since Wayne insisted—despite overwhelming evidence to the contrary—that "there was no blacklist at that time, as some people said." Nor did his denial explain what Foreman was doing in England, where he arrived in 1952, or why his passport was lifted on the following July 4.

Whatever forces had driven Foreman out of Hollywood, however, had not quarantined him from the movies. He continued to write screenplays—including another much-honored film for Columbia Pictures, *The Bridge on the River Kwai* (1957). Both Foreman and Michael Wilson, the scenarist for *Salt of the Earth*, actually co-wrote it while on the blacklist, even though novelist Pierre Boulle, who could not then write in English, won an Oscar for his adaptation. By suggesting irrational folly ("madness . . . madness, madness") when an Allied commando team blows up the railroad bridge that British military prisoners had constructed for the Japanese, *The Bridge on the River Kwai* was rare for the 1950s in its criticism of the high price of military values during World War II—"the good war." (The officers whose values are questioned are, of course, British, not American.) Though the film's only American character (played by William Holden) is a hero, he distrusts heroics and sensibly wants out of the war. In this sense, *Kwai* beams a message that is very different from *High Noon*, which makes a case not only for courage but for violence, which Mrs. Amy Kane, a declared Quaker, adopts by shooting one of the outlaws (in the back, incidentally).

However divergent the slants of the two films, the blacklist had kept only Foreman's name from the screen, not his ideas. That left the mass audience presumably in danger of ideological contamination—and not only from Foreman. Scenarist Dalton Trumbo of the Hollywood Ten earned an Oscar under a pseudonym for *The Brave One* in 1957, and the following year the opening shots of a prison truck in Kramer's *The Defiant Ones* tipped off the cognoscenti. The credits "Written by Nathan E. Douglas, Harold Jacob Smith" were superimposed on the faces in the front seat, seen through the windshield. "Douglas" himself was on the left, a *nom de plume* for Nedrick Young, who was blacklisted. That year both scenarists won Oscars, which generated such confusion that director Billy Wilder wisecracked, "Blacklist, shmacklist, as long as they're all working." Foreman himself asked for his passport three years after its annulment. When his attorney convinced a judge that the opposing State Department brief was so sloppy that the government would be downright embarrassed to have its objections on the record, Foreman got his passport back. The same attorney also arranged with HUAC's Francis Walter that, in executive session, his client would denounce himself and the Party that he had long ago repudiated. But he would name no one else and would not take the Fifth Amendment. Though the case set no precedent, Foreman was back at work—without having to become an informer.

The blacklist was enfeebled but still in effect when the planet's most powerful Communist arrived in Hollywood in 1959. The film community responded neither with ostracism nor with outrage, nor did its elite vow to run Nikita Khrushchev out of town. Instead, its leaders jostled with one another to sup with the devil, scrambling for invitations to dine with the erstwhile "butcher of Budapest." The kingpins of an industry that did not permit Ring Lardner to write under his own name or the face of Zero Mostel to appear on the screen were thrilled to welcome the ruler of the movement that nearly all the blacklist victims had quit long before. Khrushchev stayed in the Schine family's hotel in Los Angeles, and his already hectic schedule broke down at one point because Gary Cooper insisted on a little showdown. The star of *Man of the West* (1958) told the man of the East of his pleasure in listening to Soviet promises to surpass the prosperity and power of the United States, because "that's a capitalist idea—I mean competition—and I'm glad to see that you are a capitalist." Cooper's dialectical skills did not dazzle the Soviet premier, who began to give an elaborate rejoinder. But the actor walked away while the translation was still in progress, and later explained: "This fellow Khrushchev didn't seem to understand that this wasn't a working day and that he was overtime. I wasn't going to stand there and listen to that stuff."

Though the genre of the Western that Cooper personified was important to television programming in that era, such films were about to head toward the last roundup. In the same year as Khrushchev's visit, for example, Wayne starred in Howard Hawks's *Rio Bravo*, a partial response to the "un-American" communal betrayal that *High Noon* had depicted. In this Warner Brothers release, the sheriff does not throw down his tin star at the end. And whereas Marshal Kane rejected the proffered aid of an old man, a kid, and a drunkard in Hadleyville, Wayne relied on the resources of Walter Brennan, Ricky Nelson, and Dean Martin. In 1969 even an alumnus of the blacklist made a Western. Abraham Polonsky's *Tell Them Willie Boy Is Here* starred an actor who seemed so comfortable in a Western setting that he might have been the natural successor to Cooper. The sheriff whom Robert Redford plays is even named Coop. But Polonsky's main subject is racial prejudice (against Indians) and the phoniness of white liberalism that Coop personifies. Redford thus broke the mold of the hero, even playing an amoral, unreformed bandit that same year in *Butch Cassidy and the Sundance Kid*. The rigid distinctions that this supremely American genre once maintained between good and evil, white and Indian, wilderness and civilization, cowpunchers and sodbusters, lawmen and outlaws, had dissolved. The ideological consensus that the film industry itself promoted—in its images and its politics—could no longer cohere.

7

BOXED-IN: TELEVISION
AND THE PRESS

The crisis of the Cold War coincided with the emergence of a technological novelty called television, an inescapable medium that quickly rivaled the power of movies, radio, and mass-circulation magazines to transmit ideas and images. In 1950, 3.1 million television sets could be found in American homes. By 1955, the figure was already up to 32 million, and ten thousand Americans a day were buying their first TV sets. Already by 1953 half of all families owned a set, an instrument that was permanently altering the nation's entertainment preferences and habits of acquiring information.

The results could be readily measured. Movie houses, for example, closed in droves. In 1950–51, the last picture shows were exhibited in 134 cinemas in southern California, 61 in Massachusetts, 55 in metropolitan New York. In 1951, ninety million Americans were still going every week to the movies. By the end of the decade, weekly attendance had been sliced in half, down to forty-three million. Radio also lost much of its audience. Comedian Bob Hope's radio ratings were 23.8 in 1949, 12.7 two years later, and only 5.4 by 1953. A 1959 poll indicated that, as a popular source of news, television had already vastly surpassed magazines and the radio and had matched newspapers in terms of popular trust.

Television was crucial to the destruction of the general magazines (the *Saturday Evening Post, Collier's, Look, Life*) that had been pitched to the middle-class audience. In one six-month period in

1954, the newsstand circulation of *Life* skidded 21 percent, as the moving images that flickered inside most American homes made its famous photographs seem anachronistic. And because those houses were increasingly located in suburbs, the voices of newsboys screaming the evening headlines were stilled. Potential customers were no longer implored to "read all about it" when "it" could be seen and heard—and updated—on the tube at home. Because commuting was commonly done on highways, where it was impossible to drive cars and read simultaneously, fewer customers dropped by the subway newsstands or the neighborhood variety stores for the latest newspaper or magazine. As the general magazines headed toward extinction, others—aimed at newer styles of leisure and entertainment—were born, such as *TV Guide*, which in 1954 gained 98 percent in circulation.

The pioneers of the medium that *TV Guide* made its beat were eminently respectable (unlike the moguls who built the movie industry), and the network bosses therefore quickly acknowledged their political responsibilities during the Cold War. Frank M. Folsom, president of Radio Corporation of America (RCA), claimed in 1951 that television was a vital source of information "when swiftly changing events may otherwise cause confusion and alarm to the detriment of unity of purpose in safeguarding the democratic institutions of our land and our determination to assist other freedom-loving people against aggression." RCA's subsidiary, NBC, joined its major competitor, CBS, in August 1951 in an attempt to spike Soviet influence during the World Festival of Youth in East Berlin. The Department of State asked the networks to put up huge color television screens in West Berlin, hoping to counter—by this demonstration of American technological superiority—the spread of Communist propaganda among the two million young people in attendance. In the early 1950s, the networks also cooperated closely with the federal government in airing civil defense programs. Rather than adopting a detached or independent position, which the First Amendment presumably permitted, television tended to vindicate a militaristic response to the Soviet challenge. Live telecasts of nuclear explosions in Nevada were welcomed by the Pentagon, which wanted to reassure viewers of American nuclear superiority. One atomic blast was even "sponsored" by the Advertising Council. Such live coverage tended to reinforce an uncritical attitude toward American foreign and military policy, foreclosing consideration of alternatives to an expanding arms race based on ever-more-destructive nuclear weapons.

Since dissent seemed to slide so uncomfortably close to disloyalty, since controversy had become a code word for trouble (rather than an inevitable feature of democratic dialogue), official views were rarely and insufficiently challenged on television. When disagreements were presented, the framework of analysis was so narrowly circumscribed that television became a custodian of the cultural Cold War. Its viewers were boxed-in to a tight consensus. Radio had offered a less constricted political perspective during the Great Depression, when socialist tribunes like Norman Thomas and feisty libertarians like Roger Baldwin were included in the range of legitimate opinion. *America's Town Meeting of the Air* had begun on ABC radio in 1935, without unsettling audiences or inspiring social revolution. Fifteen years later, this show established a beachhead on television as well. But the availability of a forum for left-wing opinion might generate unnecessary friction, might even appear vaguely unpatriotic when unity against Communism was so urgent. *America's Town Meeting of the Air* was dropped from television in 1952, though the radio version of this public affairs program hung on for a few more years. NBC's *American Forum of the Air* lasted longer but offered even fewer divergent opinions, as the guest slots for Norman Thomas and other non-Communists on the left disappeared. The spectrum of acceptable views thus narrowed; the air became thinner.

Fear of the off-center pervaded the medium. James Wechsler had been a regular panelist on a television show, *Starring the Editors*, that Grand Union grocery stores sponsored. But because the editorial page of the *New York Post* was firmly liberal and anti-McCarthy, Wechsler was attacked by a rival newspaper, Hearst's *Journal-American*. That made Wechsler "controversial"—a word, historian Jacques Barzun complained, that had come to mean "something (or someone) about which we cannot afford to engage in controversy— virtually the opposite of the former meaning." Wechsler was dropped from *Starring the Editors*. "Such furtive pressure was operating all over the TV-radio world," the editor commented. "An accuser did not feel morally obligated to prove a case; by merely bringing any charge, he made his victim 'controversial' and this was sufficient ground for exclusion." Television programming thus fit— and contributed to—the proclivity to hang a giant Do Not Disturb sign over the nation, what CBS commentator Edward R. Murrow in 1958 called "a built-in allergy to unpleasant or disturbing information. . . . Television in the main is being used to distract, delude, amuse and insulate us." Such functions were more consistent with the needs of the sponsors who determined programming than with the purposes of the First Amendment.

To be sure there was "no room for a crusading journalist" in Russia, as Justice Douglas had proclaimed in a speech at Occidental College. But on American television there was no room for a crusading journalist either. The prime example of the species began his own four-page radical newsletter in 1953: *I. F. Stone's Weekly*. Its eponymous editor-publisher-sole contributor had no difficulty securing a second-class mailing permit, and the five thousand subscribers he attracted were enough to pay the bills. In two years his readership doubled, to about .00006 percent of the American population—few if any of whom exerted clout in Washington. Stone was so much of a loner that even his fellow journalists in the National Press Club banished him, after he had invited a black to lunch there. In researching his own articles, Stone turned his hearing defect into an advantage, as he made himself a close reader of government documents and the daily press. (He especially cherished the excitement of reading the *Washington Post*, "because you never knew on what page you would find a page-one story.")

Obscure but not obstructed, Stone was a throwback to the dissident pamphleteers who are exalted in histories of the press. His impassioned, don't-tread-on-me tenacity contrasted sharply with the mainstream media. A veteran of left-wing newspapers over two previous decades, Stone was not much of an anti-Communist and did not seem morally vexed by the character of Soviet society or its champions. He pleaded instead for adapting to reality. "We must live with the revolution in peace or destroy our own society in a futile effort to smash it," he argued in 1952. "Coexistence and the peaceful competition of diverse societies represent the only sane and humane solution. . . . Communism is in the world to stay, and we must reconcile ourselves to it, as the crowned heads of Europe had to reconcile themselves to republicanism and democracy." Though Stone's newsletter was to survive and even prosper for nineteen years, his heresy was never expressed on television in the 1950s.

1

Amplification of the Cold War consensus was especially apparent in television's coverage of international relations. In the articulation of foreign policy, no one besides Eisenhower bestrode the video colossus more formidably than Secretary of State Dulles, who was given eighteen separate opportunities in less than seven years of office to report to viewers on the state of the planet. His speeches were televised (live or on film) not only when he addressed the UN General Assembly but also when he spoke before the American Le-

gion and the 4-H Clubs. Rarely was he countered with a contradictory opinion on his conduct of foreign policy. His diplomacy seemed
the projection of the national purpose that brooked no second-guess-
ing or partisan criticism, and his views and visage were so ineluc-
table a part of news coverage that he seemed almost like a serial
character. It was fitting that both CBS and NBC canceled their regular daytime programming in May 1959 to televise his funeral.

By then Dulles had traveled over half a million miles as secretary
of state, and trips to forty-seven nations had provided plenty of opportunities to make "departure statements" and "arrival statements" from the collapsible lectern that was taken on his flights.
Television and film cameramen were often encouraged on these
occasions to shoot their peripatetic subject from a low angle, giving
Dulles a redoubtable "American eagle look." When he happened to
be in Washington and gave a press conference, any film of the event
had to secure his approval; he insisted on the right to examine the
transcript and to make cuts. Certain journalists were given off-the-
record "background" sessions, with Dulles serving as the "high government source" who was quoted or paraphrased. The consequences, as television historian Erik Barnouw pointed out, were that
viewers tended to see international affairs "through the eyes of
Dulles. . . . A filmed press conference excerpt, or a newsman's report
'from a reliable source,' or a filmed statement by Dulles from a
lectern at the edge of an airstrip, *became* the news. For networks
he often seemed a welcome *deus ex machina*. In a fifteen-minute
newscast, a ninety-second report on Southeast Asia by the Secretary
of State himself seemed grand and took care of Southeast Asia
nicely," since the networks had no bureaus close enough to film
anything in the jungles of Indochina.

If American statecraft in that era has appeared in retrospect to
have been less interventionist and militarist than under the presidents who succeeded Eisenhower, that is largely because the CIA
was then deployed so completely outside of public—or even congressional—scrutiny. Because the agency's director was Allen Dulles,
foreign policy was an instrument of brotherly love of sorts. The
combination may have thrown America's enemies off balance, and
it has bemused later historians. For one brother had a habit of denouncing the deceitfulness of "atheistic communism" with such
moralistic fervor that Ike compared him to an Old Testament
prophet. The other brother, also a quondam partner in the Wall
Street law firm of Sullivan & Cromwell, engaged in such cunning
and morally hazardous methods that, according to Senator Richard

Russell (D-Ga.), "it almost chills the marrow of a man" to hear about them.

The classic case of such operations—immune from serious journalistic scrutiny or criticism—was Guatemala, where the CIA arranged the overthrow of the government of Jacobo Arbenz Guzman in 1954. In June, mercenaries invaded from bases in Nicaragua and Honduras, countries whose dictators were friendly to the United States. Four American pilots also flew P-47 Thunderbolts over the capital, Guatemala City. Colonel Carlos Castillo Armas, who had been trained at Fort Leavenworth, arrived from exile in the plane of the American ambassador. With notable bamboozlement, John Foster Dulles then proclaimed that the intolerable situation that the Arbenz government had created was "being cured by the Guatemalans themselves." After Arbenz fled, Armas seized power, imprisoned thousands of political opponents, disenfranchised three-fourths of the voting population, ended the secret ballot for the rest, abolished all political parties and independent trade unions, canceled Arbenz's agrarian reform law, and governed by decree. The American government rewarded Armas with ninety million dollars in aid in his first two years in power, though he was assassinated soon thereafter.

What crime had his predecessor committed to require the clandestine intervention of the United States? Arbenz had not illegally seized power, having become president of Guatemala, Allen Dulles conceded, "through the usual processes of government and not by any Communist coup." And even though Ike had called Arbenz's regime "a Communist government," Communists did not serve in the presidential cabinet. Only four served in the congress (out of fifty-six members), though they were important in the land-reform and education programs. Arbenz's real crime was different: in one region of Guatemala, he had expropriated 234,000 acres of uncultivated banana land belonging to the United Fruit Company. He had offered compensation, but United Fruit rejected the proposal. Meanwhile, he had begun action to expropriate another 173,000 acres of the company's land in another part of Guatemala. Perhaps it was only coincidental that United Fruit was a client of the law firm of Sullivan & Cromwell. In any event, Armas revealed the purposes of this particular application of the Monroe Doctrine by restoring ownership of the expropriated land to United Fruit and by abolishing the tax on interest and dividends that had been imposed on foreign investors.

Secretary of State Dulles managed to explain these startling events without mentioning the role of the CIA, as though a spontaneous popular uprising indigenous to Guatemala had pitched "red colonialism" out of the Western hemisphere. "It is the policy of the United States not to intervene in the internal affairs of other nations," his department insisted. "This policy has repeatedly been affirmed under the present administration." Dulles told a television audience that the Arbenz policies were part of "the evil purpose of the Kremlin to destroy the inter-American system." Though the Soviet Union undoubtedly harbored such a design, no evidence suggested that the government of Guatemala intended to be its instrument. Never in its news digests did the Voice of America refer to the hand of the CIA, while Ambassador Henry Cabot Lodge replied to protests at the UN by categorically denying any American involvement in the sudden collapse of the Arbenz regime. No American correspondent pursued clues of CIA involvement, and, though the United Fruit Company was treated as a reliable source, the counterclaims of the legitimate government of Guatemala were not reported. Thus, the press never challenged the "cover story" (a euphemism for mendacity). Hadn't George Kennan persuasively argued in "The Sources of Soviet Conduct" (1947) that "the secretiveness, the lack of frankness [and] the duplicity" of the Russians distinguished their diplomacy from ours?

Dulles was even more effective in restricting information about mainland China. The United States did not get around to rapprochement until 1973, exactly two decades after the Republicans took over the executive branch with the accusation that the Democrats "lost" China. Ever since the Red Army had entered Peking in October 1949, no subject of political conversation was more sensitive. Indeed, Dulles snubbed Premier Chou En-lai in 1954 by refusing to shake his hand during the Geneva conference that confirmed the French expulsion from Vietnam. Though Justice Douglas called for recognition of the Communist regime in China in the fall of 1951, the proposal only heightened his reputation as a maverick and proved that he no longer hoped to be president. Public discussion of the question was virtually closed. Except in high school debate contests, which formally required two sides to every question, China meant only Chiang and his forces, which were confined to Formosa (the Japanese word, then in common use, for Taiwan).

With some exceptions, the American press concurred in this denial of reality. Television was not the only medium that downplayed or ignored the less pleasant side of the story of how and why the Kuomintang regime had lost the civil war to the Communists, after nearly half of its own soldiers had defected by early 1948. The United States had given Chiang two billion dollars in aid, and yet about 80 percent of the equipment that it donated had somehow disappeared—either sold on the black market or transferred to Mao Tsetung. One American ambassador was candid enough to call Chiang "the best asset the Communists have." But the generalissimo was a convert to Christianity and he hated Communism, and to pick apart his defects as a statesman was to forfeit serious public attention.

Dulles's most important journalistic ally was not any of the network executives but the head of Time, Inc., Henry Luce, who liked to tell friends that "the only ambassadorship I would take is to a restored democracy in China." Such an appointment was not within the power of even a Republican administration to make. But the single most powerful influence on right-center opinion—that is, on American public opinion—remained haunted by the country where he had been born and raised, as the son of Presbyterian missionaries. Indeed, by the time the Nationalist government had fallen, Chiang had appeared on the cover of *Time* more often than anyone else— even more frequently than Roosevelt or Churchill or Hitler. Sprucing up the virtues of the Kuomintang became an obsession of the Luce publications. John Hersey, who was also the Chinese-born son of missionary parents, had covered China during World War II for *Time*. But so altered were his dispatches that he told Luce to his face that the weekly was no more truthful in its reporting than *Pravda*.

In Chungking, Hersey had hired Luce's other star correspondent in China, Theodore H. White, who had studied the Chinese language at Harvard. Luce considered him the most talented correspondent he had ever employed, and White became the first reporter ever to get a by-line in *Time*. But he resigned after the magazine refused to publish his reports on the depth of popular disaffection with the Kuomintang. (Luce was not alone in refusing to believe White's gloomy reporting from China. The other impediment was Chambers, *Time*'s foreign editor.) Chiang's loss of the mandate of heaven, through ignorance and corruption, was presciently treated in *Thunder out of China*, the bestseller that White and Annalee Jacoby coauthored in 1946. Seven years later, after Cohn and Schine discovered *Thunder out of China* in the Berlin library of the International Information Agency, the copies of this Book-of-the-Month Club selection were burned.

Having quit Time, Inc., in 1946, White found himself "being nipped at for my past reporting of China. Even my old friends at *Time* magazine referred to me in their columns as 'pinko' Teddy White. . . . The harassment of others was closing both my movements and my outlets." Fearing that "no large or distinguished magazine or newspaper would hire a known 'left-wing' writer," he joined "a marginal news-feature service called the Overseas News Agency, a service which was still unafraid of the growing paranoia against liberal journalists." The account of White's pariahdom in his autobiography is overly dramatic and not strictly true. For he wrote on politics for the Sunday magazine of the *New York Times*, served as national political correspondent for the *Reporter* (circulation almost 200,000), and then repeated the same assignment for the mass circulation (4.3 million) *Collier's*. Luce even invited him back to Time-Life, an offer the journalist declined. And though CBS producers informed White that he could not be cleared as a guest on any of its network shows, his claim was much exaggerated that he "had become an outcast of American journalism early in the McCarthy years." White's analysis of postwar European politics, *Fire in the Ashes*, became a Book-of-the-Month Club selection in 1953, when McCarthy was very much on the warpath. White nevertheless wrote nothing on China from 1954 till 1972, and only four articles on Vietnam—in part because of his own uncertainty, in part because of self-censorship. He also avoided defense or foreign policy, because "too much danger lurked there."

At least Hersey and White had gotten the chance to report directly from China. By the 1950s, American reporters could not cover the mainland at all. The obstacle was not only totalitarian xenophobia. Peking offered to admit American journalists in August 1956, provided that their own government reciprocate by allowing in their Chinese counterparts to cover the United States. Dulles adamantly refused and then, after strong criticism, acknowledged that such Chinese reporters might be admitted—provided that they were not Communists! Such a condition was, of course, unacceptable. Three plucky American reporters nevertheless decided to defy the State Department ban by visiting the world's most populous nation. Among them was the *Baltimore Afro-American*'s William Worthy, whose short-wave broadcast from Peking was picked up by CBS. An undersecretary of state thereupon phoned William Paley, the network's chairman of the board, urging him to carry no further broadcasts from China. Not only did Paley promise that this breach of political decorum would not happen again, but CBS also silenced its own commentator, Eric Sevareid, who had wanted to blast the administration's effort to maximize American ignorance. Never before had Sevareid's entire program been scuttled. Murrow tried to save the network's honor by addressing the issue on his own radio program, for which CBS in turn rebuked him. He also wanted to contribute a brief in Worthy's behalf, when the reporter's passport was revoked upon his return from behind the "bamboo curtain." But Worthy lost his suit against the Department of State in 1959.

In 1956, Murrow again risked official and corporate displeasure when *See It Now* interviewed Chou En-lai, whom Luce's *Life* magazine had two years earlier called "a political thug, a ruthless intriguer, a conscienceless liar, a saber-toothed political assassin." But Murrow and his partner, producer Fred W. Friendly, protected themselves from charges of providing a conduit for Communist propaganda by capping the interview with a live panel consisting of two fierce anti-Communists: Carlos P. Romulo, the Philippine ambassador to the United States, and T. F. Tsiang, the Nationalist Chinese delegate to the UN. A wall of silence had been at least momentarily pierced, however. After Marshal Tito of Yugoslavia was interviewed on *See It Now* the following year, another impeccable live panel was arranged. It included Clare Boothe Luce, then the U.S. ambassador to Italy; Hamilton Fish, the editor of *Foreign Affairs* and director of the Council on Foreign Relations; and the *New York Times*'s William Lawrence. Also in 1957, CBS's *Face the Nation* dared to give an hour to Khrushchev, who was interviewed by three journalists, *without* a live panel afterwards—just as it did with more conventional political figures.

This willingness to trust viewers to make up their own minds infuriated the commander of the Catholic War Veterans, who wired CBS to cancel *Face the Nation*. Three days later, President Eisenhower dismissed the show as a stunt, because "a commercial firm in this country [is] trying to improve its commercial standing" (a peevish objection from the head of so pro-business an administration). Interestingly enough, the commercial firm's two rivals, NBC and ABC, did not defend CBS's right to telecast the interview. It was left to network president Frank Stanton to assert that "Khrushchev and his views are of great importance to our world and the world of our children. The less this man . . . remains a myth or a dark legend or a mystery to the American people, the more certain they are to size him up correctly."

The need to make so obvious a statement suggested how limited an effort television made to enlighten its audience, which was thus unprepared in the ensuing decade for any critical assessment of the military intervention in Southeast Asia. An audience that got the impression that a secretary of state's pronouncements were sacrosanct, that had rarely been challenged by a wide diversity of opinions, and that confused credulousness with patriotism was easily misled as the disastrous involvement in Vietnam deepened. Though

democratic institutions were supposed to require an informed citizenry, the torpor of television programming had helped atrophy
whatever mental habits of skepticism and independence the mass
audience might have cultivated. Television reporting and commentary need not be singled out as the only culprit in journalism. But
the case of television was the most acute, and its failure probably
the most consequential.

2

Because of the political emasculation of television, which hesitated
to adopt the independent perspectives that the First Amendment
sanctioned, the medium faced its earliest—and greatest—test not
in the labyrinths of foreign policy but in the domestic Cold War.
That test was personified by McCarthy, who was peculiarly a creature of the media attention that he seems to have craved more than
power itself. No politician of his time was craftier at exploiting the
habits of the press for his own self-aggrandizing ends. In *The Fourth
Branch of Government* (1959), Douglass Cater explained how, "late
one afternoon, Senator McCarthy might name a person, more likely
a series of them. All through the evening the accused's telephone
kept ringing. He was told briefly the nature of the charge against
him—let us say, 'top Soviet agent'—and asked for a brief reply. But
the dilemma for the reporter and the headline writer remained.
McCarthy's charge was controversial and unexpected—a news
count of two. The denial was controversial and completely expected—a news count of one. Both were equally lacking in proof.
Nobody carried credentials on his person to prove that he is *not* the
'top Soviet agent.'" So the lies became amplified.

Though reporters were often stymied in their efforts to combat
such methods, McCarthy's unscrupulous demagoguery also met
much spirited resistance. From virtually the beginning of his career,
he was subjected to severe journalistic criticism, beginning with the
two most important newspapers in his home state, the *Milwaukee
Journal* and the *Madison Capital-Times*. The *New York Post's*
"Smear, Inc.: Joe McCarthy's One-Man Mob" called him "the hoax
of the century." This seventeen-part exposé torpedoed his preten-
sions as an authority on Communism and defined McCarthyism as
a sort of "Political Murder, Inc." That is why the *Post's* editor was
hauled before McCarthy's committee, and why Wechsler told the
senator: "The *Post* has been fighting Senator McCarthy for a long
time. Our editorial page, I am happy to say, has never wavered on
this point. It is not going to change now."

Within the limits of the ideal of "objectivity," reporters like Philip Potter of the *Baltimore Sun* and Murrey Marder of the *Washington Post* were critical as well. The editorial antagonism of the *New York Times* was consistent. Not only the liberal press (such as the weekly journals of opinion) but also the Luce magazines were forthright in their opposition. Columnist Drew Pearson was so hostile that McCarthy once kicked him in the groin (and then, with a malevolent cackle, boasted about the incident). Martin Agronsky skewered McCarthy on ABC radio in 1953 and was nearly fired after the senator pressured more than half the local sponsors to withdraw. Commentator Elmer Davis attacked McCarthy with impunity, as did Walter Lippmann, the century's most cerebral journalist. Indeed, one of the last holdouts among the elite of the Fourth Estate was Murrow, whose impact was magnified because his resistance stiffened in the glare of national television.

When the chairman of CBS's board was once asked at a stockholders' meeting why his salary was lower than Murrow's, Paley shrugged and said, "I guess he's worth more." Murrow's broadcasts during the Battle of Britain in 1940 ("This . . . is London") had made him the most famous foreign correspondent ever to work on radio. He then made himself into the most admired journalist ever to work on television. Though his *See It Now* developed into the preeminent weekly public affairs program, its corporate origins were somewhat less exalted than the legends of crusading liberalism might suggest. In 1951, Alcoa had decided to sponsor the show because the company, which controlled 90 percent of the aluminum market, had just lost an antitrust suit and needed to scrub up its image. In a celebrated assurance, Alcoa president Irving W. Wilson told Murrow and Friendly: "You do the programs, we'll make the aluminum. Don't tell us how to make the aluminum, and we won't tell you how to make the programs." The promise was kept. But except for a four-minute segment a month after *See It Now* began, Murrow and Friendly did not tackle McCarthy directly until the spring of 1954, having ducked opportunities to do so for well over two years.

The method that they employed was the evidently fair one of letting the senator impale himself, showing him in his characteristic poses. For over a year, *See It Now* had been saving film clips for "A Report on Senator Joseph R. McCarthy" (March 9, 1954). But the corporate leadership of the network put daylight between itself and the program. CBS ran no advertisement to promote it. Nor did it permit Murrow and Friendly, who put up their own money and signed their own names to an ad, to use the CBS logo. The company's public relations unit was also thoughtful enough to cable the FBI, notifying Hoover about the upcoming program about his friend. Though this particular exposure of McCarthy became in retrospect the most important single show in the history of television, saving from utter disgrace a medium that had evaded the central issue of fear that he engendered, CBS took no pride in the journalistic achievement of *See It Now*. Indeed, a frightened Stanton told Friendly soon thereafter that, because of the political pressures that could be applied through the Federal Communications Commission (FCC), "You may have cost us the network." The CBS president also showed Friendly the results of a poll: more Americans found McCarthy credible than Murrow. After McCarthy had used free air time to call Murrow "the leader and the cleverest of the jackal pack which is always at the throat of anyone who dares to expose individual Communists and traitors," a third of those polled believed that Murrow was either a Communist or a Communist sympathizer.

After the evisceration of McCarthy on *See It Now*, Alcoa received plenty of hate mail, felt pressure from its dealers, and was sharply criticized by conservative columnists. Aluminum companies such as Alcoa also marketed fluorides, which right-wing fanatics regarded as a Communist plot; but curiously enough, little seems to have been made of such products in the attacks on *See It Now*. Perhaps the timing was merely coincidental, but Alcoa withdrew its sponsorship a year after "A Report on Senator Joseph R. McCarthy"; the show limped along with only partial or occasional sponsorship for the next three years. CBS slashed its hours, altered its time slots, changed its name, separated Murrow from Friendly, and in 1958 finally dropped *See It Now*. "Alcoa's fidelity in the face of pressures remains legendary," Professor Barnouw noted, but then raised some pertinent questions: "Must the existence of such a series, which leading critics considered a historic contribution to the democratic process, and which had apparently helped mitigate prevailing hysteria—must such a series depend on the appearance of a courageous sponsor? Or on a sponsor with image problems? Is television journalism to be a by-product of public relations crises?"

Murrow himself complained in 1959 that "the timidity of television in dealing with this man [McCarthy] when he was spreading fear throughout the land is not something to which this art of communication can point with pride, nor should it be allowed to forget it." It was more a matter of blind luck, and McCarthy's own self-destructiveness, that the army hearings in the spring of 1954 were conducted at all. But they gave television an opportunity to show what Joseph Welch called the "recklessness" and "cruelty" of the junior senator from Wisconsin. The only two networks that carried the hearings live (ABC and Dumont) were the weakest, lacking virtually any other morning or afternoon programming. NBC presented the army-McCarthy hearings live for only two days, at a cost of $125,000 in lost advertising revenue. The network opted thereafter for a late evening summary. CBS never showed the hearings live at all because its schedule was swollen with heavily sponsored soap operas and game shows, and only CBS viewers who remained awake at 11:30 P.M. were informed of what had happened that day in the Senate Caucus Room. Local variations also affected this diagnostic test of democratic institutions. The afternoon hearings were not shown in Cleveland because the machinations of the most dangerous demagogue of the era were not permitted to preempt the baseball games of the Indians, then a pennant contender. Local affiliates in Baltimore also considered the fate of the Orioles more important. Thus, the hearings eventually reached only 60 percent of the television market. Later reminded that licensees were expected to satisfy "the public interest," CBS's Stanton told the FCC that "a program in which a large part of the audience is interested is by that very fact . . . in the public interest."

3

Though television was inadvertently pivotal in dooming McCarthy, it rarely challenged the operations of McCarthyism, and indeed contributed to the sour and irrational vindictiveness that he incarnated. The fledgling industry demonstrated its commitment to the Cold War by participating in the blacklist that also affected films and radio. Because the three major networks were themselves beholden to advertisers, the effects of such political purification rites were perhaps even more severe than in the movies. From network executives down to local affiliates, from sponsoring corporations to advertising agencies, virtually everyone cooperated. The primary form of cohesion was the loyalty oath, which NBC, for example, had compelled its new employees to sign since the mid-1940s. In 1950, CBS went even farther in its assessment of the dedication of its work force to "the American way of life." Though presumably without access to classified or militarily sensitive information, the employees of a private corporation were expected to respond to the following questions:

(1) Are you now, or have you ever been, a member of the Communist Party, U.S.A., or any Communist organization?

(2) Are you now, or have you ever been, a member of a Fascist organization?

(3) Are you now, or have you ever been, a member of any organization . . . which has adopted a policy of advocacy or approving the commission of acts of force or violence to deny other persons their rights under the Constitution of the United States, or seeking to alter the form of government of the United States by unconstitutional means?

The network fired anyone who did not cooperate in the completion of this questionnaire or did not resign. Of the three major networks, the most resistant to imposing such political tests was ABC, which won a special Peabody Award in 1951.

But since authentic Communists might well have signed such loyalty oaths or denied Party membership anyway, independent monitoring of political reliability had to be added to the arsenal of the networks. In June 1950, a new publication appeared entitled *Red Channels: The Report of Communist Influence in Radio and Television*. Its authors were three former FBI agents who formed American Business Consultants, Inc., which was financed by Alfred Kohlberg (a key figure in the pro-Chiang "China Lobby" and a fervent McCarthyite). According to *Red Channels*, anyone in broadcasting who promoted civil rights or opposed the fascism of Franco's Spain could be considered traitorous. This 213-page booklet, which identified 151 entertainers as "subversives," became one of the most consulted reference works of the cultural Cold War.

Impresario Ed Sullivan, for example, discovered that a tap dancer named Paul Draper and a harmonica player named Larry Adler were "pro-Communist in sympathy." Since both had already appeared on Sullivan's variety show, *Toast of the Town*, he quickly offered a public apology to his possibly compromised sponsor and to its possibly embarrassed ad agency. To his distress, Sullivan had booked "performer[s] whose political beliefs are a matter of controversy." Realizing that future guests on his show would need clearance, he eventually urged the entertainment industry to establish a committee to review the political loyalty of performers, so that "if they can't clear themselves, the industry can blacklist them with a clear conscience." Draper, an unusual showman who tap-danced to the music of Brahms, Handel, and Bach, had aroused the ire of the ever-irate columnist Westbrook Pegler, who called him a "mincing twerp" with "twittering toes." Draper exiled himself to Switzerland, and Adler never played his harmonica again on television. When the music he had written for the film *Genevieve* (1953) was nominated for an Oscar, the conductor of the orchestra was listed as the composer instead of Adler, who became an expatriate in England. The blacklist victims had committed no crimes and were never put on trial, imprisoned, or deported. They were only deprived of the fullest opportunity to cultivate and exercise their talent and to be rewarded for it.

Red Channels and the newsletter *Counterattack*, which American Business Consultants also published, were more than guides to employers. They were instruments of political shame and economic reprisal as well. Take the case of the Block Drug Company, which made the chlorophyll toothpaste Amm-i-dent. In 1950, the company began sponsoring *Danger* on CBS, and within a year the product jumped to second among the hundred versions of toothpaste on the market. Over the next five years, the company poured twenty million dollars into television. Then Leonard Block got a letter from Laurence Johnson, an officer in the National Association of Supermarkets. Johnson noted that some of the cast of *Danger* included actors and actresses who were listed in *Counterattack* as politically unreliable. His letter then made an offer. In his supermarkets in Syracuse, Johnson would arrange side-by-side displays of Amm-i-dent and its leading rival, Lever Brothers' Chlorodent. A sign in front of Chlorodent would announce that Lever Brothers paid only for "pro-American actors" and eschewed "Stalin's little creatures." The Amm-i-dent sign would attempt to justify why Block was willing to use "communist fronters"; Block himself would be free to write the copy. Johnson asked, "Would not the results of such a test be of the utmost value to the thousands of supermarkets throughout America?" Block surrendered immediately and checked cast lists thereafter against the personnel standards acceptable to the vigilant grocer. Since 60 percent of broadcast revenues came through supermarket sales, other sponsors yielded as well. Such pressures were so threatening that the advertising agency supervising a Theater Guild series, sponsored by the giant U.S. Steel, omitted all race relations stories. Even *interest* in the topic might be symptomatic of Red leanings.

Political intimidation nearly sandbagged the most wildly successful entertainment series of the era. Gazetteer Walter Winchell hit his readers with a shocker in 1953 when he announced that "America's top comedienne has been confronted with her membership in the Communist Party." The headlines were implausible but true: LUCILLE BALL NAMED RED. For indeed she had told HUAC in 1952 of having registered as a Communist in 1936 "to please my grandfather." The committee cleared the comedienne; and because the ratings of *I Love Lucy* were so phenomenal, her sponsor (Philip Morris) continued its support. Though President and Mrs. Eisenhower were fans of the program, public reaction was uncertain. Before that week's episode started, her husband, Desi Arnaz, made an emotional appeal to the live audience at the Desilu Playhouse: "Lucille Ball is no Communist. Lucy has never been a Communist, not now and never will be. I was kicked out of Cuba because of Communism," the bandleader exclaimed. (When the Arnaz family fled to Miami in 1933, Fidel Castro was all of six years old.) "We both despise the Communists for everything they stand for. Lucille is 100 percent American. She's as American as Barney Baruch and Ike Eisenhower. Please, ladies and gentlemen, don't believe every piece of bunk you read in today's papers." The audience arose and cheered Arnaz, who called for his sobbing spouse to come onstage: "And now I want you to meet my favorite wife—my favorite redhead—in fact, that's the only thing red about her, and even *that's* not legitimate."

Intimidation and suspicion were claiming the most unlikely victims—the apolitical and the harmless. But somehow the folly of including Lucille Ball did not stanch the flow of maliciousness. A case of mistaken identity—long after careers, reputations, sanity, and the ideal of freedom were damaged—finally broke the system. In 1955, a Texas raconteur named John Henry Faulk brought a damage suit against Johnson and Hartnett for libel and conspiracy to defame, after their Aware, Inc., publicized his "Communist associations" and the radio and television stations that once welcomed Faulk's humorous stories fired him. Murrow gave him $7,500 to help pay for the defense that ace attorney Louis Nizer mounted, which took seven years before the broadcaster finally won the largest sum that a jury had ever awarded in a libel suit ($3.5 million, later much reduced). Johnson died during the trial, and Hartnett spent the rest of his life sending small checks to Faulk. Once the blacklist was no longer profitable, it was eliminated.

4

A medium consecrated to reducing the friction of politics, to amusing audiences rather than presenting ideas, cannot be analyzed only by an examination of its public affairs programming. The commitment of television to the Cold War consensus can also be found in the popular, apolitical genres of entertainment, which indicated how pervasive were the values that have been charted in earlier chapters. Shows that on the surface had nothing to do with foreign or domestic policy nevertheless reinforced the faith in "the American way of life" that Communism seemed to threaten. Game shows demon-

strated that ordinary people could seize the fabulous economic opportunities that capitalism promised; situation comedies and soap
operas showed that personal conflicts could be resolved with laughs
and love, without any recourse to institutional change; and the stal-
wart cops and detectives who always captured thugs in twenty-eight
minutes subtly fortified confidence in an infallible criminal justice
system. Without having to refer to a specific set of beliefs, or to
make assumptions explicit, an ideology was thus shaped. Two programming sensations of the 1950s illustrate this special atmosphere.

The Emmy winner as 1952's "Outstanding Television Personality" was a Roman Catholic monsignor whose show, *Life Is Worth
Living*, was "sponsored by God" (as well as by the Admiral Corporation). The program enjoyed a spectacular run for half a decade,
primarily because its star cut such a striking and confident figure.
He wore a black cassock that was streaked with red piping, a scarlet
cape that flowed from his shoulders, and a large gold cross that dangled from his chest. With candles as well as a statue of the Virgin
and Child glistening behind him, he spoke for twenty-eight minutes
without using cue cards, notes, or script. Nor was any musical background necessary to intensify the emotions that *Life Is Worth Living* was designed to convey. His long, elegant fingers sometimes
touched the chain of his cross, or soared upward in supplication, or
sliced the air to emphasize a point. But perhaps most impressive
were his piercing eyes. Wearing light tan powder over his makeup
base, he insisted that his eyes be underlit, to make them glow like
burning coals.

Fulton J. Sheen had received a doctorate in philosophy from the
University of Louvain in 1923, and for the next quarter-century
taught at the Catholic University of America. He first appeared on
radio with *The Catholic Hour* in 1930 and soon thereafter was warning against the evils of Communism, which he equated with Nazism. Sheen backed Franco's Falangist rebels during the Spanish Civil
War (as did Hitler), reasoning that "we cannot breed rats in abundance without being obliged to use rat poison, and so neither can
we breed Communists without being obliged to use the poison of
fascism."

If Spellman was the chief political paladin of Catholic anti-Communism, its major ideologue was his New York assistant and auxiliary bishop. Sheen's prolific array of sermons, articles, speeches,
and fifty books, demonstrating that Communism was the antithesis
of Roman Catholicism, appeared decades before Joe McCarthy demanded to know who promoted Peress. In 1937 alone, Sheen published four works on the topic. *Communism and the Conscience*

of the West (1948) also presented a case for defining Communism
as a sort of secular religion, making it an especially difficult adversary to combat. Sheen argued that, in the paraphrase of one of his
interpreters, "modern Christians have truth, but no zeal; the Communists have zeal, but no truth. . . . They have passion but no ideals;
we have ideals but no passion." The director of the Pontifical Society
for the Propagation of the Faith was passionate and zealous enough,
however, to lure celebrity converts to the church. The souls that he
won included Congresswoman Luce, industrialist Henry Ford II, and
journalist Heywood Broun, plus a brace of former Communists who
became famous as informers: Louis Budenz, ex-managing editor of
the *Daily Worker*, and Elizabeth Bentley, ex-espionage courier.
Sheen's importance was not only political, however. Along with the
Reverend Peale and Rabbi Joshua Loth Liebman, he contributed to
the nondenominational postwar literature of reassurance in the age
of anxiety: his *Peace of Soul* ranked ninth on the bestseller list in
1947.

In 1952, having presented *The Catholic Hour* on NBC radio for
twenty-two years, Monsignor Sheen switched to television, where
he was showcased not at some obscure, ungodly hour but in prime
time (8–8:30 on Tuesday evenings). Every week Sheen faced a live
audience of over a thousand, plus three cameras. But the Dumont
network also raised the ante by pitting the bishop against NBC's
"Mr. Television" himself, comedian Milton Berle. Within a year,
Sheen's fluent combination of biblical tales, moral exhortations,
theological musings, and appeals for charity garnered Nielsen ratings that overwhelmed "Uncle Miltie," who gallantly conceded defeat: "If I'm going to be eased off TV by anyone, it's better to lose
to the One for Whom Bishop Sheen is speaking." The program became so successful that ABC picked it up from Dumont, and by
1954 Sheen was reaching about twenty-five million Americans a
week. Eventually 170 outlets in the United States, plus 17 in Canada, became stations of the Cross when they carried *Life Is Worth
Living*. When its star picked up an Emmy on the same evening as
Bob Hope, who had paid tribute to his gag writers, Sheen humbly
announced, "I want to thank my writers too—Matthew, Mark,
Luke, and John." Their stuff was not only better than Hope's; it was
better than virtually anyone else's on television. For almost two
years the monsignor almost beat out Lucille Ball in the ratings—in
an era when Americans may have liked Ike, but they *loved* Lucy.

In 1953 a Sheen spinoff book entitled *Life Is Worth Living* reached
the fifth spot on the bestseller lists. Nor did it hurt early that year
when Stalin died only two weeks after Sheen delivered on television

an anticipatory eulogy for the tyrant. But despite Sheen's importance in arousing ideological hostility to Communism and in embodying the political edge that Catholicism gave America during the Cold War, he himself took no interest in pursuing the domestic adherents and sympathizers of Stalinism. He was never a McCarthyite (and never even met McCarthy); and though Sheen naturally found Communism hateful, he insisted that Christianity required love of the Communists themselves. He also argued that, like secularism itself, Communism perpetrated "the lie that men will never be better until they make society better." Sheen's claim was consistent with the belief in the redemptive possibilities of divine grace. But his plea for political passivity also conformed neatly with the self-satisfaction of the era and undoubtedly contributed to his huge popularity. *Life Is Worth Living* was eventually canceled not because of bad ratings but because of bad relations with the jealous Spellman, who silenced him from television.

5

The ideological emphasis upon American rectitude that television so smugly promoted faced its biggest threat, however, not from Communism but from within. The source of the trouble was not some external peril that television had either ignored or inflated but rather some of the very forces that were integral to the medium— and, indeed, to a society driven by what Tocqueville had called "the commercial passions." One of the most riveting dramas of the late 1950s not only broke on television but existed *because* of television, and it marked something of a caesura in the story of American innocence.

Radio had introduced "the $64 question" and made it part of the language. Certain forms of knowledge were tested under conditions that required quickness of mind and precision of recall, but the rewards were comparatively modest. This genre was readily transferred to television, which had programmed over twenty quiz shows by the mid-1950s. Their titles often reflected the avaricious frenzy that disturbed right-wing moralists from Billy Graham to John Foster Dulles: *The $64,000 Question, The $64,000 Challenge, The Big Surprise, Tic Tac Dough, High Finance, Treasure Hunt.* Murrow himself was appalled when he first watched one of the shows and realized that his own public affairs program would be a casualty of such hucksterism. For the stakes had gotten higher—a thousand times higher. *The $64 Question* on radio became *The $64,000 Question* on television, in which the losers got the "consolation prize" of a Cadillac. The shows sprang from the immediate need of one cosmetics giant, Revlon, to top the lipstick sales of rival Hazel Bishop. The cultural meaning was enormous, however. The ideological commitment to consumption that defined American supremacy over the Soviet system had found its perfect expression on television, where the contestants became recipients of sudden prosperity without having "produced" anything. They were the stars of a consumer society devoted to the marketing of still more lavish goods.

To make the shows more exciting, potential gladiators were required to submit to detailed exams that clued in quizmasters to the contestants' breadth of knowledge. These screenings were sometimes compared to Ph.D. orals: one show imposed a 363-question exam that lasted four hours. A television producer later explained how simple the technique was: "To keep a contestant winning, all you have to do is figure out how not to hit a question he doesn't know. That's the basis of all quiz shows." On *The $64,000 Question*, Revlon's blue-chip bank was shown going through an elaborate weekly ritual, with a pair of armed guards and a pair of bank officials bringing up the questions from a locked vault. The audience was not given credit for wondering who had the key to the locked vault (where the producer had, of course, already deposited that week's questions, specially designed for the big-money contestants).

As early as 1956, one disgruntled loser complained publicly that a program called *The Big Surprise* had been fixed. No one seemed to listen. The following year, the *New York World-Telegram and Sun* hinted that other quiz shows were faked. Not even the FCC officials who were supposed to be monitoring the air seemed to have read the newspaper's front-page articles. On April 22, 1957, *Time* asked, "Are the quiz shows rigged?" Its own answer to what the magazine called "The $60 Million Question" was ambiguous. Even when *Look* ran a similar story, posing the same query, the likelihood of an affirmative answer was ignored. Attention was paid only in the summer of 1959, when a former nightclub comedian named Eddie Hilgesheimer tried to reveal that *Dotto* was fixed. Hilgesheimer sold his account to the *New York Post,* which was so afraid of publishing the scoop that it turned its material over to Frank Hogan, the Manhattan district attorney. The sponsor of *Dotto* heard what was happening and panicked, canceling the program. The abrogation of *Dotto* was news, which gave the *Post* a rationale for publishing Hilgesheimer's exposé.

Soon the net seemed to be cast as far as the most famous contestant of them all. In the spring of 1957, Charles Van Doren had survived fourteen nerve-wracking weeks on NBC's *Twenty-One* and had earned $129,000. He had quoted lines of John Milton's poetry that a former college president could not recall and had identified the heavyweight (Bob Fitzsimmons) who had whipped Gentleman Jim Corbett for the championship in 1897. Van Doren could name the three baseball players who were credited with more than thirty-five hundred hits ("Ty Cobb, Cap Anson, and [*pause*] Tris Speaker"); and he knew the role for the aria "Sempre libera" in Verdi's *La Traviata* ("She sings it right at the end of the party given by . . . What's her name! Soprano. Her name is [*pause*] Violetta"). Sometimes the answers were snapped back immediately. With other questions, however, Van Doren would bite his lips, clench his fists, roll his eyes, suffer aloud. The beads of sweat would be visible. Then— an agonizing split-second before time was called—the correct response would be summoned from what an awestruck *Time* magazine, putting him on its cover in 1957, called "his phenomenal mind."

Few young Americans seemed more destined for intellectual distinction than Van Doren, who had studied at St. John's College, Cambridge University, and the Sorbonne and was teaching literature at Columbia when NBC plucked him from the classroom and placed him in its isolation booth. His mother was a novelist and an editor of the *Nation;* his father was a celebrated poet and teacher of literature at Columbia; his uncle was a highly regarded critic and biographer. In 1953, Mark Van Doren and Carl Van Doren—both Pulitzer Prize winners—had appeared on Senator McCarthy's list of authors whose books should not be shelved in the State Department's worldwide libraries, which was further proof of the contribution that his family had made to American civilization. Grayson Kirk, who had replaced Eisenhower as president of Columbia, praised Charles Van Doren as "an able and exciting teacher," for which the university paid him forty-five hundred dollars a year. Perhaps because his salary was so modest, perhaps because he seemed so completely a legatee of the high culture of the nation's intelligentsia, Van Doren did not own a television set.

Other than that odd lapse, he seemed so personable—so engagingly all-American—that twenty-five million viewers would *want* him to triumph, as associate producer Al Freedman immediately realized. He confided to Van Doren that the show's current champ, Herbert Stempel, was so brilliant that he was virtually invincible. But Stempel, a squat ex-G.I. from Queens who was working his way through City College, simply wasn't popular. He wasn't clean-cut. He had to be eliminated. Freedman envisioned a series of nail-biting ties, and then Stempel would—in the contestant's own later phrase—"take a dive." Such fixes were customary on the quiz shows, Freedman assured Van Doren, whose victory "would be doing a great service to teachers."

Thus the bargain was struck. The humiliated but compliant Stempel was instructed to forget the title of *Marty*, one of his favorite movies. That defeat enabled *Twenty-One* to become the hottest quiz show in history, as NBC was inundated with thousands of letters of gratitude and admiration. Soon after Van Doren failed to name the reigning king of Belgium, he signed a five-year exclusive contract with NBC for nearly fifty thousand dollars per year, as a commentator on the *Today* show. The announcement of the network contract came when he had just finished writing an essay for the U.S. Information Agency, "What Is American Culture?" On August 28, 1958, a couple of New York newspapers broke Stempel's story of how he had been told to walk the plank. Van Doren denied any knowledge of any fraud on *Twenty-One*, and in 1959 he went on to earn his Ph.D. and to become an assistant professor of English at Columbia. He was such a gentleman. It seemed inconceivable that shows like *Twenty-One* could have been as faked as the professional wrestling that was presented outside of prime time.

Frank Hogan persisted, however, as did Congress (which had gotten into the habit of extensive investigations without obvious legislative implications). The district attorney speculated that, of the 150 television figures who had been summoned to give evidence before the grand jury, at least a hundred were lying. In November 1959, Van Doren confessed to the House Subcommittee on Legislative Oversight, "I have deceived my friends, and I had millions of them." He claimed that he had engaged in the deception because "it was having such a good effect on the national attitude to teachers, education, and the intellectual life." Both Columbia and NBC quickly sacked him. Though Van Doren had been involved in the elaborate fraud from the beginning and then had covered up by lying to a New York grand jury (and to his own attorney), many viewers remained sympathetic to the earnest young swindler. Having pleaded guilty to perjury charges, he and nine other contestants received suspended sentences in 1962. Van Doren eventually became a vice-president of the company that published the *Encyclopaedia Britannica*. Hogan had been right after all: about a hundred producers, contestants, and others had lied to the grand jury. Charles and Martin Revson, the brothers who ran Revlon, often decided which contestants on *The $64,000 Question* should win or lose.

The scandals exerted an immediate impact on television. With the networks' advertisers in revolt, NBC canceled those shows that were admittedly fraudulent. CBS went even farther, dropping all of its quiz shows and even prohibiting its comedians from using canned laughter. The networks also showed how responsible they were by adding a full hour of public programming per week, which was drastically cut back when the flap died down about a year later. These "public interest" shows were not sponsored, in part because Alcoa's experience with *See It Now* made other companies wary of documentaries that occasionally raised troubling questions about American society. All three networks nevertheless realized the prestige value of documentaries, so *CBS Reports, NBC White Paper,* and ABC's *Close-Up* were useful in beefing up the corporations' reputations for gravity. CBS also began conducting annual interviews with Lippmann, not long after the veteran pundit had denounced television as "the creature, the servant, and indeed the prostitute of merchandising."

The most important political effect, however, was that NBC offered free time for a series of presidential debates the following year, an invitation that the Republicans and Democrats accepted. But the Great Debates still smacked of the shows that they were designed to repudiate. A format of quick answers ricocheting between two adversaries under the klieg lights meant "reducing great national issues to trivial dimensions," Professor Daniel Boorstin complained. "With appropriate vulgarity, they might have been called the $400,000 Question (Prize: a $100,000-a-year job for four years)." The prize that this "political quiz show" awarded to a smart, handsome young senator from Massachusetts was an unforeseen consequence of TV's self-inflicted wound.

The scandals also provoked considerable soul-searching, a fear that the nation that thought of itself as goodness incarnate had gone astray. The Gallup Poll discovered more widespread awareness of the fraud than of any other subject on which Americans had ever been queried. Not since the Black Sox scandal of 1919—to which Eisenhower compared it—had there been so widespread a sense of violation of public faith. These duplicitous shows, the president added, were "a terrible thing to do to the American people." Even if the hoax that the networks concocted "breached no law," the *Washington Post* opined, "it nevertheless robbed people of a kind of faith which it is dangerous to destroy in a democracy." Innocence itself had been shaken. The complacency of the 1950s, the public trust in the integrity of American institutions, were somewhat undermined by this evidence of what editor Ralph McGill called "our deep psychological lust for material 'things.'"

John Steinbeck discerned an America that was noteworthy for "our wealth, moral flabbiness, uncertainty and TV scandals," as his correspondent Adlai Stevenson put it. "On all levels it is rigged, Adlai," the novelist had written. "A creeping, all pervading, nerve-gas of immorality . . . starts in the nursery and does not stop before it reaches the highest offices, both corporate and governmental." Steinbeck feared that Americans were "having too many THINGS. They spend their hours and money on the couch searching for a soul." The pride of the 1950s was thus very much to blame. "If I wanted to destroy a nation, I would give it too much and I would have it on its knees. . . . Mainly, Adlai, I am troubled by the cynical immorality of my country. I do not think it can survive on this basis. . . . By our very attitudes we are drawing catastrophe to our-selves. What we have beaten in nature, we cannot conquer in our-selves." Steinbeck's letter, plus Stevenson's prefatory note, was pub-lished in *Newsday* late in 1959. Political scientist Hans J. Morgenthau was even more disturbed, calling the scandal "a great event in the history of America," for "the betrayal of truth for the sake of wealth and power" might well signify "the beginning of the end of civilized society." Another expert in foreign affairs, Senator J. William Fulbright (D-Ark.), told his colleagues that "the question of the moral strength of our people is not just an internal domestic matter. It has grave possibilities in our international relations. . . . What seems to be new about these scandals is the moral blindness or callowness which allows those in responsible positions to accept the practices which the facts reveal."

Perhaps the quiz show scandals hit so hard because they were so enmeshed in the mania for money, in the pecuniary sensations of the 1950s. Sputnik did not streak across the skies until half a year after Van Doren lost, and therefore the jolt that the Soviet tech-nological feat administered to American assurance cannot directly account for the popularity of shows that seemed to reward mental prowess. But the sense that intellect itself had to be drafted into the Cold War, which was one general consequence of sputnik, may ex-plain why the scandal was so reverberant. "The appeal of the pro-grams, with the rising challenge of Soviet brain power as a backdrop, was ultimately patriotic," novelist John Updike conjectured in 1959. "The contestants were selected to be a cross-section of our nation just as deliberately as the G.I.'s in a war movie are." Van Doren had come to symbolize the national hope of permanent superiority over the Soviets, and instead he joined the "phonies" who so repelled Holden Caulfield in *The Catcher in the Rye*. The integrity of American life that was supposed to sharpen the contrast with the Soviet Union thus looked dubious. Nor could the sincerity of American motives any longer be taken for granted as proof of eventual triumph. The buzzer of the tarnished isolation booth tolled the close of an era.

8

DISSENTING:
PITY THE LAND

When traitors in high places, atomic spies, security risks, subversives, propagandists, and atheists were somehow, sometimes linked together, almost any objections to the status quo from the left might be interpreted as Communistic activity. As early as 1949, an aide to Truman realized that social and political reform could not breathe in such a climate. "The consuming fear of communism," Stephen Spingarn wrote, "has led many sincere persons into the belief that . . . change (be it civil rights or a compulsory national health program) is subversive and those who urge it are either communists or fellow travellers." The atmosphere of suspicion led Sidney Hook, who defined himself as a social democrat, to carve a distinction between conspirators and heretics. The former "play outside the rules of the game, sometimes with deadly effect." Since Communists might try to destroy open societies, exploiting the advantages that democracy provides, conspirators should not be tolerated. Heretics deserved the full protection of the First Amendment, however, for their criticism is "essential to the health of a democratic community."

This distinction was blurred in the 1950s. The conspirators—as even the course of the Smith Act prosecutions indicated—did not act according to the Marxist script of violent revolutionary activism, and the Supreme Court began to disregard Hook's dichotomy and to move eventually toward the conclusion that Communists should enjoy the same political rights as everyone else. Yet, paradoxically, the public culture also depreciated heresy—not always, not systematically, not decisively—but at least often enough to worry anyone who cherished civil liberties. Wechsler wrote that "our republic is haunted by two kinds of silence—the calculated reticence of those who have something to hide and the deepening timidity of others who have nervously concluded that it is safer to have nothing to say." Though the silencing was rarely complete, non-Communists and anti-Communists, Communists and communists, found their right to speak challenged and restricted.

Not everyone groveled. When McCarthy asked the artist Rockwell Kent, "Have you contributed . . . money to organizations that have been officially listed by the Attorney General as fronts for doing work for the Communist Party?" Kent replied: "The fact that they are listed by the Attorney General or by anyone else as subversive does not sway me to any degree. I am a man who makes up his own mind, and if I believe that they are serving a good cause and know what that cause is, then I will join them." Such organizations were "working for the Negroes, for freedom, for the poor, for good legislation. . . . What would America be without these so-called Communist fronts?"

Although the distinguished firm of Little, Brown forced out editor-in-chief Angus Cameron after Budenz denounced him, the publishing industry was largely immune to the intimidations of the Red Scare. Serious social and political criticism was freely articulated in the decade, even if not as heeded as its authors wished. For in such straitened times, Professor Galbraith wrote, "even the mildly critical individual is likely to seem like a lion in contrast with the general mood"; and he warned readers of *The Affluent Society* that its "negative thoughts" might "strike an uncouth note in the world of positive thinking." Indeed, fear of conformity encouraged the sales of books understood to be critical of it, like *The Lonely Crowd* and *The Organization Man*—two titles that the nascent radical Tom Hayden cited in 1960 to help explain the stirring of his own "generation[,] which cannot avoid reading criticism of itself and its fathers." McCarthy himself was forcefully attacked while he was in power, as was McCarthyism itself. Elmer Davis's libertarian tract, *But We Were Born Free*, was a bestseller in 1954, and other liberal anti-Communists faced no obstacles in finding publishing houses or readers. But Communist authors, or those reputed to be Communists, or writers who contradicted too directly the Cold War consensus (or who showed insufficient enthusiasm for it), had to settle for obscure outlets or go abroad to find publishers.

Political censorship did not affect the theater. A metropolitan, generally liberal clientele supported Broadway, while off-Broadway appreciated whatever attention a right-wing picket line might provide. *The Threepenny Opera* became the longest-running musical up to that time in American history, with over two thousand performances in Greenwich Village from 1954 until 1961. Recordings of the signature song from the show, "Mack the Knife," sold ten million copies—a total that only "White Christmas" surpassed. The playwright and lyricist who was responsible for such a theatrical/ musical triumph was Bertolt Brecht, probably the most authentic Stalinist—and certainly the most towering artist—ever to testify before HUAC. (The committee was aware of neither attribute.) Brecht was the eleventh—and most ingratiating—of the Hollywood Ten and had explored in his play *Galileo* (1947) the failure of the will to resist unjust authority. "Pity the land that has no heroes," an observer remarks upon learning that the astronomer had caved in to the Inquisition. But Galileo himself responds, "Pity the land that has *need* of heroes."

J. Robert Oppenheimer was shown no instruments of torture, nor was he required to recant his scientific theories. But late in 1953 President Eisenhower had ordered a "blank wall" to separate the government's files of classified information from the "father of the atomic bomb," who had been responsible at Los Alamos for many of those very secrets. The next year, a panel under the aegis of the Atomic Energy Commission conceded that Oppenheimer had shown himself a loyal citizen who had never divulged any secrets, but declared him a "security risk," primarily because he opposed both the air force's reliance on strategic bombing and the development of the hydrogen bomb. The criteria and methods that the AEC accepted in reaching such a verdict provoked its former chairman, David Lilienthal, to exclaim: "There hadn't been a proceeding like this since the Spanish Inquisition." Oppenheimer was humiliated and stripped of his influence in the formulation of weapons policy, while the morale of scientists was widely felt to have suffered. A poor witness in his own behalf, a full participant in the labyrinthine security apparatus that entrapped him, the physicist was scarcely a hero. It would be just as misleading, however, to view him as a martyr. Oppenheimer lost neither his freedom nor his livelihood— only his government consultantship. He remained the director of the Institute for Advanced Study at Princeton, explained physics to viewers of CBS, and could pack lecture halls in Europe. Though one air force general remarked that such experts were supposed to be "on tap, not on top," Oppenheimer's awesome stature remained largely intact in the scientific community.

1

Other limitations upon the scope permitted to dissidence were less ambiguous, however. Since the Cold War consensus was grounded so deeply in faith in the FBI, skepticism about its methods and motives represented a threat that the bureau itself hastened to counter. Though publication of Max Lowenthal's *Federal Bureau of Investigation* in 1950 could not be halted, the campaign to discredit the book revealed the limits of criticism that domestic anti-Communism tried to establish. A lawyer with a long record of government service, Lowenthal was also a friend of President Truman's. He construed a powerful civil libertarian case against the bureau. The 563-page *Federal Bureau of Investigation*, which included eighty-three pages of citations, "constituted a rigorously argued and documented brief..., a marshalling of all the evidence that had been excluded by the mythologizers of the FBI legend," according to one historian of the bureau.

The general accuracy of the book could not be rebutted. But in an era in which criticism of Hoover was iconoclastic in the precise sense of the term, it was all too easy to impugn Lowenthal's patriotism. Indeed, a speech by George Dondero (R-Mich.) belongs in a sequel to *Studies in Hysteria*. Taking to the floor of the House of Representatives in September 1950—two months before the book was to be published—Dondero pinned its author at the center of an ominously anti-American conspiracy: "When he is caught the revelation will be a bigger shock to this nation than the exposé of Benedict Arnold. It must be done. The nation can take it. But it cannot win the war of survival with Russia if this man is allowed to continue his clever, diabolical scheme to undermine our national security." Dondero considered the author more than an attorney; he was a movement. "Every person still in the Government who has had a Lowenthal endorsement," the congressman warned, "should be identified and their [sic] loyalty determined."

HUAC investigators applied pressure too. They visited William Sloan, the publisher of *Federal Bureau of Investigation*, and subpoenaed the author himself. They even urged his attorney—former senator Burton Wheeler—not to represent Lowenthal at the executive session, which was timed to coincide with Dondero's assault. HUAC's questions were designed to stigmatize Lowenthal as a devotee of unsavory leftist causes. The hostility of the interrogation was as patent as the thinness of the accusations, and the transcript of the hearings was made public exactly two days before the publication of the book. Professor Robert K. Carr concluded: "That the

Committee had any legitimate basis for questioning Lowenthal even in executive session is doubtful, in view of the questions actually put to him; that it had any justification for making public his testimony, beyond a desire to tar him as a person who had been investigated by the Un-American Activities Committee, is in no way apparent."

Even though the bureau could not prevent publication of so sinister a threat to the Republic, it also campaigned against the book by providing reviewers with boilerplate condemnations of *Federal Bureau of Investigation*. To coincide with its publication, the bureau distributed a reassuring *Reader's Digest* reprint entitled, "Why I No Longer Fear the FBI," by ACLU co-counsel and national board member Morris Ernst, who was then secretly giving the bureau reports of ACLU meetings as well as the names of ACLU members whom he considered sympathetic to Communism. Lowenthal's book had a negligible impact, whatever the reasons. It found few readers—and even among these may not have changed many minds about the bureau's image as a bulwark against subversion. When the danger of Communism loomed larger than the value of the Bill of Rights, any exposure of police methods as resembling those of the enemy was unwelcome. Widespread interest in the subject seemed dormant. Although the *Nation* devoted a full issue to an exposé of the FBI on October 20, 1958, it was not until journalist Fred J. Cook enlarged his *Nation* material into a book six years later—accurately entitled *The FBI Nobody Knows*—that another assault appeared in print. In that fourteen-year interregnum, criticism of the command post of the domestic Cold War was silenced.

The novelist Nelson Algren was neither a Communist nor a supporter of Communism. But the FBI had a file on him (as it did on many other leading writers), and one of its informants claimed that Algren had contributed a "left-wing article" for—of all journals—the travel magazine *Holiday*. The punishment was therefore appropriate: in 1952 the State Department denied Algren a passport. Ex-radical journalist Dwight Macdonald was permitted to go abroad, however, where he helped edit *Encounter* in London. Upon his return, and from his new perspective, Macdonald submitted a caustic overview entitled "America! America!" to the magazine, which rejected it. *Dissent*, a social democratic quarterly, published it instead in New York in 1958. Formally, then, Macdonald's rights of expression were not infringed. But, as was the custom with "controversial" writers, a British magazine that reprinted the essay had to reassure its readers that Macdonald was a "good American"—to which Macdonald wondered whether his criticisms of his country would somehow have been invalidated if he were *not* a "good American." He preferred to consider himself a "critical American." A decade later, the radical magazine *Ramparts* disclosed that CIA subsidies had kept *Encounter* afloat. (And when the exposure cut off CIA funding, the Ford Foundation picked up the tab.) With such techniques, government agencies ensured that some ideas were more equal than others.

Sometimes a negative cultural condition cannot be directly attributed to the opposition of authorities or the tyranny of the majority, or even the weakness of ideas. Sometimes an audience has not (yet) emerged that can appreciate or understand what an author is trying to express. In the history of Western thought, Spinoza, Vico, and Kierkegaard were uncelebrated while alive, though posthumously their ideas became deeply embedded in Western philosophy. In the 1960s, Paul Goodman emerged as an emblematic intellectual. A decade earlier, his anarchism, pacifism, utopianism, and radical skepticism seemed merely a rude interruption of the great yawn. In the 1950s, he put his thoughts in notebooks (*Five Years*) because "I had no one else to write for or talk to." Even his practical schemes fell on deaf ears; a dozen publishers rejected *Growing Up Absurd* (1960). His "crazy young allies" were yet to grow up absurd themselves. When they did, Goodman would reach into his trunk, would pull out another manuscript to give to Random House, and—without a noticeable change in "lifestyle"—rose from the poorest stratum to the upper brackets, from obscurity to esteem and influence.

Even apolitical figures could be affected by the intolerance that the Cold War exacerbated. An authority on the gall wasp, Alfred Kinsey was an entomologist who hardly exuded the fiery defiance of a heretic. He was a scholar drawn to issues of measurement, not to problems of injustice. But Kinsey's efforts to record and quantify human sexual behavior aroused enormous controversy in an era that politicized—and idealized—the family as a haven against subversion and unwelcome social change. Since 1920 he had taught and conducted research at Indiana University, whose president, Herman B. Wells, was a friend who both protected his academic freedom and the welfare of the Institute for Sex Research, which was founded in 1947. Wells also urged him to get a medical publisher rather than a trade publisher, and if possible to have *Sexual Behavior in the Human Male* (1948) published sometime other than during the sixty-one days when the Indiana state legislature was in session. Despite the scientific nimbus surrounding the book, the *New York Times* refused to review or accept advertising for what came to be called the Kinsey Report. The blackout was ineffective, and even inconsistent, since the *Times* listed *Sexual Behavior in the Human Male* among its bestsellers.

Life magazine blamed the messenger when it condemned the report as "an assault on the family as a basic unit of society, a negation of moral law, and a celebration of licentiousness." In a June symposium, the *Reader's Digest* asked, "Must We Change Our Sex Standards?" The editors' idea of balance was to solicit opinions that were predictably hostile to change, or to ask sexologists whose credentials were—to put it mildly—impeachable: the Reverend Peale, the national commander of the Salvation Army, and a couple of bachelors—Father Edward J. Flanagan of Boys Town and the ubiquitous Hoover. A Gallup Poll nevertheless disclosed that 58 percent of men and 55 percent of women approved of the validity of conducting such research. That year it also occurred to Kinsey to interview Communists in New York City for his institute. He asked his attorney, Morris Ernst, to secure Hoover's approval, as well as his assurance that the bureau would not seek to violate (further) the privacy of the subjects of the interviews. Kinsey's colleague and biographer claims that the FBI did not interfere, but that too few sexual histories were taken to justify any generalizations about Communists.

Five years later, Kinsey and his staff published *Sexual Behavior in the Human Female*, revealing that a quarter of all white, middle-class women had committed adultery by the age of forty, and that nearly half had experienced intercourse before marriage. No wonder, then, that an Oklahoma senator remarked, "Dr. Kinsey and Senator McCarthy have one thing in common. They both claim to have uncovered a lot of domestic disloyalty." By then the Red Scare was flourishing, and whatever undermined family unity might be interpreted as Communistic. A Utica woman took it literally, and in 1950 was granted an annulment—not a divorce—solely because her husband was a Communist.

In part because Kinsey's sexual histories were of women in an era when the double standard was pervasive, in part because the prestige of religion had become virtually unchallenged as well as unrivaled, the criticism directed at *Sexual Behavior in the Human Female* was livelier than the attacks on his earlier report. Not far from the Indiana University campus itself, for example, the minister of the Second Presbyterian Church in Indianapolis preached a sermon, "The Celestial Fire," after having read a *Life* review of the second Kinsey Report. Dr. Jean S. Milner informed his congregation of "a fundamental kinship between that thing and Communism. . . . The influence of this report, though it may seem to be a thousand miles from Communism, will in time contribute inevitably toward Communism, for both are based on the same basic naturalist philosophy." An editorial in the weekly newspaper of the Indiana Roman Catholic archdiocese charged that Kinsey's studies "pave the way for people to believe in communism and to act like Communists." A later headline in the same Bloomington newspaper read: KINSEY'S SEX BOOKS LABELED 'RED' TAINTED. The Indiana University chapter of the American Association of University Professors felt obliged to rebut the Catholic attack, calling the association of his work with Communism "a deliberate and deplorable appeal to emotionalism, which if successful could only undermine the democratic functions of the American university." President Wells also forthrightly defended Kinsey, pointing out that one difference between the American and Soviet systems was untrammeled freedom of research.

Louis B. Heller (D-N.Y.) nevertheless urged Postmaster General Summerfield to ban from the mails a book that Heller himself had never seen, much less read. Its author, the congressman asserted, was "hurling the insult of the century against our mothers, wives, daughters and sisters." The Reverend Graham, who had been unknown to the general public when *Human Male* was published, found it "impossible to estimate the damage this book will do to the already deteriorating morals of America." The president of the Union Theological Seminary considered "the current vogue" of Kinsey's work symptomatic of "a prevailing degradation in American morality approximating the worst decadence of the Roman era. The most disturbing thing is the absence of a spontaneous, ethical revulsion from the premises of the study."

Such attacks should not be confused with the serious methodological and philosophical objections that Kinsey's work generated. Lionel Trilling's famous criticism in *Partisan Review* (1948), for example, underscored the failure of the report to connect quantitative facts to personal, social, and cultural meaning and pointed out the disguised assumptions and attitudes lurking behind the pose of objectivity. But Trilling did not traduce Kinsey's right to pursue and disseminate his research, nor suggest its abridgement because of projected consequences. But religious and congressional pressure caused the Rockefeller Foundation, which had helped finance Kinsey's pioneering inquiry, to buckle; in 1954, the foundation balked at further funding. Its head, Dean Rusk, claimed falsely that the Institute for Sex Research had secured other sources of aid. The Rockefeller Foundation, without identifying Kinsey's mysterious benefactor, announced around the same time its own huge grant (over half a million dollars) to the Union Theological Seminary "to aid in the development of vital religious leadership."

Indiana University itself held firm until the National Institute of Mental Health provided a grant to continue the research, which remained at its Bloomington base. Kinsey himself died in 1956, the same year that Spellman tried to strangle *Baby Doll* in her cradle. But Kinsey's work had already helped make his society more tolerant in its approach to sexuality. The following year—to pick one example—a French film was released which, though its title mentioned the divinity, was more about eros than agape. *"And God Created Woman* is an assault on each and every woman of our community and nation, living or dead—our mothers, sisters, wives and daughters," the Reverend James T. Lyng of Lake Placid, New York, complained. Banned in cities as diverse as Philadelphia, Fort Worth, Abilene, Memphis, and Providence, the movie that uncovered Brigitte Bardot quickly recovered its $400,000 investment, grossing ten times that amount. This time the cardinal did not even try to stop it, as the gap seemed to widen between the actualities of sexual practice that Kinsey had sought to delineate and the commandments that the church promulgated. On May 10, 1960, the *New York Times* buried a story on page 75 that would have even greater repercussions for the certitudes of sexual morality that the 1950s were supposed to encode: the Food and Drug Administration had approved an oral contraceptive (Enovid) as safe. The reputation of a scholar like Alfred Kinsey for controversy would henceforth seem increasingly quaint, a relic of the repression that was not supposed to be confined to politics.

2

Not even the most famous person on the globe was exempted from persecution during the Cold War. Perhaps the greatest genius to work in films was deeply affected by the relentless and philistine hostility to "Reds." Already during World War II the reputation of Charlie Chaplin had changed from a clown into a controversialist, when an aspiring actress named Joan Barry filed a paternity suit against him. He was tried under the Mann Act. Though Chaplin won an acquittal on the charge of having transported her across state lines for immoral purposes, he lost the paternity suit. Three physicians concurred that he could not have been the father of Barry's child. But blood tests were not admissible evidence in California courts, and the jury held him liable for child support. The highly publicized details of his private life made him vulnerable to pressure from groups that resented his leftist sympathies as well.

"Cynical pessimism" was Chaplin's own description of the mood that suffused *Monsieur Verdoux* (1947), a film that was critical of both capitalism and war and that ran into early trouble with censorship. The movie industry's own Breen Office was particularly troubled by the apparent anti-Catholicism of *Monsieur Verdoux* and invited members of the Legion of Decency to screen it. They approved it only reluctantly, especially after one censor announced, "Well, it's okay by me, there's no cleavage." But the Catholic War Veterans were unappeased, and they became actively involved in harassing Chaplin, who had lived in America for four decades without ever bothering to apply for citizenship. Perhaps even more damaging was the hostility that he aroused from the American Legion, which could boast over three million members, many auxiliaries, and formidable influence. Legionnaires included President Truman and five members of his cabinet, three justices of the Supreme Court, forty-four senators, and 195 congressmen. The Legion's Counter-Subversive Activities Committee in Washington was especially vigilant. If Legionnaires and their allies disliked the credits on particular films and set up picket lines outside movie houses, financiers would not associate themselves with such names in the future, distributors would refuse to handle such films, and most projectionists would decline to screen the work of "subversives." American Legion demonstrations outside cinemas that exhibited *Monsieur Verdoux* forced the film to be withdrawn from circulation.

Whether Chaplin's foes resented his sexual freedom more than his dissident political values is not easy to determine, and the distinction may not have mattered anyway. In the same breath, HUAC's John Rankin condemned the comedian for his taste for the left-wing art of *New Masses* magazine and for "his forcible seduction of white girls." The solution was Chaplin's deportation. His life, according to another congressman in 1947, "is detrimental to the moral fabric of the nation." Two years later, a senator charged that Chaplin's "public utterances provide a series of eulogies for the Stalinist dictatorship." The creator of the Tramp had come "perilously close to treason." In fact, though the comedian was highly critical of American foreign policy, defended the civil liberties of Communists, and favored Henry Wallace in the 1948 campaign, Chaplin always denied that he was a Communist. Despite many rumors to the contrary, the FBI never found any evidence of contributions to the Communist party and its causes. Beginning in 1947, HUAC announced that it would ask Chaplin to testify, postponed three times calling him as a witness, and then never did. Chaplin tele-grammed the committee in 1947 that he had never "joined any po-litical organization in my life." But the beloved comic was being transformed into a dangerous Commie, and the drumbeat of intim-idation continued.

In *Limelight* (1952), Chaplin played an aging clown named Calvero who realizes that, "as a man gets on, he wants to live deeply. A feeling of sad dignity comes over him, and that's fatal for a comic." When his protégée (Claire Bloom) remarks on "what a sad business it is, being funny," Calvero agrees: "Yes, it is—when they don't laugh." For Chaplin's own relationship with his audience had changed. The American Legion instituted a campaign of picketing theaters that had booked *Limelight*, without even having to dem-onstrate that it contained any unwholesome themes; major chains such as Loew's, Fox, and RKO withdrew the film after initial show-ings. Since accusations of Communism could wreck an industry that was losing its vast audience to television, *Limelight* was shown in relatively few cities. The American Legion and the Catholic War Veterans also dissuaded many theater owners and some television stations from reviving Chaplin's classic silent films too—some dat-ing back to 1916–17.

The FBI's failure to link him to Communism did not prevent the bureau from feeding malicious items to Hollywood gossip column-ists Louella Parsons and Hedda Hopper. In May 1952, Senator Nixon agreed with Hopper that "the way the Chaplin case has been handled has been a disgrace for years. Unfortunately, we aren't able to do much about it when the top decisions are made by the likes of Ache-son and [Attorney General James] McGranery." Nixon expressed the hope that if the Republicans took power the following January, they would "apply the same rules to Chaplin as they do to ordinary cit-izens."

By September the attorney general had gotten the message; while Chaplin was sailing in the mid-Atlantic, McGranery rescinded his reentry permit. The attorney general ordered the Immigration and Naturalization Service to detain Chaplin for hearings, should he attempt to return to the United States. Aliens could be barred be-cause of "morals, health or insanity, or for advancing Communism or associating with Communist or pro-Communist organizations." The attorney general explained that Chaplin was "an unsavory char-acter" alleged in the press to be a member of the Communist party (which the FBI knew to be false). "He has been charged with making leering, sneering statements about the country whose gracious hos-pitality has enriched him," McGranery added. That month Hopper told readers of her nationally syndicated column, "Good riddance to bad rubbish," while another columnist dismissed Chaplin as "never more than a custard-pie comedian" anyway. He thus became a victim of sullen nativism as well as right-wing animus.

When the *Queen Elizabeth* arrived at Southampton, the writer-director-star of *The Great Dictator* (1940) stated: "I've never been political. I have no political convictions. I'm an individualist, and I believe in liberty." An editorial in the *New York Times* supported him: "No political situation, no international menace, can destroy the fact that he is a great artist who has given infinite pleasure to many millions, not in any one country but in all countries. Unless there is far more evidence against him than is at the moment visible, the Department of State will not dignify itself or increase the national security if it sends him into exile."

In fact, the invisible evidence against Chaplin was no more damning than the visible. His FBI file had been inaugurated three decades earlier, and it eventually ran over nineteen hundred pages. The bureau had vainly pursued a lead that the comedian was "engaged in Soviet espionage"—which, if true, would have made him the most conspicuous spy in history. When Oona O. Chaplin went back to Los Angeles to pick up her husband's assets, she learned that the FBI had interrogated the servants about moral turpitude in the household. Taxpayers had also unwittingly subsidized the bureau's fascination with the intricacies of his second marriage to teenager Lita Grey over a quarter of a century earlier, third wife Paulette Goddard's Mexican divorce in 1942, and once again Joan Barry's charge that Chaplin had been the father of her child. Indeed, even if the sixty-three-year-old entertainer had made "leering" and "sneering" statements, his right to do so was presumably among the prerogatives which a free society ensures—and which was readily granted to the sensationalist press that employed and enriched Hedda Hopper and Louella Parsons. The FBI also learned that, in blocking Chaplin's reentry, the INS conceded that its case would be insufficiently strong if he were to challenge the ban.

But Chaplin did not try. In April 1954, he formally returned his American reentry permit, claiming to "have been the object of lies and vicious propaganda by powerful reactionary groups who, by their influence and by aid of America's yellow press, have created an unhealthy atmosphere in which liberal minded individuals can be singled out and persecuted." He decided to sit out the Cold War in Geneva, where he lunched with Chou En-lai during the conference that arranged for French withdrawal from Indochina. Also in 1954, Chaplin accepted a prize from a Communist peace organization but gave most of the five thousand pounds away. Two years later, he met Khrushchev and Soviet premier Nikolai Bulganin in London. But Chaplin's most important political statement came in 1957, when he wrote, directed, produced, scored, and starred in a film that attacked the Red Scare more directly than any American movie of the era. Produced by the British film company Archway, *A King in New York* did not premiere in the United States until 1976.

Chaplin played the refugee king of Estrovia, who emigrates to the United States when a revolution drives him from the throne. Penniless, he is reduced to making television commercials. The film's obvious satire of American popular culture switches to a tone of terror, however, when King Shahdov befriends a runaway boy named Rupert (played by Chaplin's own son Michael), whose parents are under surveillance because of their political affiliations. Their summons to testify before HUAC has caused their neighbors to ostracize them as Communists, and such prejudice forces the child to become a fugitive. Shahdov's efforts to calm him result in the king's own summons to a HUAC interrogation, according to the doctrine of guilt by association. But he manages to turn the hearings into a shambles by squirting a fire hose at the pompous inquisitors.

A King in New York hardly concludes on a comic note, however. Rupert is advised that his parents will be released from their difficulties if he will provide the names of their political colleagues. Nearly hysterical, the ten-year-old buckles under the strain and becomes an informer. He is ashamed, even though the school to which he returns is proud of his heroism and patriotism. Fortunately, his parents are cleared when they turn out to be merely believers in the right to privacy and in freedom of association, and not Communists after all. But America is not supposed to honor children for divulging the political contacts of their parents, and the king—saddened by the suspiciousness and hatred that he has encountered here—hastily returns to Europe to find a home.

Reviewing Chaplin's eightieth film in the *London Evening Standard*, John Osborne noted that "in some ways *A King in New York* must be his most bitter film. It is a calculated, passionate rage." Unfortunately, Chaplin fudged the moral and constitutional issues that HUAC inquisitions raised by making the victims completely non-Communist and therefore "innocent," instead of citizens with past actions to be confronted or disguised or regretted. *A King in New York* was, in short, politically simplistic—and therefore aesthetically insipid. In any event, Chaplin knew that he had forfeited the American market. When he gave a press conference in Paris for the film, he petulantly confirmed the anti-Americanism that had partially animated *A King in New York* by banning all newsmen from the United States. They were barred from the Paris premiere as well. When Murrow nevertheless managed to ask him why his treatment of the nation where he had lived since 1910 was so one-sided, Chaplin replied: "If you give both sides, it becomes bloody dull. I'm not a highbrow—I'm an instinctive artist. Whatever I do is for effect." But the effect was coarse and unambiguous; the instinct was propagandistic.

In 1972, Chaplin finally returned to the United States—after its ambassador in Switzerland had telegrammed the attorney general and an undersecretary of state, recommending a quick waiver of Chaplin's ineligibility to return. Since Brandeis University was planning to give him an award, the ambassador feared unfavorable publicity. After an absence of two decades, Chaplin also visited Los Angeles, where plans for a "Walk of Fame" on Hollywood Boulevard had been announced in 1958. The fifteen hundred bronze stars embedded in the sidewalk honored all sorts of forgotten actors and actresses, but somehow his name was not among them. Yet "the incalculable effect he has had on making motion pictures the art form of the century" was the citation on the special Oscar that he earned in 1972, and he was in tears when he attended a tribute at the Lincoln Center Film Society in New York. Upon his death in Switzerland in 1977 at the age of eighty-eight, Laurence Olivier eulogized Chaplin as "perhaps the greatest actor of all time."

3

If ever one case could be made for the national faith in individual opportunity, as well as for the blazing talent that the eclipse of racism might unleash, the defense would rest with Paul Robeson. The son of a runaway slave who had served in the Union Army in the Civil War, Robeson was an All-American end at Rutgers, where he was also elected to Phi Beta Kappa. In 1923, he received a law degree from Columbia, where one of his professors was Harold Medina, and where Robeson paid for his tuition by playing professional football on weekends. Though admitted to the bar in New York, he joined the Provincetown Players and starred in Eugene O'Neill plays like *The Emperor Jones* (1924). He sang "Ol' Man River" in *Show Boat* (1928) and in 1943 became the first black actor to star in an *Othello* in New York, where its 295 performances set a Broadway record for Shakespeare. Robeson was also featured in eleven films and made more than three hundred recordings as a concert singer. It would be hard to imagine a more versatile and astonishing career.

He seemed so much larger than life that, when HUAC asked Adolphe Menjou to define their common ideological foe, the dapper actor replied, "A Communist is anyone who attends any meeting at which Paul Robeson appears—and applauds." Though Robeson was a faithful fellow traveler who testified under oath in 1946 that he was not a Party member, no distinction was ever finer. He defended Stalin's purges as suitable punishment for "counter-revolutionary assassins" and justified the Nazi-Soviet Pact of 1939 as "defensive." He publicly opposed the restoration of civil liberties to the American Trotskyists in 1949, though the Stalinist leadership was facing the same Smith Act penalties inflicted on the Socialist Workers party, eighteen of whose leaders had been jailed during World War II. He also refused to testify about Party membership after 1946. When the Soviet government gave him the Stalin Peace Prize six years later, the regime also showed its appreciation of his services by naming a Russian mountain in his honor, implanting a bust of Robeson on its summit.

Such recognition was intimately connected with the demolition of his career and reputation in the United States. Local politicians canceled his concerts in Peoria, Illinois, and Albany, New York, in 1947. At Peekskill, New York, two years later, Robeson attempted to give a concert in support of the Party leaders on trial in Foley Square (with Judge Medina presiding). Legionnaires hurled stones at the visitors and burned sheet music after barricading the approach roads. The Civil Rights Congress, which sponsored the event, then vowed to hold a second concert a week later. This time a thousand state troopers were on hand, permitting Robeson to sing "Ol' Man River" and "Peat Bog Soldiers" without interruption. Afterwards, however, about one hundred fifty concertgoers were injured in ambushes. Few missed the irony that the assailants were primarily proletarians—war veterans and their allies. Though Robeson sued two veterans' groups and Westchester County officials, a grand jury found them blameless. FBI agents watched his home and monitored his activities, which enabled the Department of Justice to complain later that, during his concert tours, he "has repeatedly criticized the conditions of Negroes in the United States."

Then, in a speech in Paris, Robeson's fidelity to the Party line went beyond recovery when he asserted: "We shall not make war on anyone. We shall not make war on the Soviet Union." The Associated Press blatantly misquoted him, however. The wire service reported that Robeson found it "unthinkable that American Negroes would go to war on behalf of those who have oppressed us for generations" against the Soviet Union, a nation which "has raised our people to the full dignity of mankind." This a priori refusal to join with one's countrymen in a war against the USSR was the official position of the French and Italian Communist parties, and Robeson's adoption of that stance subjected him to a hailstorm of outrage. Anti-Communists fighting for civil rights were especially worried at the windfall that such irresponsibility provided bigots. The militant black labor leader A. Philip Randolph, for example, had also insisted that "no intelligent Negro is willing to lay down his life for the United States as it presently exists." But in 1949 Randolph criticized a segregated army because it was segregated—not because it would be primed to fight the USSR.

One headline read, "Jackie Hits Robeson's Red Pitch." For star athletes of the era did not confine themselves to endorsing Wheaties, if the Cold War required it. Testimony in Washington was included among off-the-field duties of Jackie Robinson, who was the perfect foil for Robeson. The second baseman was then leading the National League with a .360 batting average and had made all Communists who followed baseball into Brooklyn Dodgers fans when he integrated the national pastime in 1947. Even from her cell in Sing Sing, Ethel Rosenberg could praise the team for an "indomitable spirit that has endeared them to so many. But it is chiefly in their outstanding contribution to the eradication of racial prejudice that they have covered themselves with glory."

Yet Robinson had not crossed the color line to submit to a Party line. He told HUAC in July 1949 that Robeson's utterance was "very silly to me," after Dodgers president Branch Rickey released the infielder from his pledge to eschew politics upon entering the major leagues. In a statement written with Rickey's help, Robinson made clear to HUAC that equality for American blacks remained the primary issue: "The fact [that] it is a Communist who denounces injustice in the courts, police brutality, and lynching when it happens doesn't change the truth of his charges. Just because Communists kick up a big fuss over racial discrimination when it suits their purposes, a lot of people try to pretend that the whole issue is a creation of Communist imagination." But he added that "they are not fooling anyone with this kind of pretense, and talk about 'Communists stirring up Negroes to protest' only makes present misunderstanding worse than ever. Negroes were stirred up long before there was a Communist Party, and they will stay stirred up long after the party has disappeared—unless Jim Crow has disappeared by then as well."

Robeson himself did not testify before HUAC until 1956, and by then the sword that he had given his enemies had been slashingly effective. The passport that he had held since 1922 had been revoked in 1950, in part because of "the appellant's frank admission that he has been for years extremely active politically in behalf of independence of the colonial peoples of Africa." (Longstanding imperialist nations like France, England, Portugal, and Belgium were needed as allies against Soviet-style imperialism.) Without a passport, Robeson was blocked from making concert appearances abroad, where he was still very much in demand. Three years earlier, he had earned $104,000. In 1950, his income had dropped to $2,000. His name was even erased from the official list of All-Americans for 1917 and 1918 (reducing those dream squads to ten men). Langston Hughes, who was also being subjected to inquisitorial pressures, excised Robeson from his book *Famous Negro Music Makers* in 1955.

The blanket of nonpersonhood was temporarily lifted the following year with his HUAC testimony, which demonstrated the validity of Koestler's definition of Communism as not left but east. When a congressman asked Robeson, who claimed that he felt like a full human being only in the Soviet Union, whether he had been shown the forced labor camps, the son of a slave changed the subject and instead attacked the degradation of blacks at home, where "the slaves I see are still in a kind of semi-serfdom. I am interested in the place I am, and in the country that can do something about it. As far as I know, about the slave camps, they were Fascist prisoners who had murdered millions of the Jewish people, and who would have wiped out millions of the Negro people, could they have gotten a hold of them. That is all I know about that."

By professing concern only about his own country, Robeson logically should have excluded himself from the anticolonialist struggle that had stirred the enmity of the Department of State and should never have joined the anti-Fascist campaigns of the 1930s and 1940s. His response also constituted a macabre libel on millions of Soviet political prisoners, including the future memorialist of these *zeks*, Alexander Solzhenitsyn. Robeson's testimony represented a willful and perverse refusal to imagine one day in the life of Ivan Denisovich. Though the witness had answered all questions, HUAC recommended that the House of Representatives cite him for contempt. He *was*, of course, contemptuous of Congress, but it took no action.

Two years later, Robeson's autobiography appeared. The publisher of *Here I Stand* was unusual: "Othello Associates," with no street address listed. In 1958, the State Department returned his passport to him, after the Supreme Court determined that such cancellations were unconstitutional. But by then his health was destroyed, curtailing his opportunities to sing and receive honors abroad (especially in Britain and East Germany). The silence surrounding him on native grounds was lifting by the time of his death in 1976, at the age of seventy-seven. To measure the wreck of so remarkable a career, Franz Kafka can be quoted: "It is enough that the arrows fit exactly in the wounds they have made."

4

By 1953, thirty-six million people were annually visiting about two hundred International Information Agency libraries overseas, and among them that year were Cohn and Schine. After a whirlwind tour of seven European countries, McCarthy's most notorious aides claimed that thirty thousand books—out of two million on the shelves—were by "pro-Communist" writers. The works of about forty authors were withdrawn. Banned "pending further examination" were the books of some twenty others who had not been candid about their Communist affiliations when testifying before Senate investigating committees. When Cohn had landed in Frankfurt, for example, he had asked the director of America House where the Communist authors were hidden. None was available in the library, the official recalled assuring Cohn, who "then asked where I kept the Dashiell Hammett books. I led him to the shelf where *The Maltese Falcon* and *The Thin Man* were. He turned to the reporters and announced triumphantly that this was proof that there were indeed Communists represented in the American library."

Cohn's trophy was a novelist who happened to have seen the most primitive face of American capitalism. As a Pinkerton detective, Hammett had been used as a union-buster before World War I. He later claimed that an official of the Anaconda Copper Mining Company had offered him five thousand dollars to murder a radical union organizer named Frank Little, a crippled Wobbly whom vigilantes finally lynched in Montana in 1917. Such violence continued even after World War I, with hoodlums hired by Anaconda shooting fifteen union pickets. By the end of the 1920s, Hammett had become a writer of detective stories. He served in World War II and, when the Cold War dawned, was lecturing on mystery writing in New York at an institution that the attorney general listed as subversive. The Jefferson School of Social Science taught Marxism as "the philosophy and science of the working class." When Hammett's conservative brother asked him directly if he were a Communist, the reply was cryptic: "I'm a Marxist." The catalogue of the Jefferson School described his course as "a practical workshop in the writing of novels and short stories." But Hammett also lectured on "the history of the mystery story, the relationship between the detective story and the general novel and the possibility of the detective story as a progressive medium in literature."

No one was more qualified to offer such instruction than the chief inventor of the tough, cynical, and laconic fictional detective whose characterization evoked so much interest abroad, where Hammett was appreciated early. His first novel, *Red Harvest* (1929), was hailed by British critic Cyril Connolly as a key work of the interwar period. In 1942, French novelist André Gide commented: "In English, or at least in American, many subtleties of the dialogue escape me; but in *Red Harvest* those dialogues, written in a masterful way, are such as to give pointers to Hemingway and even to Faulkner. . . . In that very special type of thing it is, I really believe, the most remarkable I have read." Such sympathetic readers could not have realized that, by 1934, Hammett had already published his last short story, as well as his last novel, *The Thin Man*. As a creative figure he had become a burnt-out case by the onset of the Cold War, during which Spillane was to vulgarize the archetype of the hard-boiled private eye that Hammett had largely created. The earlier protagonists had barely been heroes at all but isolated, rather seedy detectives who pursued too many questions and answered few themselves. Spillane's protagonist was an unreflective crusader, a brutal self-parody of machismo who asked questions only after shooting numerous villains. Sam Spade could face the murky terrors of modern society because he had recognized his own inner demons; Mike Hammer was so preposterously hard-boiled that he was slightly cracked. Hammett from the left as well as Spillane from the right wrote from an implacably antiauthoritarian perspective, laying bare a society that their private eyes knew to be corrupt and evil. But it was Spillane whose work tapped the rancid frustrations and the buried rage of the Cold War, which struck Hammett directly in the wake of the Foley Square prosecutions.

He was then serving as president of the Civil Rights Congress, a nonprofit trust fund and a Communist front in an era when virtually no one else was willing to put up bail for Stalinists enmeshed in the criminal justice system. To free the eleven Party leaders who were appealing their criminal conspiracy convictions, the Civil Rights Congress had allocated $260,000. In 1951, soon after the Supreme Court had denied their appeal, four of them jumped bail, believing that they would have to guide their comrades from abroad when the American fascists began the mass roundups and concentration camp detentions. The bail fund trustees were then subpoenaed to account for the background of the fund and to disclose what they knew about the whereabouts of the four convicted leaders. As chairman of the bail fund committee, Hammett was assumed to bear a greater responsibility to divulge information than were the other trustees. Irving Saypol, the U.S. district attorney who had successfully prosecuted the Rosenbergs four months earlier, interrogated Hammett. The novelist refused to answer questions and was therefore given a six-month sentence for contempt of court.

The primary source for a heroic interpretation of Hammett's conduct was Hellman's memoir, *An Unfinished Woman* (1969), in which she claimed that his jail sentence pivoted on a point of honor. Hammett had refused to identify the other contributors to the fund, even though he allegedly did not know their names anyway and had never even been in the Congress office. When Hellman asked her lover why he would not plead ignorance, Hammett replied, "I can't say that." He explained that keeping his word was something that mattered. "I hate this damn kind of talk," he added, "but maybe I better tell you that if it were more than jail, if it were my life, I would give it for what I think democracy is, and I don't let cops or judges tell me what I think democracy is."

Even if Hammett's response sounds suspiciously lifted from the third act of a Hellman play and cannot be easily reconciled with adherence to a patently antidemocratic movement, the transcript of the court proceedings is more prosaic than melodramatic. The witness was never directly asked to identify the contributors to the fund, so he was not charged with contempt of court for refusing to name names. Hammett declined to cooperate at all, invariably "on the ground that the answer may tend to incriminate me"—even when Saypol asked him to acknowledge his service as one of the five trustees of the fund, even when questioned whether the initials "D.H." on documents were his. When Hammett was asked if he knew any of the four who had jumped bail, which the Civil Rights Congress had put up, and when he was asked whether the bail fund had a deposit box or a checkbook, he continued to plead the Fifth Amendment. Such utter intransigence—possibly due to Party discipline—was accompanied by the claim that any inquiries about the bail fund of the Civil Rights Congress were beyond the jurisdiction of the court and that the operation of the congress was unrelated to the issue of the whereabouts of the fugitives. The court did not recognize the applicability of the Fifth Amendment, however, because it deemed proper the pursuit of information leading to the arrest of the Communist leaders who had skipped bail.

Documents of the Civil Rights Congress that the court subpoe-

naed tended to undercut the inference from *An Unfinished Woman*
that Hammett's was merely a name on a letterhead. Honorary chair-
men did not customarily initial the accounts of meetings, and as a
trustee he may well have helped fashion the policies of the bail fund
committee. His response to frequent instructions to answer the
questions was not to articulate the meaning of democracy but to
take the Fifth Amendment, giving the judge little alternative. The
most unusual feature of the case was not that Hammett was sentenced for contempt of court but that he was denied bail.

He served twenty-two weeks, with four off for good behavior, first
in the West Street detention center in New York, where he did
library duty, and then in Ashland, Kentucky. Though he compared
going to jail with going home, he came out—at the age of fifty-
seven—with broken health. In the meantime, the bail fund records
that he had tried to protect were surrendered to the State Banking
Department, a presumably apolitical agency that had to sort out the
financial consequences of the four Smith Act defections. But the
attorney general of New York seized the records and, claiming "national security," turned the names of the contributors over to the
FBI, "to determine whether the lists disclose any subversive elements." The freedom of political association, for which Hammett
had in effect been imprisoned, was thereby weakened. But without
complaining about his fate, he moved to a four-room gatekeeper's
cottage that a friend provided, about twenty miles north of Manhattan. Though sick, ruined, and unable to work, he was generally
left unmolested. The FBI kept watch on him, but he must have been
aware of the surveillance. After all, as a Pinkerton detective three
decades earlier, Hammett had once tracked a suspect for a month
and a half, riding the same trains and visiting half a dozen of the
same small towns, without arousing suspicion.

In 1953, McCarthy's Senate Permanent Investigations Subcommittee called Hammett to the witness stand. Again he refused to
answer any questions about the Communist party, and again he
invoked the Fifth Amendment. McCarthy himself, as well as chief
counsel Cohn, interrogated him. When asked about the prospects
of national adoption of Communism, Hammett wryly invoked two
enduring aspects of the American sensibility—pragmatism and ma-
joritarianism—in doubting the likelihood of Bolshevization: "It
would seem to me impractical, if most people didn't want it."
McCarthy inquired, "Mr. Hammett, if you were spending, as we are,
over a hundred million dollars a year on an information program
allegedly for the purpose of fighting communism, and if you were
in charge of that program to fight communism, would you purchase

the works of some seventy-five Communist authors and distribute their works throughout the world, placing our official stamp of approval upon those works?" The witness retorted, "If I were fighting communism, I don't think I would do it by giving people any books at all."

All of Hammett's books were removed from State Department libraries. NBC had already taken *The Adventures of Sam Spade* serial off the radio in 1951, depriving the author of his chief source of income. When the film version of *The Maltese Falcon* (1941) was revived, vigilantes tore down the advertisements. His novels were not reprinted. Because Hammett had neglected his financial affairs during his military service in World War II, the Internal Revenue Service elected to compound his problems by attaching—against back income taxes of over $100,000—whatever little money came in during the Cold War, when his sources of income had evaporated. Hammett nevertheless continued to teach at the Jefferson School until 1956 but was otherwise a recluse. Beginning in 1959, he received a VA pension for respiratory illness. Two years later, having worn his country's uniform in two world wars, he was buried at his own request in Arlington National Cemetery.

Even as Hammett's politics were overshadowing his literary reputation in his own country, large numbers of foreign readers were discovering for themselves the crust and cogency of his fiction. From 1948, when the Smith Act indictments that eventually led to his own imprisonment were handed down, until his death thirteen years later, his novels and short stories appeared in sixty-eight different translations. The carapace that had obscured his work in the United States was lifted in 1961 when Permabooks published mass-market paperback editions of *Red Harvest, The Dain Curse, The Maltese Falcon,* and *The Glass Key.* And though Hammett's fiction has not since gone out of print, it seems fair to conclude that the scale of his critical reception abroad demonstrated the failure of the Cohn/McCarthy campaign to deny foreign readers access to his work. His international reputation as one of the greatest mystery writers of all time may be the firmest vindication of the hope that Hammett had expressed to his publisher Blanche Knopf in 1929, that he wished to endow the detective story with the dignity of "literature."

5

The fragility of the left-wing popular culture that faced extinction during the Cold War was symbolized by an encounter in 1956 in a New Jersey hospital. Harold Leventhal, a Communist who once plugged songs for Irving Berlin, went to Greystone Park to visit one of the inmates. A psychiatrist rummaged through the files on his desk, then exclaimed: "Guthrie, Guthrie, ah, Guthrie! A very sick man. Very sick. Delusional! He says he has written more than a thousand songs! And a novel too. And he says he has made records for the Library of Congress." Leventhal's reply was terse: "He has."

By then, ignorance of the *oeuvre* of Woodrow Wilson Guthrie was perhaps excusable. Groups like the Almanac Singers and the Weavers had been staples of "progressive" entertainment in the 1940s, and "If I Had a Hammer" had been introduced into the folk music repertory in 1949 to protest the Smith Act prosecution of the Party leadership. Then the blacklisters struck. Despite the growing popularity of folk singing by the end of the decade, so central a performer as Pete Seeger was not allowed to play his banjo and sing on network television after 1950. When he did return in 1967, five years after finally having won his appeal of a year's jail sentence for contempt of HUAC, he was at first not allowed to perform a song on CBS's *Smothers Brothers Comedy Hour* that might have been interpreted as critical of American intervention in Vietnam. After an ultraconservative group called Texans for America pressured the Texas State Textbook Committee, which was the second largest purchaser of school texts in the nation, publishers of American history textbooks excised references to Seeger as well.

The most creative figure within that particular musical tradition was also unabashedly Stalinist as well. Born in 1912, Woody Guthrie had proudly cultivated an ardent pro-Communism by the late 1930s and did not waver thereafter. The restless individualist who seemed so autochthonous a son of the Middle Border was in fact a regular columnist for *The People's World*. After Stalin and Hitler had signed their nonaggression pact in 1939, Guthrie became *more* militantly pro-Soviet, synchronizing antimilitarism with the Communist party line until Hitler violated the pact with Operation Barbarossa. After 1941, Guthrie's devotion to the working class became so tempered with patriotism that he omitted from his repertory his anthems of union organizing, since strikes would hinder the American war effort and retard the opening of a second front against the invaders of Russia. "This Machine Kills Fascists" was inscribed on Guthrie's guitar. During the Korean War, however, he did not conceal his support for the North Korean and Chinese forces. But by the late 1940s, he and the groups with which he was associated— as performer and writer—had begun to disappear. His own autobiography, *Bound for Glory* (1943), went out of print. Recordings of his work became increasingly difficult to locate. A drifter and a loner, Guthrie was even jailed and given a six-month sentence in 1948 for writing obscene letters to a Los Angeles woman. His drinking and self-destructive rages were awful preludes to the congenital disease called Huntington's chorea that would eventually deprive him of control of mind and body. The atrophy would gradually worsen until he would quiver into horrifying disintegration, his brain utterly depleted.

Guthrie was functioning well enough to attend a major concert held in New York in 1956 to honor his work. Over a thousand people filled Pythian Hall, and at the end of the program the entire cast sang "This Land Is Your Land." Guthrie sat in the balcony, and the audience cheered him when it too joined in "This Land Is Your Land." Within a few months of that consolidation of the political culture to which Guthrie had contributed for two decades, he was committed to Greystone Park, and five years later to Brooklyn State Hospital. One pilgrim who came east to visit the hospitalized Guthrie early in 1961 would quickly become his most dazzling successor, taking audiences far beyond the "progressive" confines within which Guthrie had operated. Bob Dylan idolized Guthrie, sang and dressed like him, concocted a similar past, and recorded a "Song to Woody" on his first album in 1962. Born in 1941, the University of Minnesota dropout was immune to Guthrie's pro-Soviet politics. But Dylan transmitted an outrage against social injustice and war in such early songs as "Blowin' in the Wind" and "A Hard Rain's Gonna Fall" that outstripped the appeal of Guthrie's music a generation earlier, though the successor himself soon abandoned the leftist orientation to which Guthrie himself had been so faithful.

The song that had closed the 1956 tribute to Guthrie had undergone vicissitudes of its own. First written in 1940 as "God Blessed America," mostly as a riposte to Irving Berlin, Guthrie had described "a big high wall that tried to stop me / A sign was painted said: Private Property," and observed that in a "relief office I saw my people— / As they stood there hungry." He recorded it in 1944, giving it a new title, "This Land Is Your Land," and repeated a new line after each verse: "This land was made for you and me." Before the disease deprived him of the power of speech, he taught his son Arlo the original 1940 lyrics, afraid that the left-wing thrust of the song would become blunted into a patriotic hymn. Arlo Guthrie barely knew his father prior to the bouts of hospitalization, and he learned his father's style of singing (as Dylan had) mostly from records. But he included the verse about private property as he made the song his own. "This Land Is Your Land" was often mentioned in the 1960s as an alternative national anthem, since all but the most ardent jingoists admit to the musical limitations of "The Star-Spangled Banner." Both United Airlines and the Ford Motor Company turned Guthrie's ballad instead into an advertising jingle. Versions of "This Land Is Your Land" were also recorded by Bing Crosby, Connie Francis, Paul Anka, the New Christy Minstrels, and the Mormon Tabernacle Choir—all of whom were thus pouring into mainstream culture a Marxist rebuttal to "God Bless America." In 1966, a year before Guthrie died, the Bonneville Power Authority named one of its substations after him.

"Collapsed ideologies are not blown away by the winds," the critic Harold Rosenberg once remarked. "On the contrary, they spread throughout our society and take the form of popular culture." The careers of Communists like Guthrie, Robeson, and Hammett, and of non-Communists like Chaplin, permit other brief generalizations. In the 1950s, when dissent was too easily equated with disloyalty, the influence of such figures sharply diminished. As a result, talents were thwarted, creative possibilities were stifled, and the development of a more vital and various national culture was unrealized. Yet the loss of imaginative vigor cannot be attributed solely to politics, but in some instances to individual desiccation as well. The reconciliations and rehabilitations that began in the 1960s were not only signs of artistic appreciation but—whatever the sectarian motives of many listeners and readers—also a claim that a political definition of what audiences had the right to confront would no longer be sovereign. Political considerations would continue to affect judgments, but right-wing criteria would cease to intimidate and circumscribe art and thought. When *The End of Ideology*, dedicated to Sidney Hook, was published in 1960, Daniel Bell still felt obliged to defend political controversy: "One can be a critic of one's country without being an enemy of its promise." It was revealing that the case for dissent still had to be made. So sophisticated a thinker still had to deny that criticism meant deracination or might "influence intellectuals in Asia and Africa to be anti-American." But as the fear of conspiracy ebbed, the intolerance of heresy weakened too. Without such anxieties to define the national purpose or darken the national prospect, the culture of the Cold War could no longer be sustained.

9

THAWING: A SUBSTITUTE
FOR VICTORY

From external blows as well as self-inflicted wounds, American Communism was never to recover its status as a minor political force and ideological irritant, as the case for stigmatizing and fearing the Party became increasingly shrill, musty, and finally irrelevant. Though the Soviet Union remained a dangerous and thoroughly undemocratic foe, it became detotalitarianized around 1956 with the repudiation of some of Stalin's excesses. Its leaders, especially after Khrushchev's boisterous visit in 1959, gradually seemed less demonic. It was difficult to foresee a future in which Soviet Communism would be radically dislodged, overthrown, or transformed, which meant that the nuclear age—contrary to General MacArthur's assertion—required a substitute for victory. The culture of the Cold War decomposed when the moral distinction between East and West lost a bit of its sharpness, when American self-righteousness could be more readily punctured, when the activities of the two superpowers assumed greater symmetry.

1

Two British novels, *The Quiet American* and *The Spy Who Came in from the Cold,* transmitted early signals of geopolitical change that even some dissident Americans were reluctant to accept. By blurring the moral categorizations of East and West and by questioning the very desirability of a clear-cut triumph, these books were harbingers of thaw.

Greeneland was the terra incognita of the Cold War. Early in the postwar era, the State Department had blocked Graham Greene from entering the United States because (mostly as a joke) he had joined the Oxford University Communist Club for a month in 1923. In 1952 the novelist got his visa and three years later his revenge, for *The Quiet American* was a prescient—that is, an unheeded— exploration of the national determination to defeat Communism with ethically confused means. Its protagonist is Alden Pyle, who is involved in counterterrorism that kills and maims innocent civilians. The journalist-narrator describes him as "impregnably armoured by his good intentions and his ignorance," a deceiver who ends up deceiving himself, as his country was to do in the next decade on a far more massive and bloody scale in Vietnam. The sincerity of American motives, which was supposed to vindicate one side in the bipolar conflict, was depicted as conducive to evil results, and thus the novelist anticipated the tragedy to come. The film version of *The Quiet American* (1957) misses the point. For director-scenarist Joseph L. Mankiewicz switches Pyle from a CIA agent to an employee with a private U.S. aid mission and turns Greene's anti-American ending into a anti-Communist final reel instead.

In literary merit and in political judgment, *The Quiet American* was vastly superior to *The Ugly American* (1958), which was so popular a bestseller (number six) that even Ike read it on vacation. Authors William J. Lederer and Eugene Burdick made image-making and practical know-how so decisive in the struggle for the allegiance of neutral countries that they missed the ideological dangers lurking in the real Asian versions of Sarkhan. In *The Ugly American*, the good guys get out into the field and show the natives how to make things work better; the bad guys are the bureaucrats who get in the way of hands-on economic development. The novel offered unexceptionable proposals for an improved Foreign Service (language training, knowledge of the writings of Asian Communists, personal modesty). But the two authors did not consider the military context of foreign aid, and they missed almost completely the role of intense nationalist feelings in igniting the political revolutions that the United States faced.

Greene had based the lethally innocent Pyle in part on an enterprising CIA agent in Vietnam, Colonel Edward Lansdale, who was switched into a hero (Colonel Edwin Barnum Hillindale) in *The Ugly American*. Thus, its readers did not have to face the moral quagmire into which the CIA was then getting sucked in Indochina. Not long thereafter, for example, seven hundred American troops under CIA auspices were dropped into Laos to organize an army of about forty thousand Meo tribesmen as mercenaries against the Communist Pathet Lao, in exchange for Meo control of the lucrative opium traffic in Southeast Asia's "Golden Triangle." These were among the ugly political choices that *The Ugly American* did not adumbrate, for the novel's tepid criticism of American foreign policy remained imprisoned in orthodoxy. *The Quiet American* proved far more illuminating in its consideration of how high a price would be paid for the illusion that the United States was equipped to defeat Communism in Vietnam.

In 1963, Graham Greene hailed "the best spy story I have ever read": John le Carré's *The Spy Who Came in from the Cold*. Written in less than five months by a junior diplomat in the British embassy in Bonn, it became the first thriller ever to outsell all other works of fiction. Two hundred thirty thousand copies of *The Spy Who Came in from the Cold* were sold in American bookstores in 1964. The next year, over two million more were purchased in paperback, which is also when Paramount released its film version. In the 1956 film *Storm Center*, Bette Davis had played a librarian falsely accused of being a Communist. But what if she *had* been one? Within a decade, le Carré provided the answer: Liz Gold makes no secret of her membership in the British Communist party while working in a London library. Her employer grants her a brief leave to visit East Germany as part of a cultural exchange program to promote peace. There her idealism and love for Alec Leamas, a British intelligence operative who pretends to have defected, embroil her in a convoluted plot that implies a kind of moral equivalency between East and West. In East Germany the brutal Hans-Dieter Mundt, an alumnus of Hitler Youth, is actually on Her Majesty's payroll. Leamas is only a pawn who is being manipulated to eliminate Jens Fiedler, the Jewish second-in-command in the East German Abteilung, who has correctly suspected Mundt of being a double agent. But at the end of the novel, an East German working for the British kills the innocent Liz Gold as she tries to climb over the Berlin Wall to safety in the West. Leamas, disgusted by the corruption and treachery of his own side, goes back over the eastern side of the wall to join her fleetingly before he too is shot.

Earlier in the novel, Control in London has told Leamas that the methods and techniques of the West must sometimes be as ruthless as the other side's, though Western policy remains defensive. *The Spy Who Came in from the Cold* is hardly pro-Communist. The

East Bloc agents stationed in London are bullies who disdain their underlings; and the East Germans treat Liz, a believer in "History," just as cynically as the British Cold Warriors who operate from the Circus. But though life in the East is bleak and drab, the West may have its own spiritual hollowness and nagging conscience to confront. Fiedler, a gracious and attractive person, does not understand how Leamas can disclaim any ideals, how he can declare that operations from West Berlin had been just a job. Fiedler wonders how Leamas can sleep nights. Le Carré traced the novel's origins to his own "great and abiding bitterness about the East-West ideological deadlock," and he wanted his readers to ask, "for how long can we defend ourselves . . . by methods of this kind, and still remain the kind of society that is worth defending?" No wonder that Richard Helms, who was then in charge of undercover operations for the CIA, detested *The Spy Who Came in from the Cold*. For its unprecedented popularity signified a downshift in the ideological intensity that the novelist blamed for "political misery."

2

The disintegrating culture of the Cold War coincided with a transfer of political power, as the then-oldest president in history yielded in 1961 to the youngest elected president ever. The dramatic discontinuities should not be exaggerated, however. McCarthy and McCarthyism still shadowed the 1960 campaign, having touched what was to become the most famous and glamorous of political families.

Since Nixon, the Republican candidate, was a known quantity from the Cold War, liberal suspicions were directed at Kennedy, whose father had liked McCarthy and invited him a couple of times to the family compound in Hyannis Port, Massachusetts. A younger brother of the Democratic nominee had worked as assistant counsel to the McCarthy committee for six months before resigning and then returning as counsel for the Democratic minority. In his major task, an investigation of Western shippers to China, Robert Kennedy had not been careless with facts, however. Nor did he traduce the loyalty of the subjects of his investigation—in marked contrast to McCarthy himself and to Cohn, with whom intense antagonism erupted. Robert Kennedy nevertheless did not sever personal relations with McCarthy himself, who had also dated two of Joseph P. Kennedy's daughters, Pat and Jean. When the senator from Wisconsin married someone else, in 1953, both John and Robert Kennedy showed up at the wedding (as did Vice-President and Mrs. Nixon).

Perhaps largely because of such personal ties, McCarthy had kept out of Massachusetts in 1952, when John F. Kennedy ran successfully for the Senate. Like other liberal Democrats, JFK supported the Communist Control Act two years later, and he consistently declined the opportunity to tackle McCarthy himself. Late in 1954, when the Senate confronted the issue of censure, Kennedy was hospitalized for a serious back operation and could have been paired with another senator. Instead, he became the only Democrat not to vote against McCarthy. Apparently unmoved by the moral issues that the censure implied, Kennedy later explained, "Hell, half my voters in Massachusetts look on McCarthy as a hero." Since liberals were so much quicker to forgive Senator Humphrey for his efforts to placate McCarthyism, the author of *Profiles in Courage* (1956) probably paid a certain price for the title of that book. Kennedy's exculpation—"I didn't have a chapter in it on myself"—did not dispel the doubts to which Eleanor Roosevelt gave voice in her memoirs: "A public servant must clearly indicate that he understands the harm that McCarthyism did to our country and that he opposes it actively, so that one would feel sure that he would always do so in the future."

In the 1960 presidential campaign, voters might have had a hard time deciding which candidate was the more aggressive Cold Warrior. Kennedy charged that the Republican administration had permitted a dangerous "missile gap" to exist. (It would quickly disappear after the inauguration.) Though the candidate had apparently been briefed about CIA invasion plans for Cuba (to be implemented at the Bay of Pigs), he blamed the GOP for allowing Communism to lurk only ninety miles from Florida. The famous television debates swirled around foreign policy, while his campaign raised the possibility of fresh thinking at home. Kennedy aroused a certain hope that social and economic problems would no longer fester and that an awareness of them would no longer be a sign of treason. His youthful bravura and lively intelligence, perhaps more than anything he actually said, reopened discussion of topics like the decay of cities, the decline of the schools, the persistence of hunger and poverty and bigotry, and the eclipse of idealism and purpose. Of Americans eligible to vote in 1960, 63.8 percent did so—a proportion that has been unequaled since then, and the highest percentage since William Howard Taft defeated William Jennings Bryan in 1908. Over six million more ballots were cast in 1960 than four years earlier. But the election was so breathtakingly close that hanky-panky was used in the vote counting. "With a little bit of luck and the help of a few close friends," Mayor Richard J. Daley of Chicago assured Kennedy by phone during the cliffhanger, "you're going to carry

Illinois." He did. Had Kennedy lost that state and Texas, Nixon would have become the thirty-fifth president instead of the thirty-seventh. The Republicans actually gained twenty-one seats in the House and two in the Senate. Yet the political climate had been irrevocably altered.

Kennedy's inaugural address was the most memorable of the century (other than Roosevelt's in 1933), but it promised a continuation of the Cold War. Addressed "to friend and foe alike," the speech called upon a prosperous nation to sacrifice itself and to "bear the burdens of a long twilight struggle, year in and year out." The president was about to launch the biggest arms race in history, inevitably provoking the Soviet Union into matching the massive military buildup. Yet two rhetorical pivots hinted that earlier rigidity was about to be superseded. On the advice of Walter Lippmann, who had popularized the phrase "Cold War" in 1947, Kennedy referred to the Soviets not as the "enemy" but as an "adversary." The rumbling about "massive retaliation" and "national liberation" would be evicted from the vocabulary of American diplomacy when Kennedy proclaimed, "Let us never negotiate out of fear. But let us never fear to negotiate."

Two years later, in the president's own Massachusetts, his brother Edward was elected to the Senate, easily defeating an independent whose candidacy epitomized the thaw. In what was once probably the most McCarthyite state in the union, Professor H. Stuart Hughes warned that the threat of atomic catastrophe transcended the political differences between East and West. Unlike the Progressive party or American Labor party candidates who ran during the early phases of the Cold War, Hughes was unsympathetic to Soviet foreign policy. Yet the Harvard historian had never been, by his own admission, "a strenuous anti-Communist" either, even during the moral nadir of Stalinism. The 1962 senatorial campaign that he conducted (Abbie Hoffman was among its organizers) was so strongly influenced by pacifism that the foreign policy Hughes advocated approached neutralism and isolationism. As national cochairman of the National Committee for a Sane Nuclear Policy (SANE), he even proposed unilateral disarmament as "a dramatic gesture of conciliation," believing that Soviet leadership had emerged more fully from its totalitarian past than was widely believed. The hints in Kennedy's inaugural address had become the birthmarks of a "new politics."

By then, the pursuit of peace (rather than national liberation behind the Iron Curtain) had become sufficiently legitimated that Sargent Shriver could overrule objections to the name of the federal agency that he directed: the Peace Corps. The president's brother-in-law thus deprived the Communists of their virtual monopoly of the word "peace." Only six years earlier the army had distributed a pamphlet, *How to Spot a Communist,* that warned its inductees that use of the word betokened Communist inclinations. In 1961, Nixon grumbled that the Peace Corps might become a haven for draft dodgers. By ignoring such warnings, the Kennedy administration helped weaken the Cold War mentality itself. Within three years of the inaugural would come the atomic test ban treaty that had eluded Eisenhower in the interlude after Dulles's death, and the "nuclear sword of Damocles" that President Kennedy warned against at the United Nations was slightly blunted. The brink of catastrophe to which the planet had been brought over Soviet missiles in Cuba in 1962 forced both superpowers to realize how little room to maneuver they enjoyed. With monolithic Communism disrupted by China's break with the Soviet Union, the Kremlin itself felt less fear to negotiate, especially since underground testing could continue unabated after the limited test ban treaty. Indeed, the United States managed to test *more* atomic weapons in the five years after the 1963 Treaty of Moscow than it had in the previous five years.

The Kennedy administration also decided to award the Fermi Prize, for the highest achievement in nuclear energy, to J. Robert Oppenheimer. In fact, the president was intending to confer the award in the White House, shortly after returning from Dallas in November 1963. Instead, Kennedy's successor made the presentation to Oppenheimer, who expressed appreciation to Lyndon B. Johnson, since "it has taken some charity and some courage for you to make this award today. That would seem to be a good augury for all our futures." The gesture redressed a palpable individual injustice that the Atomic Energy Commission had perpetrated almost a decade earlier in denying him security clearance. A less timorous administration may also have realized that the most hard-line stance on the arms race—which Oppenheimer had vainly opposed—would not necessarily and always be in the national interest.

3

Popular culture also registered a change in the temperature of the Cold War. Consider, for example, two movies that John Frankenheimer directed.

United Artists' *The Manchurian Candidate* (1962), based on Richard Condon's 1959 novel, has been judged the last as well as "the most sophisticated film of the cold war." It reworked the family dynamics of *My Son John*—"an intrusive, sexually unsatisfied mother, a weak father, and a cold, isolated son"—into a "demonologically explicit" thriller. Michael Paul Rogin called *The Manchurian Candidate* "a brilliant, self-knowing film. But far from mocking the mentality it displays, it aims to reawaken a lethargic nation to the Communist menace." This interpretation is dubious. From the opening scene of libidinous G.I.'s carousing with Korean bargirls beneath a stern photo of General MacArthur, Cold War conventions are shaken. The bizarre plot centers on Sergeant Raymond Shaw (Laurence Harvey), who is brainwashed during captivity in the Korean War. Programmed to kill when he hears a certain phrase, Shaw is released and repatriated to the United States, where he is turned over to a top Soviet agent—his own mother (Angela Lansbury). She intends to use her son the somnambule to assassinate the presidential nominee from a booth high above Madison Square Garden. A clear path to the White House would thus be blazed for her husband, Johnny Iselin (James Gregory), a nutty right-winger who is the party's vice-presidential candidate. This calamity is avoided only when Major Ben Marco (Frank Sinatra), who had been captured in Shaw's unit in Korea but has emancipated himself from the subjugation of Communist brainwashing control, picks open the lock of Shaw's mind as well. Marco races to the booth just as the trigger is about to be squeezed, but Shaw assassinates his mother and stepfather on the podium before killing himself. (The film deviates from the novel, in which Marco orders the mother and stepfather to be executed.)

In the form of a weird espionage nightmare, *The Manchurian Candidate* shows the diabolical cunning of the Eastern Bloc. But what made the film so disorienting is its satire of McCarthyism as well. Shaw's stepfather is obviously modeled on the Wisconsin demagogue; they even share a spurious war record. In first running for the Senate, "Tail Gunner Joe" had himself photographed in the cockpit of a plane that he had never flown in combat, while Iselin likewise became a "one-man battleship" by testing some navy guns on harmless targets. Senator Iselin accuses the secretary of defense of harboring fifty-seven Communists—a figure derived from spotting a bottle of catsup. A drunken ignoramus who cannot remember the numbers he invents, Iselin is also a blackmailer who dominates the fanatical and paranoid environment that he has helped to create. The movie version of *The Manchurian Candidate* omits much of the novel's spoof of right-wingers bristling with "opinions they rented that week from Mr. Sokolsky, Mr. [David] Lawrence, Mr.

Pegler, and that fascinating younger fellow who had written about men and God at Yale," William F. Buckley. But the film is unsparing in its demonstration that, while Communism is fiendish and still dangerous, the far right is hypocritical and foolish.

The director recalled that "at one stage we were going to be picketed by both the American Legion and the Communist Party at the same time, which we tried to encourage of course; after all, the whole point of the film was the absurdity of any type of extremism." When the Communists felt free to picket again, when a movie director could welcome such controversy, and when the American Legion was considered as "extremist" as the Communists, the 1950s were going into remission. But then something terrible happened. One year after *The Manchurian Candidate* was released, a young ex-military man who had returned to the United States from a Communist nation carried a rifle outfitted with telescopic sights up several flights of steps, intending to shoot through the window at a presidential target surrounded by a crowd below. This time no savior rushed up to stop the assassin, a loner whose name—Lee Harvey Oswald—even bore an eerie resemblance to actor Laurence Harvey's, and who fit D. H. Lawrence's definition of the archetypal American soul as "hard, isolate, stoic and a killer." Sinatra blocked the commercial re-release of the film for the next quarter-century.

Frankenheimer's next film was another political thriller, *Seven Days in May* (1964), based on the novel by Fletcher Knebel and Charles W. Bailey II that had been the number seven bestseller two years earlier. In this tale, a marine colonel (Kirk Douglas) foils a coup d'état designed to block what a right-wing air force general (Burt Lancaster) perceives to be appeasement of the Soviet Union. Made without the cooperation of the Department of Defense, *Seven Days in May* enjoyed the behind-the-scenes encouragement of the White House, from which Kennedy promised to absent himself on a weekend if Frankenheimer wished to shoot on the premises. The film certainly showed that not all officialdom championed peace, and that the military included elements that were hostile to it. But the happy ending of the movie saved audiences from worrying whether counterparts to the film's General James Mattoon Scott required close civic supervision. *Seven Days in May* was released before publication of *Thirteen Days*, Robert Kennedy's memoir of the Cuban missile crisis of October 1962. He disclosed the belief of one member of the Joint Chiefs of Staff in "a preventive attack against the Soviet Union. On that fateful Sunday morning when the Russians answered that they were withdrawing their missiles, it was suggested by one high military adviser that we attack [Cuba] in any case."

Another novel, published in paperback in the same year as *Seven Days in May*, quickly sold over two million copies and became far more of a milestone in revising attitudes toward war. "A difficult situation or problem whose seemingly alternative solutions are logically invalid" is how the *American Heritage Dictionary* defines "catch-22," which became a catchword as well. The rules of World War II permitted only flyers who were crazy to be grounded, and yet "a concern for one's own safety in the face of dangers that were real and immediate was the process of a rational mind"—hence missions had to be flown. Joseph Heller's unique novel crossed the wires of zaniness and dread, as though the dialogue that Sergeant Bilko's motor pool crew delivered in the 1950s television comedy starring Phil Silvers had suddenly been altered by a new team of writers named Dostoevsky and Kafka. Unlike Senator McCarthy, the author of *Catch-22* really had flown B-25s in World War II combat missions. Yet so faithfully did the novel anticipate the bureaucratic texture of an escalating war that "grunts" in Vietnam were observed wearing helmets on which the phrase "catch-22" had been painted.

The novelist later explained the genesis of *Catch-22* within the culture of the Cold War itself. "Virtually none of the attitudes in the book—the suspicion and distrust of officials in the government, the feelings of helplessness and victimization, the realization that most government agencies would lie—coincided with my experience as a bombardier in World War II," Heller noted. "The anti-war and anti-government feelings in the book belong to . . . the Korean War, the cold war of the fifties. A general disintegration of belief took place then, and it affected *Catch-22* in that the form of the novel became almost disintegrated." The comic assault that *Catch-22* mounted against the Army Air Corps used World War II as a metaphor, a backdrop. It drew far more directly from the postwar era, during which it was written, which is why Heller "deliberately seeded the book with anachronisms" to tip off readers that "*Catch-22* wasn't really *about* World War II."

For example, the enemies of the protagonist, Captain John Yossarian, include Captain Black, an intelligence officer who knows that one corporal was "a subversive because he wore eyeglasses and used words like *panacea* and *utopia*, and because he disapproved of Adolf Hitler, who had done such a great job of combating un-American activities in Germany." It is Black who comes up with the Glorious Loyalty Oath Crusade, based on the premise that "the more loyalty oaths a person signed, the more loyal he was. . . . He had

Corporal Kolodny sign hundreds with his name each day so that he could always prove he was more loyal than anyone else. . . . Men were tied up all over the squadron signing, pledging and singing [the national anthem], and the [combat] missions took hours longer to get under way." Black also "scrupulously reinforced each day the doctrine of 'Continual Reaffirmation' that he had originated, a doctrine designed to trap all those men who had become disloyal since the last time they had signed a loyalty oath the day before."

Then there was Major Major, who had "majored in English history, which was a mistake. '*English* history!' roared the silver-maned senior Senator from his state indignantly. 'What's the matter with American history? American history is as good as any history in the world!' Major Major switched immediately to American literature, but not before the FBI had opened a file on him. There were six people and a Scotch terrier inhabiting the remote farmhouse Major Major called home, and five of them and the Scotch terrier turned out to be agents for the FBI." He started his army career as a private and was promoted to major four days later by an IBM machine, leading "Congressmen with nothing else on their minds" to "go trotting back and forth through the streets of Washington, D.C., chanting, 'Who promoted Major Major? Who promoted Major Major?'"

Perhaps the most striking political feature of the novel is its apparent repudiation of the automatic justice of the Allied side—at least when Yossarian is asked to exceed his quota of combat missions. When Major Danby announces that World War II differs from World War I—"we're at war with aggressors who would not let either one of us live if they won," Yossarian agrees. But he adds: "I've flown seventy goddam combat missions. Don't talk to me about fighting to save my country. I've been fighting all along to save my country. Now I'm going to fight a little to save myself. The country's not in danger any more, but I am." In recognizing that his own side—exemplified by Colonel Cathcart and other officers—is very willing to have him killed, that these superior officers are in fact his enemy, the protagonist undercuts the moral asymmetry that sanctioned the Cold War as well. When the psychiatrist, Major Sanderson, diagnoses Yossarian as suffering from "a bad persecution complex. You think people are trying to harm you," Yossarian replies, "People *are* trying to harm me." To which the psychiatrist offers a rejoinder: "You see? You have no respect for excessive authority or obsolete traditions." Sanderson considers Yossarian "immature. You've been unable to adjust to the idea of war. . . . You have deep-seated survival anxieties." Thus was satirized the suspicion of nonconformity that pervaded the 1950s, as well as the psychiatric tendency to assume that adaptation was the only way to respond to society—instead of resisting it or withdrawing from it or trying to change it. In refusing to fly any more combat missions and in trying to make his separate peace, Yossarian was, according to his superiors, "jeopardizing his traditional rights of freedom and independence by daring to exercise them."

Such dissidence was puzzling. When Major Major asks, "Would you like to see our country lose?" Yossarian responds: "We won't lose. We've got more men, more money and more material. There are ten million men in uniform who could replace me. Some people are getting killed and a lot more are making money and having fun. Let somebody else get killed." Major Major counterpunches with a version of Kant's categorical imperative: "But suppose everybody on our side felt that way." Yossarian gives a conformist 1950s response: "Then I'd certainly be a damned fool to feel any other way. Wouldn't I?" He realizes that, in World War II, "only a fraction of his countrymen would give up their lives to win it, and it was not his ambition to be among them. . . . History did not demand Yossarian's premature demise, justice could be satisfied without it . . . [and] victory did not depend on it. That men would die was a matter of necessity; *which* men would die, though, was a matter of circumstance, and Yossarian was willing to be the victim of anything but circumstance. But that was war."

Since *Catch-22* is something of a catalogue of the political culture of the decade in which it was written, big business is also harpooned. The slogan of Milo Minderbender's ambitious and utterly amoral syndicate, for instance, is "What's good for M & M Enterprises is good for the country." Through the growing doubts of the chaplain who tries in vain to comfort Yossarian, Heller also confronts the power of religion—not cynically but sympathetically. The trust that the Reverend A. T. Tappman "had placed in the wisdom and justice of an immortal, omnipotent, omniscient, humane, universal, anthropomorphic, English-speaking, Anglo-Saxon, pro-American God . . . had begun to waver." For "there were no miracles; prayers went unanswered, and misfortune tramped with equal brutality on the virtuous and the corrupt." Yet "mystic phenomena" have kept the chaplain from relinquishing his vocation. Such tender passages are rare in this savage, unsettling comedy, which pushed into new territory the radical individualist opposition to military authority of earlier war fiction. *Catch-22* became the most popular "serious" novel of the 1960s, spinning off bumper stickers like "Better Yossarian Than Rotarian" that uncovered a wide cultural chasm as well.

Other artifacts early in the decade presented war as more fearsome than Bolshevik conspiracies. Antimilitarism surfaced as a successor to anti-Communism in such books as Jules Feiffer's *Munro*, which the cartoonist had tried to get published after leaving the military in 1952. A satire on the army that had drafted a four-year-old by mistake, *Munro* was animated by the same antibureaucratic, antipatriotic passions as *Catch-22*. "You couldn't even think for a moment that the army, like your mother, meant for your best, that the army was out for your interest," Feiffer recalled. "The army was basically out to kill you—it didn't care whether it did or it didn't." Perhaps because editors could not figure out whether his book was a *jeu d'esprit* for children or a bitter political satire for adults, *Munro* was published only at the end of the decade. The movie version won an Academy Award in 1961, the same year that *Catch-22* was published.

The prestige of the military was further eroded in 1965 with the release of James B. Harris's *The Bedford Incident*, a rejoinder to *The Caine Mutiny* (also by Columbia Pictures). Captain Erik J. Finlander (Richard Widmark) commands a nuclear submarine in the North Atlantic, tracking its Soviet counterpart in the territorial waters off Greenland. But even after the Russian prey returns to international waters and apparent tranquillity, Finlander continues the pursuit, insisting that the enemy be forced to the surface. Like Queeg, the skipper of the *Bedford* has lost touch with reality, largely because of the constant frustration and remorseless pressure of command. Unlike the captain of the *Caine*, however, Finlander apparently suffers from an ideological tic as well: he *hates* Communism. Wouk's novel and Dmytryk's film had attempted to vindicate the necessity of obedience—even when leadership is mentally unbalanced. *The Bedford Incident*, made without navy cooperation, warns that such deranged authority could unleash nuclear war, which happens accidentally. When Finlander explains that his submarine would not initiate hostilities but would retaliate against the enemy ("The *Bedford* will never fire first. But if he fires one, I'll fire one!"), the weapons officer misinterprets his testy commander. He hears only the phrase "Fire one!" and the fatal button is pressed. Detecting the sound of the American missile heading in its direction, the Soviet submarine then fires its own nuclear torpedoes at the *Bedford*, which does not take evasive action when Finlander realizes the horrible price of his obsession. Both submarines explode; it is The End. Though Widmark was quite experienced in playing psychopaths, he deliberately based his portrayal of Finlander on

Barry Goldwater's mannerisms and rhetoric in the 1964 presidential campaign.

4

Of all the filmmakers to transform the vision of war and to treat with skepticism the "long twilight struggle" that Kennedy's inaugural address had promised, by far the most important was Stanley Kubrick, whose dissidence had surfaced as early as 1957. In depicting a mutiny in the French army in 1916, his *Paths of Glory* pierced through the callous irresponsibility of military leadership and the desperate madness of combat. So graphic a message of the folly of war was an astonishing exception to the Cold War consensus, and *Paths of Glory* would not have been made had Kirk Douglas not agreed to star in it. Naturally, the film posed no questions about the caliber of *American* generals; and it might have helped rinse the film of any radical taint that Menjou, one of HUAC's friendliest witnesses, played a villainous general. Even then United Artists released *Paths of Glory* with a disclaimer: the incident on which the film was based was unrepresentative of the splendid conduct of millions of other French troops during the Great War. The movie was banned in France anyway.

Kubrick's next work, also starring Douglas, was a spectacle set in the ancient world. But it diverged sharply from the typical epic of the 1950s. Films like *The Robe* (1953) or *The Silver Chalice* (1954) had been reverent, and they were usually adapted from the most popular American novels (even when rights to option the Bible were free). It was fitting that De Mille, the director who specialized in projecting religiosity on the big screen, was also consummately right-wing. He complained, for example, that criticism of his *Samson and Delilah* (1949) was Communist-inspired. De Mille also campaigned for a loyalty oath for fellow members of the Screen Directors Guild, threatened to tell Senator McCarthy which of his colleagues opposed such an oath, and proposed a "loyalty index" for actors and actresses as well. In the prologue to *The Ten Commandments* (1956), the director tells the audience directly that "the theme of this picture is whether men are to be ruled by God's law—or whether they are to be ruled by the whims of a dictator. . . . Are men the property of the state? Or are they free souls under God? This same battle continues throughout the world today."

Men are literally the property of the state in Kubrick's *Spartacus* (1960), for they are Roman slaves in the first century before Christ. But at the end of this Universal-International film, they are crucified not for their religious faith but for the political challenge that they hurled down to the most powerful empire of their time. Spartacus, the Thracian leader of the insurrection, was long included in the pantheon of Communist heroes. (Rosa Luxemburg, also martyred, had spearheaded the German *Spartakusbund* in the era of World War I, for instance.) Kubrick's film was based on Howard Fast's best-selling 1951 novel, which Little, Brown had first agreed to publish and then rejected, as did six other houses. Having written *Spartacus* mostly in jail, Fast felt compelled to publish it himself. (The Russian word for "self-publishing" would become widely known a decade later: *samizdat*.) A winner of the Stalin Peace Prize in 1954, he repudiated a decade's allegiance to Communism two years later. Kirk Douglas, who produced *Spartacus* as well, then compounded the risks of drawing upon so "progressive" a source. By hiring an ex-convict from the Hollywood Ten to adapt the novel to the screen, Douglas helped break the blacklist by announcing Dalton Trumbo's authorship (and thus forestalled Kubrick's attempt to grab credit for a screenplay that the director had not written). The demonstrations erupted from a predictable quarter. But President-elect Kennedy and his brother, the future attorney general, were not petrified. By crossing an American Legion picket line to see *Spartacus*, they eroded the legion's power to inspire fear in Hollywood and to define the politically permissible.

Even before Kubrick was hired to direct *Spartacus*, he had become intrigued as a citizen by the problem of nuclear war and deterrence. He talked to strategists Thomas Schelling and Herman Kahn and then, upon the recommendation of Alastair Buchan, director of the Institute of Strategic Studies in London, came across a 1958 novel entitled *Red Alert*. Its author, Peter George, was a retired Royal Air Force pilot who imagined a psychotic general unleashing a squadron of American bombers against the Soviet Union. Kubrick read *Red Alert* in 1961, among the approximately seventy books that he devoured on the subject of the Bomb, and decided to make George's suspense thriller the basis of a screenplay. Two years later the director wrote, "It was very important to deal with this problem dramatically because it's the only social problem where there's absolutely no chance for people to learn anything from experience." While writing the scenario, the artist discovered something happening that the citizen had not anticipated. Swirling up from his unconscious, the worst catastrophe looming over the planet was coming out funny. "As I kept trying to imagine the way in which things would really happen," he recalled, "ideas kept coming to me which I would discard because they were so ludicrous. I kept saying to myself: 'I can't do this. People will laugh.' But after a month or so I began to realize that all the things I was throwing out were the things which were most truthful." Kubrick thus realized that "the only way to tell the story was as a black comedy, or better, a nightmare comedy, where the things you laugh at most are really the heart of the paradoxical postures that make a nuclear war possible."

The director apparently did not even bother to request the assistance of the air force. Thus, the sole technical adviser was not a Pentagon public relations officer but Stanley Kubrick, drawing on memories of a Bronx boyhood partly spent watching World War II movies. Since officialdom had never admitted that an underground crisis center in the Pentagon even existed (much less released a photograph of it), he designed the war room out of his own and his art director's imagination. From an unauthorized photo in an aviation magazine, Kubrick constructed a B-52 cockpit. The result was *Dr. Strangelove*, which Columbia Pictures released early in 1964. Nominated for Academy Awards in such categories as Best Picture, Best Director, and Best Screenplay (though it won no Oscars), *Dr. Strangelove* deserves to be ranked among the most important achievements in the history of movies.

It is nevertheless based on a premise that the air force stoutly insisted was false. Presumably the commander of a Strategic Air Command base could not on his own have ordered a squadron to initiate war upon the Soviet Union, and only the president or his surrogate could have relayed the attack code to such a commander. Air force officials also claimed that the Positive Control System was impossible to subvert; it was "fail-safe." Yet *Dr. Strangelove* is not thereby deprived of its power to shock. For the film belongs to a quaint phase in the military history of deterrence, since manned bombers rather than missiles allow some time to modify and perhaps correct human error. It could be argued that the discrepancy between the complexity and speed of the technology of extinction and the fallibility of human judgment and control has since become far greater than when the film was conceived. Had it been primarily a critique of inordinate faith in technology, *Dr. Strangelove* would hardly have been so distinctive or so memorable. But in the unsettling form of a pitch-black comedy, it also mocked the paranoid hostility to Communism and the patriotic verities of the Cold War that the film—more than any other—transcends.

To be sure, *Dr. Strangelove* hardly shows the chief adversary of the United States in a benevolent or neutral light. The Soviet ambassador sneaks a hidden camera into the underground war room in Washington. And the plot requires the "mad fools" in his government to be powerful enough to order construction of a Doomsday device that will lead to nuclear catastrophe. In *On Thermonuclear War* (1960), Kahn had speculated on the radical possibility of a Doomsday Machine. Such a device would have the ideal characteristics of a deterrent: "frightening," "inexorable," "persuasive," "cheap," and "relatively foolproof." But it would not be "controllable," which is why he had concluded that the machine would be an unsuitable deterrent. That, at least, was the consensus among the American scientists and engineers whom Kahn consulted, in behalf of the RAND Corporation. Some of them, he reported, nevertheless appeared "attracted to the idea" of such a device—an attitude that Kahn, himself a calculator of "megadeaths," found "disquieting." In the film the operational readiness of this absolute weapons system is to be announced at the forthcoming Soviet Party Congress. In *Dr. Strangelove*, duplicity and apocalyptic irresponsibility thus characterize the Soviets, whose hard-liners worry about falling behind in the arms race and apparently itch for a fearful end rather than live in endless fear.

But the demented air force general, Jack D. Ripper (Sterling Hayden), dominates the first third of the film, and his lunacy therefore becomes its primary image of anti-Communism. The general has given the B-52s the "go" code and refuses to recall them because he wants to preserve "our precious bodily fluids." Ripper asks RAF Group Captain Lionel Mandrake (Peter Sellers): "Have you ever seen a Communist drink a glass of water? Vodka, that's what they drink, isn't it? Never water—on no account will a Commie ever drink water. . . . Have you ever heard of a thing called fluoridation? Do you realize that fluoridation is the most monstrously conceived and dangerous Communist plot we've ever had to face?" It began in 1946, Ripper tells Mandrake. (Transposing the last two digits gives the release date of the film that composed a comic obituary to such paranoia.)

General Ripper's superior, General Buck Turgidson (George C. Scott), personifies what the radical sociologist C. Wright Mills called "crackpot realism." Once Ripper has initiated hostilities from Burpleson Air Force Base, Turgidson favors a full-scale assault on the Soviet Union. The crew-cut, gum-chewing Turgidson earnestly believes that World War III is winnable. Though conceding that we might "get our hair mussed," he assures the other officials in the crisis center of a maximum of "10 to 20 million [Americans] killed, tops—depending on the breaks." In fact, Turgidson's rousing war room advocacy of a massive first strike borrows from a section in *On Thermonuclear War* on "Tragic But Distinguishable Postwar

States," leading Kahn, after the film was screened at his think tank, to ask Kubrick for a royalty. It is also relevant to the Cold War satire that the two air force generals are the only religious characters in the film. Ripper is chillingly confident that in the afterlife he will be able to answer for unleashing World War III, while the far more worldly Turgidson impulsively—and, as it turns out, prematurely—leads a public prayer of thanks that the "Angel of Death fluttering over the Valley of Fear" had spared the planet.

If there is a sympathetic character in this giddy and gruesome film, it is President Merkin Muffley (Peter Sellers). Bald and bespectacled as an egghead, apparently a liberal, he seems modeled on Adlai Stevenson, though, given the choices that the psychotic Ripper has left him, the president acts far more decisively than Stevenson was reputed to manage. But despite Muffley's decency of purpose and clarity of mind, his failure to avert Doomsday marks the radical distance that *Dr. Strangelove* achieves over other Hollywood films. For democratic statesmanship has been unable to control the aggressive madness of the military and the inexorable destructiveness of machines in the service of "crackpot realism." Muffley too is subject to the sinister domain of Dr. Strangelove (Peter Sellers), whose dark wavy hair, eyeglasses, and German accent conjure up Henry Kissinger, the Harvard political scientist who was then best known as a theorist of nuclear strategy. Dr. Strangelove's definition of deterrence ("the art of producing in the mind of the enemy the fear to attack you") compresses the more academic version in Dr. Kissinger's *Nuclear Weapons and Foreign Policy* (1957)—"the attempt to keep an opponent from adopting a certain course of action by posing risks which will to him seem out of proportion to any gains to be achieved."

The title character is undoubtedly drawn as well on the expatriate rocket scientist Dr. Wernher Von Braun. When Strangelove (*né* Merkwürdigliebe) addresses the president as "Mein Führer" and gives him the Nazi salute, the Good War itself—or at least its final phase—is seen in a different light. Audiences might also have recalled that John Foster Dulles, a sore loser, had conjectured immediately after sputnik orbited into space that "German scientists captured at the end of the Second World War doubtless played a big part in the Soviet achievement." Their German scientists, went one popular complaint, are better than ours. World War II is recalled as well in the figure of Major "King" Kong (Slim Pickens), the amiable but determined cowboy pilot of the lone bomber that continues its mission. Kong would have been a wild-blue-yonder hero in the action films that laureates of the Hollywood Ten had written, like Trumbo's

Thirty Seconds over Tokyo (1944), Alvah Bessie's *Objective Burma* (1945), and Albert Maltz's *Destination Tokyo* (1944) and *Pride of the Marines* (1945). But Major Kong's speech promising the crew citations—regardless of race or creed—after the completion of their bombing run stamps him as a grotesque anachronism for whom, like his air force superiors, the enormity of nuclear war is unfathomable. ("When Johnny Comes Marching Home" plays on the soundtrack.) Kong is technically resourceful and seizes the initiative, but to root for him to fulfill his assignment is to welcome the apocalypse. It was another sign of Kubrick's audacity that for once a Hollywood film did not compromise at the end, even though the bomb in George's *Red Alert* was too damaged to be detonated.

Dr. Strangelove is a satirical compendium of the ideology of the 1950s. For example, the film suggests that assertive masculinity, far from being essential to the defense of freedom, can in fact lead to the annihilation of everything. In the opening shots, while the credits roll and "Try a Little Tenderness" is heard on the soundtrack, the refueling SAC bombers seem to be having intercourse with one another. Near the very end, Major Kong, waving his stetson, rides the atomic bomb between his legs down to the targeted Soviet base at Laputa. The film also mocks the syndrome of bomb shelters, which were supposed to be havens in a heartless, radioactive world, enabling the family to reconstitute itself down below. But the civil defense shelters imagined at the end of *Dr. Strangelove* are romper rooms for lusty lads and busty maids, dooming the monogamous family unit, as Turgidson and Strangelove gleefully realize. Colonel "Bat" Guano (Keenan Wynn) has no idea that nuclear holocaust looms, since his attention is concentrated on "deviated preverts" and the sanctity of private property—of which its shrine is a Coca-Cola dispensing machine. Viewers who found this satire of free enterprise a little too obvious must have missed the cover story that *U.S. News and World Report* ran in 1961, "If Bombs Do Fall—What Happens to Your Investments." The mostly Republican readers of the weekly magazine were assured that plans were under way to permit checks to continue to be written, even if the banks were incinerated. In any event, the *Washington Post* reviewer of *Dr. Strangelove* worried that "no communist could dream of a more effective anti-American film to spread abroad than this one." The movie critic for the conservative *National Review* expressed the hope that, after *Dr. Strangelove*, Kubrick would make a film criticizing Stalinism.

General Curtis LeMay of the Joint Chiefs of Staff made it clear that his own favorite film about the air force had been released only a year earlier. *A Gathering of Eagles* (1963) showed how a valiant young colonel (Rock Hudson) takes charge of a SAC wing that had failed a surprise alert and trains his men up to the proper level of combat readiness. LeMay considered *A Gathering of Eagles* more realistic than any other film about the service, a rebuttal of the Gaither Report (1957) that Eisenhower had commissioned in an effort to build public confidence in his defense policies. The Gaither Commission had learned that, in one test of readiness, not a single SAC bomber had taken off within the requisite six hours. LeMay had seemed unruffled, however. He told the commission that, if aerial surveillance revealed that the Soviet Union seemed primed for an assault, SAC would strike first: "If I see that the Russians are amassing their planes for an attack, I'm going to knock the shit out of them before they take off the ground." When the co-chairman of the commission reminded LeMay that a preemptive strike contradicted national policy, the general responded: "It's my policy. That's what I'm going to do." (Spillane's 1950 blockbuster was entitled *Vengeance Is Mine.*) Such revelations suggested the value of widening the debate on nuclear deterrence.

The opportunity to make more discriminating judgments was the historical significance of *Dr. Strangelove,* in that no longer would official preferences throttle popular culture. It was unhealthy for a system based upon the ideal of popular sovereignty to treat political and military affairs as sacrosanct. "A movie that defied the traditions of taste and subverted our institutions implied that the Fifties were finally fading," Nora Sayre commented. The air of democratic discourse was less thin after *Dr. Strangelove.* Without any high-minded preachiness or sentimentality of its own, it helped to scrape away the inhibitions upon public discussion in the 1950s; critics, right or wrong, could breathe a little more easily. In a letter published in the *New York Times,* Lewis Mumford called *Dr. Strangelove* "the first break in the catatonic cold war trance that has so long held our country in its rigid grip." Mumford, a social critic, not a movie critic, praised the film for saying that "what is sick is our supposedly moral, democratic country which allowed this policy to be formulated and implemented without even the pretense of public debate."

By the early 1960s, that policy was undergoing more scrutiny. Eugene Burdick and Harvey Wheeler's novel *Fail-Safe* (1962) addressed the danger of accidental nuclear war. Initially serialized in the *Saturday Evening Post* in the very month of the Cuban missile crisis, the novel became the number six bestseller of 1962. Film producer Max Youngstein, to whom Condon dedicated *The Man-*

churian Candidate, had read *Fail-Safe* in manuscript. As a member of SANE, he was impressed by its deadly logic and, after meeting the authors, hired Walter Bernstein, who had been blacklisted, to write the scenario. The script follows the Burdick-Wheeler novel much more closely than *Dr. Strangelove* did with *Red Alert,* and the tone of Sidney Lumet's taut 1964 film is cold-sweat serious. The nuclear disaster is triggered by a mechanical failure rather than a psychotic general, a premise that again precluded air force cooperation. An epilogue to the credits reads: "The producers of this film wish to stress that it is the stated position of the Department of Defense and the United States Air Force that a rigidly enforced system of safeguards and controls insure[s] that occurrences such as those depicted in this story cannot happen." The Positive Control System in Omaha was designed so that a malfunctioning computer would send bombers *back* to their bases, not on the attack—for which the code had to come positively from the very top of the command structure. In an extended critique, Professor Hook also condemned *Fail-Safe.* Though his austerely logical gifts were peculiarly unsuited for confronting the exhilarating ghoulishness of a comedy like *Dr. Strangelove,* he noted the defective assumption in *Fail-Safe* that the orders to send the bombers on their mission need not be given positively.

These were among the analogues in popular culture to the view that David Riesman, himself so influential and subtle a 1950s thinker, was formulating as a way of getting out of the geopolitical impasse. In 1963, the sociologist endorsed what he took to be President Kennedy's attempt "to raise the sights of America and to ask for postponement at least of the traditional gratifications of undiscriminating hatred of the Russians (some fanatical right wingers have objected to Secretary [of Defense Robert S.] McNamara's 'no-cities' doctrine on the ground that it will spare too many Russian lives!)." Riesman added: "Not even an institution, let alone a country, can survive and prosper over any considerable period of time by serving only a single goal or purpose. If individuals try to purify their own lives to dedicate them to a single purpose only, they become fanatics."

5

Nevertheless, the legacy of the Cold War did not entirely disappear. Inheriting a war in Vietnam, President Johnson escalated it from sixteen thousand American military "advisers" in 1963 to half a million troops. He also became very receptive to the barrage of FBI reports that highlighted Communist participation in the antiwar movement itself. He vowed to two of his aides, Richard Goodwin and Bill Moyers: "I am not going to have anything more to do with the liberals. They won't have anything to do with me. They all just follow the Communist line—liberals, intellectuals, Communists. They're all the same." Such presidential conversations seemed to envision a massive Communist conspiracy, in which the Kennedy family, journalists, and other liberals were, perhaps, unwittingly implicated. In the Oval Office on July 5, 1965, Johnson told Goodwin: "You know, Dick, the Communists are taking over the country. Look here," the president announced, as he removed a manila folder from his desk. "It's Teddy White's FBI file. He's a Communist sympathizer." Several weeks later, sitting by the pool on his Texas ranch, the president continued in the same vein: "I'm going to be known as the President who lost Southeast Asia. I'm going to be the one who lost this form of government. The Communists already control the three major networks and the forty major outlets of communication. Walter Lippmann is a Communist and so is Teddy White. And they're not the only ones. You'd all be shocked at the kind of things revealed by the FBI reports." While denying any intention to become "like a McCarthyite," he warned the staffers—as well as Mrs. Johnson—that "this country is in a little more danger than we think. And someone has to uncover this information."

Later, again in the Oval Office, Johnson blamed the growing antiwar movement on the former attorney general. According to Goodwin, the president told staffers that "Bobby [Kennedy] gave the Communists the idea. Now I'm not saying he's a Communist, mind you. But they saw they might be able to divide the country against me. They already control the three major networks. . . . Hell, you can always find [Ambassador Anatoly] Dobrynin's car in front of a columnist's house the night before he blasts me on Vietnam." In August 1965, after CBS ran a film of U.S. Marines burning down the village of Cam Ne, Frank Stanton received an obscene wake-up call from Johnson, who accused reporter Morley Safer, a Canadian, of being a Communist and of desecrating the American flag. The Royal Canadian Mounted Police checked into Safer's past and family, discovering nothing suspicious. But the president's reaction was a residue of McCarthyism. Johnson continued to believe that he was fulfilling the obligations to the Republic of South Vietnam that Eisenhower and Kennedy had made, that a continuum existed through at least three American administrations that had to be honored. In this sense, there was something coextensive about the culture of the Cold War into the late 1960s and beyond as well, and Vietnam may be seen as the most tragic and costly legacy of the fear of Communism. For Johnson apparently believed in the domino theory that Eisenhower had first propounded. The loss of Indochina would mean danger to India, Pakistan, and the Pacific Rim. "We'll lose all of Asia and then Europe," he warned his biographer (and Goodwin's future wife), Doris Kearns. The result would be utter American isolation and World War III. "And when that comes to pass," the president added, "I'd hate to depend on the Galbraiths and that Harvard crowd to protect my property or lead me to shelter in the Burnet caves" (a tourist site near Johnson City, Texas).

Eric F. Goldman, a Princeton historian who served as an intellectual-in-residence, also recalled such a chat with other aides and Johnson, who exclaimed in 1966: "Liberal critics! It's the Russians who are behind the whole thing." According to the president, the Soviets were constantly in contact with antiwar senators, who partied at the Soviet embassy and whose staffers' children dated Russians. "The Russians think up things for the Senators to say. I often know before they do what their speeches are going to say." Such suspicions encouraged an atmosphere in which W. H. Auden, who had been among the judges who valiantly awarded Ezra Pound the Bollingen Prize in 1949, was denied a Presidential Medal of Freedom when a Johnson aide inspected the poet's FBI file.

McCarthyism extended beyond the president's own feverish imagination. In 1966, the White House sponsored a ceremony to highlight the program of Presidential Scholars, a talent search to encourage "the really bright kids, no matter who they are," as the official announcement had proclaimed. But what if "the most precious resource of the nation, the brain-power of its youth" happened to include an adolescent critic of U.S. military intervention in Vietnam? And what if the young lady's father had been cited by HUAC? Johnson's aide Marvin Watson phoned Professor Goldman to ensure that the "radical" parents of the scholar "absolutely should not be invited." But Goldman warned Watson of embarrassing publicity that would hurt the president, who by then was demanding complete FBI clearance of White House guests, whom Watson would then approve or reject. Watson told Goldman that the teenager, who had attended rallies against the draft and the war, was "bad enough"; her "crummy parents" were even worse. Though Johnson had not yet been informed of these potential guests, Watson added, "he would ban the girl too." In 1966 it was still necessary to tell this key White House aide, as Goldman did: "How are you going to support your charge of un-Americanism—by telling the country that you used the FBI against a bright seventeen-year-old and her parents, when she is coming to be awarded a medal she won in what the President has proclaimed to be a free intellectual competition?" Fearing adverse publicity, Watson relented. But henceforth, Goldman wrote, Presidential Scholars would be named only after the FBI checked the young winners of this intellectual competition *and* their families. Such was the pathetic coda for a program begun under a president who was himself a former schoolteacher.

The FBI director continued to seek a wider readership than the Oval Office, though a shrinking number of Americans shared his obsession with domestic subversion. Neither *A Study of Communism* (1962) nor *J. Edgar Hoover on Communism* (1969) matched the popular impact of *Masters of Deceit*. The burgeoning civil rights movement had disturbed him because of its vulnerability to Communist infiltration and control, but national attention was shifting to the persistence of racial discrimination. Attorney General Kennedy, who had become Hoover's superior in 1961, challenged the racism that had long permeated the bureau, which employed no black agents, except for the director's servants. Though Hoover resented pressure to eliminate the segregationist practices of the bureau, the fight against bigotry was no longer ominous; it had become obligatory. By then, the citadel of the domestic Cold War was finding it difficult to recruit new agents. Late in 1960, new agents' classes had to be postponed three times for lack of applicants, and the ranks of nonlawyers were quietly trolled for potential G-men. The bureau's own clerical workers were supplying over a sixth of its recruits at the beginning of the 1960s. Taking daily vitamin injections in his office, the sexagenarian Hoover nevertheless still operated on Red Alert. Haunted by the vestigial phantoms of the 1950s, he analyzed the increasing "Turbulence on Campus" in a 1966 article, calling the Party-supported Du Bois Clubs, named after the radical black intellectual W.E.B. Du Bois, "new blood for the vampire of international communism." The most frostbitten of Cold Warriors served on the national board of the Boys Clubs of America, as did Nixon, who found it pernicious that the name of the Communist youth organization sounded so much like the Boys Clubs.

Despite the ridicule with which this particular warning was greeted, Nixon did not entirely abandon the habit of inflating fears of domestic Communism. In 1965, he intervened in the New Jersey gubernatorial race because incumbent Richard Hughes defended the academic freedom of Rutgers University historian Eugene D. Genovese, a Marxist who had proclaimed that he "welcome[d] the victory of the Viet Cong." But the former vice-president was functioning in a more open political climate than in the 1950s, and threats to academic freedom did not go unchallenged. Both the president and the board of governors of Rutgers defended Genovese, a non-Communist who openly advocated opinions that had been concealed or soft-pedaled among radicals over a decade earlier. And he was more difficult to dislodge. Genovese did not go into exile, as did M. I. Finley, an earlier Rutgers historian of slavery, who was not permitted to contaminate the American classroom after taking the Fifth Amendment in 1952. (Later, as Sir Moses Finley, he taught ancient history at Cambridge University.) Genovese remained in academe, and Governor Hughes was reelected in a landslide despite Nixon's intervention. In 1966, while Genovese was teaching at the University of Rochester, a group of graduating seniors walked out of the commencement ceremony there when Nixon came to accept an honorary degree. They cited his earlier challenge to Genovese's academic freedom. Such a protest would have been unimaginable in the 1950s.

In 1968, Nixon's running mate inadvertently ended the Cold War style of partisanship. Spiro T. Agnew, governor of Maryland, called the Democratic standard-bearer, Hubert Humphrey, "squishy-soft on Communism." This smear against a sponsor of the Communist Control Act of 1954—and an indefatigable drum major for military intervention in Vietnam—was bizarre. So fully did this antipatriotic accusation appear to erase the cultivated impression of a "new Nixon" that Agnew was forced to back down. In pleading ignorance of the ugly historical implications of such a charge, Agnew was strangely convincing, since he had been a supermarket manager in 1953 and may never have learned what McCarthyism represented. Without political advantage to be derived from such accusations, the party system itself seemed at last to regain some equilibrium, as though recoiling from the excesses and obsessions of the domestic Cold War.

Its demise does not require any romanticizing of the sensibility that formed upon its ruins. Though the political milieu that displaced it was more sensitive to civil liberties and more tolerant of diversity, it was to suffer from illusions, imbalances, and dogmas of its own; and it was forced to confront challenges barely imagined in the 1950s. For in the succeeding years the confidence that had marked the public culture of the 1950s became less secure. The Korean War had been a draw—the first foreign war since 1814 that the United States had not won. The Vietnam War was a defeat—the first in American history. Nor could the CIA interventions that toppled regimes in Iran and Central America in the 1950s be duplicated in the 1970s and 1980s in those very places. Economic supremacy became increasingly eroded, as the United States lost about 10 percent of its share of the world's GNP in each succeeding postwar decade. In 1985, the United States became a debtor nation for the first time since the end of World War I, and even the American Legion imported its supplies of Old Glory from Japan. The postwar paradigm of stars and stripes forever was doomed.

The texture of "the American way of life" that the Cold War was fought to protect also underwent dramatic disintegration after the 1950s. Propensities toward violence and criminality worsened, intensified by an apparently unappeasable national appetite for drugs, while an alienated underclass threatened to become permanent. Neither the size nor the tenacity of such problems had been earlier envisaged. But perhaps the most widespread change occurred in the family and reinforced the rise of feminism that left virtually no one unaffected. Already by 1960, two women out of every five were employed, and one out of every three married women worked outside the home. Two-thirds of all new entrants into the work force were female, which altered familial, economic, and legal relations so incalculably that the Cold War ideal of a stable America—a bulwark amid global transformation, a fortress against subversive evil—could no longer be sustained. In this respect, an epitaph that Thomas Hine composed in 1986 defies paraphrase: "Rarely has an era striven so hard, in the midst of immense social change, to define the normal and the seemingly immutable." The postwar years had "confidently projected the American family—Mom, Dad, Junior and Sis—unchanged, centuries into the future, spinning through the galaxies in star-bound station wagons. And today, Mom and Dad are divorced, the factory where Dad worked has moved to Taiwan, Sis is a corporate vice president, Junior is gay and Mom's a Moonie. The American Way of Life has shattered into a bewildering array of 'lifestyles,' which offer greater freedom but not the security that one is doing the normal thing."

BIBLIOGRAPHICAL ESSAY

Historical scholarship, as in so many businesses, is not exempt from pilferage; authors steal with impunity from the works of their predecessors. I am no exception, and I can recommend the books and articles cited below to anyone who is intrigued by the political culture of the United States, 1945–60. They are, of course, only a sampling of the documentation in which *The Culture of the Cold War* is grounded and which should stimulate further research and interpretation.

General Accounts

Geoffrey Perrett's *A Dream of Greatness: The American People, 1945–1963* (New York: Coward, McCann & Geoghegan, 1979) is probably the best overall chronicle of the era, an amusing and well-researched portrait. Briefer—and still sound and immediate—is Eric F. Goldman's *The Crucial Decade—and After: America, 1945–1960* (New York: Vintage Books, 1960). Its focus is the political mainstream. William L. O'Neill's *American High: The Years of Confidence, 1945–1960* (New York: Free Press, 1986) does not quite explain whether and how the national confidence was justified. Was such pride warranted? John Patrick Diggins's *The Proud Decades: America in War and Peace, 1941–1960* (New York: Norton, 1988) also does not offer to elaborate. But both of these books represent informative and judicious scholarship. A smug, eerily unbalanced account is Jeffrey Hart's *When the Going Was Good!: American Life in the Fifties* (New York: Crown, 1982). Paul A. Carter's *Another Part of the Fifties* (New York: Columbia University Press, 1983) is idiosyncratic and surprisingly dull; its parts do not cohere. William E. Leuchtenburg's *A Troubled Feast: American Society since 1945* (Boston: Little, Brown, 1973) is a lucid and reliable general account. Howard Zinn's *Postwar America: 1945–1971* (Indianapolis: Bobbs-Merrill, 1973) and Frederick F. Siegel's *Troubled Journey: From Pearl Harbor to Ronald Reagan* (New York: Hill & Wang, 1984) are both surveys that extend past the 1950s and are written from a leftist perspective. The liveliness and liberal passion that course through

Carl Solberg's *Riding High: America in the Cold War* (New York: Mason & Lipscomb, 1973) are too little known.

Ranging from legal realism to suburban architecture to the influence of American popular culture in Austria, Lary May's *Recasting America: Culture and Politics in the Age of the Cold War* (Chicago: University of Chicago Press, 1989) may set a new standard in thematic unevenness among anthologies. Despite its subtitle, no movie, play, or painting of the period—and only one novel—is actually analyzed. But the individual essays do fuel the hope that a synthesis of the period can emerge. A transatlantic comparison can be gleaned from Robert Hewison's highly opinionated *In Anger: British Culture in the Cold War, 1945–1960* (New York: Oxford University Press, 1981).

Chapter 1: Politicizing Culture

David Caute's *The Great Fear: The Anti-Communist Purge under Truman and Eisenhower* (New York: Simon & Schuster, 1978) lacks a central idea or a compelling explanation for the excesses of anti-Communism. But no historical account is more comprehensive in the evidence that it presents of the violations of the Bill of Rights; such cumulative detail justifies Caute's *j'accuse*. A slimmed-down version is Richard M. Fried's *Nightmare in Red: The McCarthy Era in Perspective* (New York: Oxford University Press, 1990).

Stephen E. Ambrose's *Rise to Globalism: American Foreign Policy, 1938–1980* (New York: Penguin Books, 1980) includes some penetrating critical chapters on the late 1940s and 1950s. Robert A. Divine's *Eisenhower and the Cold War* (New York: Oxford University Press, 1981) is a compact and sympathetic account of Republican foreign policy. Townsend Hoopes's *The Devil and John Foster Dulles* (Boston: Atlantic-Little, Brown, 1973) takes a jaundiced view. See also Hans J. Morgenthau's "John Foster Dulles," in *An Uncertain Tradition: American Secretaries of State in the Twentieth Century*, edited by Norman A. Graebner (New York: McGraw-Hill, 1961). In *By the Bomb's Early Light: American Thought and Culture at the Dawn of the Atomic Age* (New York: Pantheon Books, 1985), Paul Boyer shows the eagerness of many Americans to normalize their post-Hiroshima world.

Biography is a necessary device for unlocking the politics of the era, though the avuncular, colorless personality of the thirty-fourth president has yet to inspire a truly first-rate portrait. The second volume of Stephen E. Ambrose's biography *Eisenhower* (New York: Simon & Schuster, 1983) is nevertheless important. Herbert S. Parmet's earlier *Eisenhower and the American Crusades* (New York: Macmillan, 1972) is rather pedestrian. How Ike wielded power has generated an interesting debate. See Fred I. Greenstein's *The Hidden-Hand Presidency: Eisenhower as Leader* (New York: Basic Books, 1982). Though tilted heavily toward the late 1960s, Garry Wills's *Nixon Agonistes: The Crisis of the Self-made Man* (Boston: Houghton Mifflin, 1970) is brilliant. The fullest scholarly account of Richard M. Nixon's Cold War career, if not a psychologically penetrating one, is the prolific Stephen E. Ambrose's *Nixon: The Education of a Politician, 1913–1962* (New York: Simon & Schuster, 1987).

As for the Democrats, see Cabell Phillips's engaging narrative, *The Truman Presidency: The History of a Triumphant Succession* (New York: Macmillan, 1966), and especially Alonzo L. Hamby's *Beyond the New Deal: Harry S Truman and American Liberalism* (New York: Columbia University Press, 1973). The agenda of liberal anti-Communism within the Democratic party is historically examined in Steven M. Gillon's *Politics and Vision: The ADA and American Liberalism, 1947–1985* (New York: Oxford University Press, 1987). Arthur M. Schlesinger, Jr., provided a key text for the ADA with *The Vital Center: The Politics of Freedom* (Boston: Houghton Mifflin, 1949). An elegant and highly admiring sketch is Herbert J. Muller's *Adlai Stevenson: A Study in Values* (New York: Harper & Row, 1967). Irving Howe caught the limitations of the Democratic standard-bearer in "Stevenson and the Intellectuals" (1954), reprinted in *Steady Work: Essays in the Politics of Democratic Radicalism, 1953–1966* (New York: Harcourt, Brace & World, 1966), a valuable collection for Howe's critique of other features of Cold War culture.

How the political system confronted or evaded social and economic problems is cogently treated in Richard Polenberg's *One Nation Divisible: Class, Race, and Ethnicity in the United States* (New York: Viking Press, 1980), which is among many accounts to tabulate the uses of anti-Communism in perpetuating bigotry. See also Wilson Record's *Race and Radicalism: The NAACP and the Communist Party in Conflict* (Ithaca: Cornell University Press, 1964). The gathering force of the civil rights movement can be fathomed in Taylor Branch's *Parting the Waters: America in the King Years, 1954–1963* (New York: Simon & Schuster, 1988). The travail of an eminent black man of letters is recorded in Arnold Rampersad's *The Life of Langston Hughes: I Dream a World, 1941–1967* (New York: Oxford University Press, 1988). The impact of a social science masterpiece is explored in David W. Southern's *Gunnar Myrdal and*

Black-White Relations: The Use and Abuse of "An American Dilemma," 1944–1969 (Baton Rouge: Louisiana State University Press, 1987). Mort Sahl's acerbic comment on race relations is quoted in Tony Hendra's study of comedy, *Going Too Far* (New York: Doubleday, 1987). Senator Eastland is quoted in John P. Roche's *Courts and Rights: The American Judiciary in Action* (New York: Random House, 1961). The politics of medical care is analyzed in Richard Harris's *A Sacred Trust* (New York: New American Library, 1966). Richard Carter chronicles the defeat of polio in *Breakthrough: The Saga of Jonas Salk* (New York: Trident Press, 1966).

George Charney traced his transformation into an ex-Communist in his memoir, *A Long Journey* (Chicago: Quadrangle Books, 1968). Robert Conquest's conversation with Tibor Szamuely is recorded in his essay "Evolution of an Exile: *Gulag Archipelago*," in *Solzhenitsyn*, edited by Kathryn S. Feuer (Englewood Cliffs, N.J.: Prentice-Hall, 1976). Philip Rahv's assessment of Communism appeared in his contribution to the symposium "Our Country and Our Culture," *Partisan Review* 19 (May–June 1952): 304–10. How much one psychotherapist liked Ike can be discerned in Myron Sharaf's *Fury on Earth: A Biography of Wilhelm Reich* (New York: St. Martin's Press/Marek, 1983). Dennis McNally's *Desolation Angel: Jack Kerouac, the Beat Generation, and America* (New York: Random House, 1979) cites the novelist's Republican preferences. James Burnham's view that World War III had already begun was presented in *The Coming Defeat of Communism* (New York: John Day, 1950). Congressman Jackson's criticism of Dmitri Shostakovich is quoted in James Aronson, *The Press and the Cold War* (Indianapolis: Bobbs-Merrill, 1970). The death and oblivion of Beria are described in Bertram D. Wolfe's *Khrushchev and Stalin's Ghost* (New York: Praeger, 1957).

Chapter 2: Seeing Red

The culture of the Cold War can be so described because of the perimeters that separated political deviants and outsiders from patriots and loyal citizens. A provocative and illuminating study of this culture is Michael Paul Rogin's *Ronald Reagan, the Movie: And Other Episodes in Political Demonology* (Berkeley: University of California Press, 1987). The hostile psychoanalytic interpretation of the domestic Cold War that Rogin offers is not confined to the cinema. Leslie Kirby Adler's "The Red Image: American Attitudes toward Communism in the Cold War Era" (1970), a doctoral dissertation in the Department of History at Berkeley, unfortunately remains unpublished. Edward A. Shils's *The Torment of Secrecy: The Background and Consequences of American Security Policies* (New York: Free Press, 1956) contains few facts or names but remains a classic comparative analysis of how British and American society differed in coping with domestic Communism.

Despite the controversy that still bedevils the case, it is hard to see how Allen Weinstein's *Perjury: The Hiss-Chambers Case* (New York: Knopf, 1978) will be surpassed as an explanation of what almost certainly happened before and after a senior editor of *Time* accused the head of the Carnegie Endowment for International Peace of having been, in effect, a Soviet espionage agent. The compelling undertow of Whittaker Chambers's *Witness* (Chicago: Henry Regnery, 1952) pulls this fascinating autobiography past the period over which it exerted such influence. Chambers's passage from apocalyptic anti-Communism to a conservative reconciliation to a citizenry that harbored no hard feelings can be traced in his *Odyssey of a Friend: Letters to William F. Buckley, 1954–1961* (New York: Putnam, 1969). See also John B. Judis, "The Two Faces of Whittaker Chambers," *New Republic*, April 16, 1984, 25–31. Though less fraught with consequences for American liberalism as such, the Rosenberg case has continued to stimulate disagreement. But a convincing historical interpretation that at least Julius Rosenberg was guilty is Ronald Radosh and Joyce Milton's *The Rosenberg File: A Search for the Truth* (New York: Vintage Books, 1984). Its chief historiographical target is the defense that Walter and Miriam Schneir mounted in *Invitation to an Inquest* (Baltimore: Penguin Books, 1973). A powerful novel inspired by the ordeal of the Rosenberg family is E. L. Doctorow's *The Book of Daniel* (New York: Random House, 1971).

The best scholarly biography of the junior senator from Wisconsin is David M. Oshinsky's *A Conspiracy So Immense: The World of Joe McCarthy* (New York: Free Press, 1983), an absorbing and disturbing work. A sharper interpretation of the demagogue's motives and character is Richard H. Rovere's *Senator Joe McCarthy* (New York: Harcourt, Brace, 1959), depicting a quest not for power but for publicity—which is also why Edwin R. Bayley's *Joe McCarthy and the Press* (New York: Pantheon Books, 1982) should help to revise certain myths about the ease with which the media were manipulated. Perhaps the best contemporary account of the journalistic brush with McCarthy is James A. Wechsler's *The Age of Suspicion* (New York: Random House, 1953). Richard M. Fried's *Men against McCarthy* (New York: Columbia University Press, 1976) should also be consulted. Thomas C. Reeves claimed that

McCarthy never found a single Communist in *The Life and Times of Joe McCarthy: A Biography* (New York: Stein & Day, 1982). Dwight Macdonald's description of McCarthy's "dead souls" appeared in a critique, reprinted in *The Partisan Review Anthology*, edited by William Phillips and Philip Rahv (New York: Holt, Rinehart & Winston, 1962), of William F. Buckley, Jr., and L. Brent Bozell's *McCarthy and His Enemies: The Record and Its Meaning* (New Rochelle, N.Y.: Arlington House, 1954), which downgraded Thoreau to a security risk.

Nicholas von Hoffman's portrait, *Citizen Cohn* (New York: Doubleday, 1988), is suitably caustic about McCarthy's chief aide. The standard scholarly appraisal of the Roman Catholic connection is Donald F. Crosby's *God, Church, and Flag: Senator Joseph R. McCarthy and the Catholic Church, 1950–1957* (Chapel Hill: University of North Carolina Press, 1978). Allen J. Matusow has summoned a range of voices—both contemporary and secondary—in his anthology, *Joseph R. McCarthy* (Englewood Cliffs, N.J.: Prentice-Hall, 1970). Michael P. Rogin's *McCarthy and the Intellectuals: The Radical Specter* (Cambridge: MIT Press, 1967) is dense but important as a challenge to the "populist" interpretation of McCarthy's appeal, in Daniel Bell, ed., *The Radical Right* (Garden City, N.Y.: Doubleday, 1963). The collection entitled *The Specter: Original Essays on the Cold War and the Origins of McCarthyism* (New York: Franklin Watts, 1974), edited by Robert Griffith and Athan Theoharis, has now been superseded in many places by more ample scholarship, but it remains useful. See especially the contributions of Ronald Lora, "A View from the Right: Conservative Intellectuals, the Cold War, and McCarthy," and Peter H. Irons, "American Business and the Origins of McCarthyism: The Cold War Crusade of the United States Chamber of Commerce."

The apprehensions of the period stirred Richard Hofstadter to explore, with his characteristic poise as well as acrid wit, *Anti-intellectualism in American Life* (New York: Knopf, 1970). See also the title essay in the same author's *The Paranoid Style in American Politics and Other Essays* (New York: Vintage Books, 1965), which puts both McCarthy and the John Birch Society into historical perspective. On the rise of the far right, see David H. Bennett's *The Party of Fear: From Nativist Movements to the New Right in American History* (Chapel Hill: University of North Carolina Press, 1988). John P. Roche's *The Quest for the Dream: The Development of Civil Rights and Human Relations in Modern America* (New York: Macmillan, 1963) is acute on the impact of the "Yahoos" on the public culture of the 1950s.

Homophobia in the 1950s is discussed in Elaine Tyler May's *Homeward Bound: American Families in the Cold War Era* (New York: Basic Books, 1988), itself an excellent general exhumation of the domesticity of the 1950s. Ambassador Bohlen's nomination process is described in Hoopes's *Devil and John Foster Dulles* and in Charles E. Bohlen's *Witness to History, 1929–1969* (New York: Norton, 1973). The salience of Mickey Spillane can be charted in Kenneth C. Davis's *Two-Bit Culture: The Paperbacking of America* (Boston: Houghton Mifflin, 1984) and in William Darby's *Necessary American Fictions: Popular Literature of the 1950s* (Bowling Green, Ohio: Bowling Green State University Popular Press, 1987).

The crisis in civil liberties can be evaluated in chapters 9–10 of Paul L. Murphy's *The Constitution in Crisis Times, 1918–1969* (New York: Harper & Row, 1972), in Milton R. Konvitz's *Expanding Liberties* (New York: Viking Press, 1967), and in C. Herman Pritchett's *Civil Liberties and the Vinson Court* (Chicago: University of Chicago Press, 1954). Stanley I. Kutler's *The American Inquisition: Justice and Injustice in the Cold War* (New York: Hill & Wang, 1982) looks sharply at particular legal imbroglios, including those of Ezra Pound and Harry Bridges. The Smith Act prosecutions have inspired two very critical historical analyses: Peter L. Steinberg's *The Great "Red" Menace: United States Prosecution of American Communists, 1947–1952* (Westport, Conn.: Greenwood Press, 1984) and Michal R. Belknap's *Cold War Political Justice: The Smith Act, the Communist Party, and American Civil Liberties* (Westport, Conn.: Greenwood Press, 1977). The far left is also the subject of Irving Howe and Lewis A. Coser's *The American Communist Party: A Critical History* (Boston: Beacon Press, 1957), written by social democrats sensitive to civil liberties. Ex-president Eisenhower's yearning to kill Communists is disclosed in *The Memoirs of Chief Justice Earl Warren* (Garden City, N.Y.: Doubleday, 1977).

Chapter 3: Assenting

The "end of ideology" was a response of certain leading intellectuals to the danger of totalitarianism, and it intensified the pragmatism and empiricism that formed the primary tradition of American political thought. The anthology edited by Chaim I. Waxman, *The End of Ideology Debate* (New York: Funk & Wagnalls, 1968), is especially valuable for stating their case, which longshoreman Eric Hoffer was perhaps the first to advance in *The True Believer: Thoughts on the Nature of Mass Movements* (New York: Harper & Bros., 1951). Totalitarianism shadowed thought and experience and heightened appreciation for "the American way of life" that this chapter is designed to elucidate. Tracing the historical meaning of the term are Les K. Adler and Thomas G. Paterson in "Red Fascism: The Merger of Nazi Germany and Soviet Russia in the American Image of Totalitarianism, 1930s–1950s," *American Historical Review* 75 (April 1970): 1046–64, and Stephen J. Whitfield's "'Totalitarianism' in Eclipse: The Recent Fate of an Idea," in *Images and Ideas in American Culture: Essays in Memory of Philip Rahv*, edited by Arthur Edelstein (Hanover, N.H.: Brandeis University Press, 1979). The starboard drift of historiography is exemplified in Daniel J. Boorstin's *The Genius of American Politics* (Chicago: University of Chicago Press, 1953). His presentation of the divergence from European ideological politics is found in *The Americans: The Colonial Experience* (New York: Random House, 1958). Such contrasts were sharpened in Will Herberg's "McCarthy and Hitler: A Delusive Parallel" (1954) in the Matusow anthology. Conyers Read's AHA address, "The Social Responsibilities of the Historian," was published in the *American Historical Review* 55 (January 1950): 275–85. The vogue of Toynbee can be gleaned not only from Whittaker Chambers's cover story, "The Challenge," *Time*, March 17, 1947, 71–76, but also in William H. McNeill's biography, *Arnold J. Toynbee: A Life* (New York: Oxford University Press, 1989). Frances FitzGerald's *America Revised: History Schoolbooks in the Twentieth Century* (Boston: Little, Brown, 1979) is a fascinating analysis by a versatile and talented journalist of how images of the American past have been conveyed and rearranged in the texts assigned in public schools.

Lionel Trilling's dismissal of the conservative tradition, in *The Liberal Imagination* (New York: Viking, 1950), proved to be premature, since the decade was soon replete with the iconography of order and authority. The firing of General Douglas MacArthur is retold in many of the synoptic works already cited. See also Richard H. Rovere and Arthur Schlesinger, Jr., *The General and the President* (New York: Farrar, Straus & Giroux, 1951), and William Manchester, *The Glory and the Dream: A Narrative History of America, 1932–1972* (Boston: Little, Brown, 1974). The plight of pacifists is recounted in Lawrence S. Wittner's *Rebels against War: The American Peace Movement, 1941–1960* (New York: Columbia University Press, 1969). In *The Organization Man* (New York: Simon & Schuster, 1956), itself a reverberant critique of the bureaucratic demands imposed upon individuality in the era, William H. Whyte, Jr., noted the authoritarianism seeping through Herman Wouk's *The Caine Mutiny* (Garden City, N.Y.: Doubleday, 1951). The only extensive critical study of this immensely popular postwar novelist is Arnold Beichman's tendentious *Herman Wouk: The Novelist as Social Historian* (New Brunswick, N.J.: Transaction Books, 1984). See also Harvey Swados, "Popular Taste and *The Caine Mutiny*," *Partisan Review* 20 (March–April 1953): 248–56. The transformation of this bestseller to the screen is recounted in Lawrence H. Suid's lively and informative *Guts and Glory: Great American War Movies* (Reading, Mass.: Addison-Wesley, 1978). Director Edward Dmytryk's film version is available on video cassette, as is Fred Zinnemann's adaptation of *From Here to Eternity*—both from Columbia Pictures.

Highlighting the bureaucratic ambitions as well as the ideological values of the director of the FBI, Richard Gid Powers draws a masterful portrait in *Secrecy and Power: The Life of J. Edgar Hoover* (New York: Free Press, 1987). The same author's earlier *G-Men: Hoover's FBI in American Popular Culture* (Carbondale: Southern Illinois University Press, 1983) is a revealing and compelling demonstration of Hoover's skill as a mythologizer. His *Masters of Deceit: The Story of Communism in America and How to Fight It* (New York: Holt, Rinehart & Winston, 1958) was the biggest nonfiction bestseller on an explicitly political topic in the era. Athan G. Theoharis and John Stuart Cox are highly critical of Hoover in *The Boss: J. Edgar Hoover and the Great American Inquisition* (Philadelphia: Temple University Press, 1988).

A genuinely fresh and delightful resurrection of material culture is Thomas Hine's *Populuxe* (New York: Knopf, 1986). Written with unusual grace and force, this self-referential coffee-table volume is also deft in its use of economic statistics to show the structural underpinning of the bourgeois style and *objets d'art* of the period (including Barbie). David Riesman's "The Nylon War" (1951) is reprinted in his essay collection, *Abundance for What?* (Garden City, N.Y.: Doubleday, 1964). More impressively than any other observer, the sociologist encapsulated an era when he published *The Lonely Crowd: A Study in the Changing American Character*, with Nathan Glazer and Reuel Denney (New Haven: Yale University Press, 1950). Riesman also became among the most sympathetic and wary critics of the very trends that he identified with such conceptual power and revelatory detail. George M. Humphrey's consternation over the popularity of Hemingway's novella is quoted in Kenneth S. Lynn, *The Dream of Success: A Study of the Modern American Imagination* (Boston: Little, Brown, 1955).

Nixon's own account of "the kitchen debate" is found in his memoir, *Six Crises* (Garden City, N.Y.: Doubleday, 1962). The homestead exemption from Communist inclinations that William Levitt granted is quoted in Eric Larrabee, "The Six Thousand Houses That Levitt Built," *Harper's*, September 1948, 79–88. The discomfort with the imbalance between private wealth and public parsimony is adumbrated in John Kenneth Galbraith's famous formulation of the liberal agenda, *The Affluent Society* (Boston: Houghton Mifflin, 1958). For references to the anxiety of affluence that both Adams and Kennedy exhibited, see Rupert Wilkinson, *The Pursuit of American Character* (New York: Harper & Row, 1988).

Chapter 4: Praying

Two insightful biographies of the most prominent churchman of the era are William G. McLoughlin, Jr.'s *Billy Graham: Revivalist in a Secular Age* (New York: Ronald Press, 1960), and Marshall Frady's *Billy Graham: A Parable of American Righteousness* (Boston: Little, Brown, 1979), which itself draws heavily upon McLoughlin's fair-minded account. Mark Silk's *Spiritual Politics: Religion and America since World War II* (New York: Simon & Schuster, 1988) is a pithy and perceptive study (especially chapters 3–5) of the entanglement of anti-Communism and religiosity. See also, for general trends, Sydney Ahlstrom's magisterial *Religious History of the American People* (New Haven: Yale University Press, 1972). In the age of anxiety, Norman Vincent Peale's *The Power of Positive Thinking* (New York: Prentice-Hall, 1952) outsold all other works of nonfiction. In a discerning and sprightly book, *The Positive Thinkers: Religion as Pop Psychology from Mary Baker Eddy to Oral Roberts* (New York: Pantheon Books, 1980), Donald Meyer resisted the temptations of condescension to put Peale in the tradition of "mind cure."

On the leading Catholic prelate of the Cold War, see John Cooney's unsympathetic biography, *The American Pope: The Life and Times of Francis Cardinal Spellman* (New York: Times Books, 1984). His role in drawing the United States deeper into the political morass of Vietnam is traced in Robert Scheer's New Left pamphlet, *How the United States Got Involved in Vietnam* (Santa Barbara, Calif.: Fund for the Republic, 1965). See also Crosby's *God, Church, and Flag* on the Catholic role in domestic anti-Communism and, on the ordeal of Cardinal Mindszenty, Hart's *When the Going Was Good!*

The stature of Reinhold Niebuhr can be discerned not only in his extensive writings but also in chapter 11 of Richard Kostelanetz's *Master Minds: Portraits of Contemporary American Artists and*

Intellectuals (New York: Macmillan, 1969) and in Richard Wightman Fox's *Reinhold Niebuhr: A Biography* (New York: Pantheon Books, 1986), which is stronger on the earlier years than on the 1950s. See also Arthur M. Schlesinger, Jr.'s influential essay, "Reinhold Niebuhr's Role in American Political Thought and Life" (1956), which is easily located in *The Politics of Hope* (Boston: Houghton Mifflin, 1963). Martin Luther King, Jr., paid tribute to Niebuhr in *Stride toward Freedom: The Montgomery Story* (New York: Harper & Row, 1958).

Boorstin's friendly HUAC testimony is extracted in Eric Bentley's anthology *Thirty Years of Treason: Excerpts from Hearings before the House Committee on Un-American Activities, 1938–1968* (New York: Viking Press, 1971). Jane Russell's description of the deity is quoted in Goldman's *Crucial Decade*. The adult campaign for wholesome music against orgiastic adolescence is amusingly reported in Reebee Garofalo and Steve Chapple's *Rock 'n' Roll Is Here to Pay: The History and Politics of the Music Industry* (Chicago: Nelson-Hall, 1977) and in Thomas Doherty's *Teenagers and Teenpics: The Juvenilization of American Movies in the 1950s* (Boston: Unwin Hyman, 1988). Senator Martin's juggling of cross and sword is cited in Solberg's *Riding High*. Dulles's opposition to compromise is articulated in *War or Peace* (New York: Macmillan, 1950), while his religious convictions are stressed in Hoopes's *Devil and John Foster Dulles*. Stevenson's providential appeal is included in the fourth volume of Walter Johnson's edition of *The Papers of Adlai E. Stevenson* (Boston: Little, Brown, 1974). Will Herberg's yearning for transcendence is noted in Adler's dissertation, "Red Image," and in Silk's *Spiritual Politics*. In "Integral Humanism" (1940), reprinted in *Reason, Social Myths, and Democracy* (New York: Humanities Press, 1940), Sidney Hook called Catholicism "totalitarian."

Chapter 5: Informing

Two volumes are indispensable for any historical consideration of the ethos of informing. To anthologize HUAC testimony was an inspired idea, which Eric Bentley executed admirably. His *Thirty Years of Treason* underscores the theatricality of the inquisitorial experience by confining the testimony almost entirely to witnesses from show business. Bentley, himself a drama specialist, also contributed a biting foreword to the book, which includes the testimony of Ayn Rand, Gary Cooper, Elia Kazan, Arthur Miller, Lillian Hellman, Paul Robeson, and Zero Mostel. Victor S. Navasky's *Naming Names* (New York: Viking Press, 1980) is a radiantly intelligent account of the rituals of denunciation, confession, and penitence to which Hollywood succumbed. Though *Naming Names* has been criticized for its lack of sympathy toward those who cooperated with the committee, the author's portrayal is nuanced and sensitive. He allows all sides to be heard without losing his moral equilibrium. Still invaluable as well is the standard historical account of HUAC: Walter Goodman's *The Committee: The Extraordinary Career of the House Committee on Un-American Activities* (New York: Farrar, Straus & Giroux, 1968). The liberal journalist published this narrative when his subject had collapsed into irrelevance.

Kazan's own version of his encounter with HUAC, and with politics generally, is told in his lapel-grabbing autobiography, *A Life* (New York: Knopf, 1988). It belongs on the shelf next to Miller's *Timebends: A Life* (New York: Grove Press, 1987), which, though less compelling and less candid, consolidates the playwright's reputation for political seriousness and decency. Despite their divergent political paths, the two erstwhile collaborators and friends are—as memoirists—gracious toward one another. A useful essay on Kazan's film, initially based on Miller's idea, is Kenneth R. Hey's "Ambivalence as a Theme in *On the Waterfront* (1954): An Interdisciplinary Approach to Film Study," in *Hollywood as Historian: American Film in a Cultural Context,* edited by Peter C. Rollins (Lexington: University of Kentucky Press, 1983). See also the afterword to Budd Schulberg's published scenario of *On the Waterfront* (Carbondale: Southern Illinois University Press, 1980). The Columbia Pictures film has also been released in video cassette. Daniel Bell's article in *Fortune* on "The Racket-Ridden Longshoremen" (1951) was revised for publication in *The End of Ideology: On the Exhaustion of Political Ideas in the Fifties* (New York: Free Press, 1962), itself one of the seminal books of the period.

The career of the most important female playwright in America has elicited two biographies: Carl Rollyson's *Lillian Hellman: Her Legend and Her Legacy* (New York: St. Martin's Press, 1988) and William Wright's *Lillian Hellman: The Image, the Woman* (New York: Simon & Schuster, 1986). Both books are correctives to her own much-touted political memoir, *Scoundrel Time* (Boston: Little, Brown, 1976), as well as *An Unfinished Woman: A Memoir* (Boston: Little, Brown, 1969). Unanswerable objections to her reminiscences are registered in Sidney Hook's "The Scoundrel in the Looking Glass" (1977), reprinted in his *Philosophy and Public Policy* (Carbondale: Southern Illinois University Press, 1980), and in Irving Howe's "Lillian Hellman and the McCarthy Years" (1976), reprinted in *Celebrations and Attacks: Thirty Years of Literary and Cultural Commentary* (New York: Horizon Press, 1979).

The legal, political, and moral issues that Miller's contempt of Congress raised are considered in Mary McCarthy's "Naming Names: The Arthur Miller Case" (1957), reprinted in *On the Contrary: Articles of Belief, 1946–1961* (New York: Farrar, Straus & Giroux, 1961), and in Richard H. Rovere's "The Conscience of Arthur Miller" (1957), reprinted in *The American Establishment and Other Reports, Opinions, and Speculations* (New York: Harcourt, Brace & World, 1962), itself a fine entree into the public culture of the period. The playwright's troubles with New York's city government are described in Walter Goodman, "How Not to Produce a Film," *New Republic*, December 26, 1955, 12–13, and cited in Eric Bentley's anthology. Cold War recriminations serve as a subtheme of Miller's *After the Fall* (New York: Penguin Books, 1964).

The brother of the actress Beatrice Straight, who was penalized for appearing in *The Crucible*, has written an interesting memoir of the period, *After Long Silence* (New York: Norton, 1983). Michael Straight was briefly implicated in the Soviet apparatus in England before eventually editing the *New Republic*. Harvey Matusow expressed astonishment at his upward mobility in his memoir, *False Witness* (New York: Cameron & Kahn, 1955). The unfavorable—and unsavory—literary criticism that FBI agents wrote during the Cold War is documented in Herbert Mitgang's *Dangerous Dossiers* (New York: Donald I. Fine, 1988). Attorney General Clark's rationale for detaining Eisler is recorded in Caute's *The Great Fear*. The significance of the release of Junius Scales is analyzed in Victor S. Navasky's *Kennedy Justice* (New York: Atheneum, 1971) and in Arthur M. Schlesinger, Jr.'s *Robert Kennedy and His Times* (Boston: Houghton Mifflin, 1978). The attorney general's admission of error is recorded in Jean Stein and George Plimpton, eds., *American Journey: The Times of Robert Kennedy* (New York: Harcourt Brace Jovanovich, 1970).

Chapter 6: Reeling

The movies of the era have stimulated two brilliant explorations of cinematic politics (including sexual politics) and social messages. Nora Sayre's *Running Time: Films of the Cold War* (New York: Dial Press, 1982) is cogent, judicious, observant, and mordant. Her book is especially useful in deciphering *On the Waterfront*. Peter Biskind's *Seeing Is Believing: How Hollywood Taught Us to Stop Worrying and Love the Fifties* (New York: Pantheon Books, 1983) is less overtly political in its interests and devotes more space to decoding the dynamics of individual films. Though less relevant for the culture of the Cold War, *Seeing Is Believing* is a splendid contribution to the interpretation of film. Other accounts include Andrew Dowdy's *The Films of the Fifties: The American State of Mind* (New York: Morrow, 1973) and Douglas Brode's *The Films of the Fifties: "Sunset Boulevard" to "On the Beach"* (Secaucus, N.J.: Citadel Press, 1976). David Manning White and Richard Averson's *The Celluloid Weapon: Social Comment in the American Film* (Boston: Beacon Press, 1972) is simplistic but relevant. Terry Christensen's *Reel Politics: American Political Movies from "Birth of a Nation" to "Platoon"* (New York: Blackwell, 1987) also lacks depth but is the only general book on the subject.

Robert Warshow's devastating essay on *My Son John*, "Father and Son—and the FBI" (1952), is reprinted in *The Immediate Experience: Movies, Comics, Theatre, and Other Aspects of Popular Culture* (Garden City, N.Y.: Doubleday, 1962). Thomas Doherty analyzes *Big Jim McLain* and *My Son John* in "Hollywood Agit-Prop: The Anti-Communist Cycle, 1948–1954," in *Journal of Film and Video* 40 (Fall 1988): 15–27. Director Leo McCarey's friendly HUAC testimony is quoted in Stefan Kanfer, *A Journal of the Plague Years* (New York: Atheneum, 1973). Betty Friedan's criticism of male homosexuality is embedded in a far more ambitious social indictment in *The Feminine Mystique* (New York: Norton, 1963). The hyperpatriotic films of the early 1950s were partly due to the ideological tenacity of the guru of "Objectivism," the subject of Barbara Branden's biography, *The Passion of Ayn Rand* (Garden City, N.Y.: Doubleday, 1986).

An adulatory portrait of the most popular actor of the era is Maurice Zolotow's *Shooting Star: A Biography of John Wayne* (New York: Simon & Schuster, 1974). The development of Ronald Reagan's politics was deeply entwined in Hollywood, which Garry Wills explores with typical originality, assurance, and insight in *Reagan's America: Innocents at Home* (Garden City, N.Y.: Doubleday, 1987). See also Rogin's *Ronald Reagan, the Movie*. One star's admiration for Lincoln Steffens is recorded in Gloria Steinem's *Marilyn* (New York: Henry Holt, 1986), while the misfortune of Kim Hunter is depicted in Murray Kempton's *America Comes of Middle Age: Columns, 1950–1962* (Boston: Little, Brown, 1963). Rosalind Russell's praise of normality is quoted in May's *Homeward Bound*. The consequences of Hollywood's realization that the age of the audience had plunged are engagingly explored in Doherty's *Teenagers and Teenpics*.

The blacklist in the movie industry has been the subject of works too numerous to mention. The interest in Dalton Trumbo's corrosive and colorful letters of the period, collected as *Additional Dialogue, 1942–1962*, edited by Helen Manfull (New York: M. Evans, 1970), may outlive the scenarios by which he earned his living. Billy Wilder's wisecrack is quoted in Kanfer's study of blacklisting. Kirk Douglas's autobiography, *The Ragman's Son* (New York: Pocket Books, 1989), also depicts the crumbling of the blacklist. Herbert Biberman of the Hollywood Ten described the difficulties of making an independent, progressive movie in *Salt of the Earth: The Story of a Film* (Boston: Beacon Press, 1965). Larry Ceplair and Steven Englund's *The Inquisition in Hollywood: Politics in the Film Community, 1930–1960* (Garden City, N.Y.: Doubleday, 1980) is oddly skimpy on the Cold War era itself.

Eisenhower's recollection of the Abilene code is recounted in Erik Barnouw's *The Image Empire: A History of Broadcasting in the United States* (New York: Oxford University Press, 1970). Carl Foreman's claim about the meaning of *High Noon* is quoted in Christensen, *Reel Politics*. Pauline Kael's interpretation of *High Noon* appears in *Kiss Kiss Bang Bang* (New York: Bantam Books, 1969). The 1952 Western has released on video cassette (United Artists). Khrushchev's rambunctious visit to Hollywood is described in Kempton, "That Day in Hollywood" (1959), reprinted in *America Comes of Middle Age*.

Chapter 7: Boxed-In

Barnouw's work, written from a vigorously liberal perspective, deserves to be better known among historians; he is the Braudel of broadcasting. See in particular *The Image Empire*, as well as *The Sponsor: Notes on a Modern Potentate* (New York: Oxford University Press, 1978). J. Fred MacDonald's *Television and the Red Menace: The Video Road to Vietnam* (New York: Praeger, 1985) is a thoughtful, invaluable account of how faithfully the television networks served as conduits for official views of the Cold War. Both of these authors sprinkle their learning with paprika.

Theodore H. White's enthralling autobiography, *In Search of History: A Personal Adventure* (New York: Harper & Row, 1978), recalls the constraints under which he operated, after covering the Chinese civil war and the triumph of Communism, as a journalist in the United States. His entrapment in the Luce organization is described in David Halberstam's *The Powers That Be* (New York: Knopf, 1979). The magazine publisher's attitude toward China is recounted in W. A. Swanberg's *Luce and His Empire* (New York: Scribner, 1972) and in Halberstam's book. Barbara Tuchman quotes *Life* magazine's low opinion of Chou En-lai in "The United States and China," in *American Vistas: 1877 to the Present,* edited by Leonard Dinnerstein and Kenneth T. Jackson (New York: Oxford University Press, 1979). On the CIA-sponsored plot that overthrew Jacobo Arbenz and the complicity of the American press, see Stephen Schlesinger and Stephen Kinzer's *Bitter Fruit: The Untold Story of the American Coup in Guatemala* (Garden City, N.Y.: Doubleday, 1982). Senator Russell's *frisson* is noted in Barnouw, *Image Empire.*

A non-Communist leftist, I. F. Stone, wrote some of the most incisive journalistic criticism of the era, republished in *The Truman Era* (New York: Monthly Review Press, 1953) and in *The Haunted Fifties* (New York: Vintage Books, 1969). The only book about him, Andrew Patner's *I. F. Stone: A Portrait* (New York: Pantheon Books, 1988), is uncritical and inadequate. Stone's plea for reconciliation with Communism was entitled "All the Canutes Lost Their Crowns" (1952) and is reprinted in *The Truman Era.*

The most comprehensive scholarly study of the most important television journalist of the era is A. M. Sperber's *Murrow: His Life and Times* (New York: Freundlich Books, 1986), which supersedes a biography by one of Murrow's former associates, Alexander Kendrick, *Prime Time: The Life of Edward R. Murrow* (Boston: Little, Brown, 1969). Note also the compelling memoir of Murrow's producer, Fred W. Friendly, *Due to Circumstances beyond Our Control . . .* (New York: Vintage Books, 1968), which also quotes Frank Stanton's definition of the public interest. Douglass Cater explained McCarthy's *modus operandi* in *The Fourth Branch of Government* (Boston: Houghton Mifflin, 1959). Barnouw's reservations about Alcoa's support of *See It Now* are ventilated in *The Sponsor.*

"The casual researcher may wonder whether the blacklist ever existed," Stefan Kanfer wrote in a bibliographic note in 1973. "Many libraries carry no listings at all under the title, and even the *Reader's Guide to Periodical Literature* missed a score of articles written for small-circulation magazines." No subsequent researcher has grounds for complaint, however, since the books of Caute, MacDonald, Barnouw, and Kanfer himself are especially useful on radio and television. Larry Adler's "My Life on the Blacklist" was published in the *New York Times,* June 15, 1975, section 2, page 19. Desi Arnaz's spirited defense of his wife, Lucille Ball, is quoted in Hart, *When the Going Was Good!* The blacklist was broken thanks to John Henry Faulk, whose harrowing account of his experience is *Fear on Trial* (New York: Simon & Schuster, 1964). A forthright but neglected novel on the political pressures in radio is Irwin Shaw's *The Troubled Air* (New York: Random House, 1951).

The only book on the preeminent Catholic television personality is D. P. Noonan's glowing biography, *The Passion of Fulton Sheen* (New York: Dodd, Mead, 1972). See also Perrett's *Dream of Greatness*, as well as the report, "Sheen Converts Communist," in *Life* magazine, October 22, 1945, 44.

The quiz show scandals have retained their fascination. See in particular the books of Perrett, Paul Carter, and Carl Solberg (cited above), plus Andrew Tobias's biography of Charles Revson, *Fire and Ice* (New York: Morrow, 1976). "The $60 Million Question," *Time* magazine, April 22, 1957, 78–82, raised the question—and then fudged the answer—of a possible fix, details of which are described in Richard N. Goodwin's memoir, *Remembering America: A Voice from the Sixties* (Boston: Little, Brown, 1988). Richard S. Tedlow's "Intellect on Television: The Quiz Show Scandals of the 1950s" (1976) crisply relates the shows to American culture and is reprinted in the Dinnerstein and Jackson anthology. See also Walter Karp's retrospective article, "The Quiz-Show Scandal," in *American Heritage* 40 (May–June 1989): 76–88. Boorstin's analogy to the presidential debates appears in *The Image; or, What Happened to the American Dream* (New York: Atheneum, 1962). One pundit's denunciation of television is quoted in Ronald Steel's *Walter Lippmann and the American Century* (Boston: Little, Brown, 1980). Steinbeck's letter to Stevenson was originally published in *Newsday*, December 22, 1959, and is accessible in *Steinbeck: A Life in Letters* (New York: Viking Press, 1975), which Elaine Steinbeck and Robert Wallsten edited. John Updike's "Morality Play" (1959) can be found in *Assorted Prose* (New York: Knopf, 1965).

Chapter 8: Dissenting

The distinction between heresy and conspiracy is presented in Sidney Hook's pamphlet *Heresy, Yes, Conspiracy, No* (New York: John Day, 1953), elaborated in his Cold War compendium, *Political Power and Personal Freedom: Critical Studies in Democracy, Communism, and Civil Rights* (New York: Criterion, 1959) and left unrevised in his autobiography, *Out of Step: An Unquiet Life in the Twentieth Century* (New York: Harper & Row, 1987). Hook was the most influential professional philosopher of the era, and his combative and gallant career very much needs a scholarly biography. Jacques Barzun dissected the corruption of cultural standards in *The House of Intellect* (New York: Harper & Row, 1959). Stephen Spingarn's statement is quoted in Polenberg, *One Nation Divisible.* Rockwell Kent's obduracy before HUAC is quoted in von Hoffman's *Citizen Cohn.*

One phase of the career of the greatest German poet-playwright of the century is traced in James K. Lyon's *Bertolt Brecht in America* (Princeton, N.J.: Princeton University Press, 1980) and in Bruce Cook's shallow *Brecht in Exile* (New York: Holt, Rinehart & Winston, 1982). The quotation from Brecht's *Leben des Galilei* is from the Suhrkamp Verlag edition (Berlin, 1964), 139–40. Philip M. Stern's *The Oppenheimer Case: Security on Trial* (New York: Harper & Row, 1969) is most effective in evoking the shamefulness and pathos of the AEC's proceedings. Efforts to throttle Max Lowenthal's criticism of the FBI are depicted in Richard Gid Powers's books. In *The Rosenberg File,* Radosh and Milton confirm that a secret life as an FBI informant was part of the importance of being Morris Ernst.

Tom Hayden's indebtedness to earlier intellectuals is recorded in James Miller's *"Democracy Is in the Streets": From Port Huron to the Siege of Chicago* (New York: Simon & Schuster, 1987). The editorial reaction to Dwight Macdonald's "America! America!" is recounted in Stephen J. Whitfield's *A Critical American: The Politics of Dwight Macdonald* (Hamden, Conn.: Archon Books, 1984). Paul Goodman's *Five Years* (New York: Brussel & Brussel, 1966) is the journal of an internal exile, while his *New Reformation: Notes of a Neolithic Conservative* (New York: Random House, 1970) reveals Goodman's estrangement from the "crazy young allies" he helped to spawn. The most influential entomologist of the century is portrayed in Wardell B. Pomeroy's *Dr. Kinsey and the Institute for Sex Research* (New Haven: Yale University Press, 1982) and Cornelia V. Christenson's *Kinsey: A Biography* (Bloomington: Indiana University Press, 1971). See also the second chapter of Paul Robinson's *The Modernization of Sex: Havelock Ellis, Alfred Kinsey, William Masters, and Virginia Johnson* (New York: Harper & Row, 1976).

Among the numerous books on Charles Chaplin, his own account, *My Autobiography* (New York: Simon & Schuster, 1964), should be supplemented with Charles J. Maland's *Chaplin and American Culture: The Evolution of a Star Image* (Princeton, N.J.: Princeton University Press, 1989) and David Robinson's *Chaplin: The Mirror of Opinion* (Bloomington: Indiana University Press, 1984). See also Polenberg's *One Nation Divisible* for a brief account of the comedian's popular decline and political eviction. The three films of the era that he starred in, wrote, directed, and scored (*Monsieur Verdoux, Limelight,* and *A King in New York*) are all available on video cassette. The scale of Martin Bauml Duberman's *Paul Robeson* (New York: Knopf, 1988) is magnificent and ambitious, befitting its subject. If the author errs on the side of undue sympathy, that comes with the territory of biographers. Note also Ron A. Smith, "The Paul Robeson-Jackie Robinson Saga," *Journal of Sport History* 6 (Summer 1979): 5–27, as well as Navasky's *Naming Names*. Ethel Rosenberg's praise of the biracial Brooklyn Dodgers is quoted in Robert Warshow's "The 'Idealism' of Julius and Ethel Rosenberg" (1953) in *The Immediate Experience*. The singular career of Dashiell Hammett has inspired three superb biographies and critical analyses of his fiction: Julian Symons's *Dashiell Hammett* (San Diego: Harcourt Brace Jovanovich, 1985), Diane Johnson's *Dashiell Hammett: A Life* (New York: Random House, 1983), and Richard Layman's *Shadow Man: The Life of Dashiell Hammett* (New York: Harcourt Brace Jovanovich, 1981). Connolly and Gide are quoted in Symons's book. A contrast between Spillane and Hammett is offered in John G. Cawelti's *Adventure, Mystery, and Romance: Formula Stories as Art and Popular Culture* (Chicago: University of Chicago Press, 1976). See also Hellman's portrait of Hammett in *An Unfinished Woman*. A splendid, scrupulous biography is Joe Klein's *Woody Guthrie: A Life* (New York: Knopf, 1980). He was a heretic—certainly not a conspirator—who ended up a heroic legend. The 1943 publication of Guthrie's own autobiography, *Bound for Glory*, preceded the era of the Cold War. See also David King Dunaway's *How Can I Keep from Singing: Pete Seeger* (New York: McGraw-Hill, 1981).

Chapter 9: Thawing

How the 1950s became the (late) 1960s is worthy of attention and wonder, since culture is more of a continuum than a caesura. It remains somewhat mysterious how the abscess of suspicion that defined the domestic Cold War was lanced. But important signs of the origins of the 1960s can be detected in Maurice Isserman's *If I Had a Hammer . . .: The Death of the Old Left and the Birth of the New Left* (New York: Basic Books, 1987) and in Morris Dickstein's *Gates of Eden: American Culture in the Sixties* (New York: Basic Books, 1977).

One English novelist—George Orwell—had envisioned an incessantly bleak totalitarian universe in *1984;* two other English novelists anticipated the end of the rigid simplifications that the twilight struggle sanctioned. Graham Greene's *The Quiet American* (New York: Viking Press, 1956) should be read, however, against an

American bestseller, William J. Lederer and Eugene Burdick's *The Ugly American* (New York: Norton, 1958), in part because both novels reinvent the career of CIA agent Edward Lansdale. The ambiguous moral geography of the Cold War is covered in John le Carré's classic thriller, *The Spy Who Came in from the Cold* (New York: Coward-McCann, 1963). The critical studies of the novelist's *oeuvre* include Eric Homberger's *John le Carré* (London: Metheun, 1986) and Peter Lewis's *John le Carré* (New York: Ungar, 1985). See also his own message "To Russia, with Greetings," in *Encounter*, May 1966, 3–6.

President Kennedy's transition from Cold Warrior to a man with a greater tolerance for diversity is treated in Arthur M. Schlesinger, Jr.'s *A Thousand Days: John F. Kennedy in the White House* (Boston: Houghton Mifflin, 1965) and David Burner's *John F. Kennedy and a New Generation* (Glenview, Ill.: Scott, Foresman, 1988). The reassuring phone call from Mayor Daley is recorded in Benjamin C. Bradlee's *Conversations with Kennedy* (New York: Pocket Books, 1976). The salience of the 1960 electoral squeaker is examined in Theodore H. White's *The Making of the President 1960* (New York: Atheneum, 1961) and in his memoir, *In Search of History*. H. Stuart Hughes's collection of essays, *An Approach to Peace* (New York: Atheneum, 1962), represents an early effort to move beyond the platitudes of Cold War hawkishness.

Director John Frankenheimer discussed his 1962 adaptation of Richard Condon's novel *The Manchurian Candidate* (New York: McGraw-Hill, 1959) in *The Celluloid Muse: Hollywood Directors Speak*, edited by Charles Higham and Joel Greenberg (New York: Signet, 1969). See also Richard Corliss, "From Failure to Cult Classic," *Time* magazine, March 21, 1988, 84. A video cassette is available (United Artists). Joseph Heller's *Catch-22* (1961) remains available in a Modern Library edition. His elucidation of the genesis of his novel is quoted in Davis's *Two-Bit Culture* and in an interview conducted in *Playboy*, June 1975, 59–76. Howard Fast's disillusionment with Communism is articulated in *The Naked God* (New York: Praeger, 1957).

Charles Maland's analysis of Kubrick's most amazing film is informative and perceptive: "*Dr. Strangelove* (1964): Nightmare Comedy and the Ideology of Liberal Consensus," in Rollins, *Hollywood as Historian*. Readers should also refer to the works of Christensen, Suid, and especially Sayre (cited above). Herman Kahn's morally unsettling magnum opus, *On Thermonuclear War*, 2d ed. (Princeton, N.J.: Princeton University Press, 1961), is parodied in the Columbia Pictures film. On Kahn himself, see Kostelanetz's *Master*

Minds. Kissinger defined deterrence in *Nuclear Weapons and Foreign Policy* (New York: Harper & Bros., 1957). "If Bombs Do Fall" was the cover story of *U.S. News and World Report,* September 25, 1961, 81–87. Lewis Mumford's admiration for *Dr. Strangelove*—now accessible on video cassette—is quoted in Stanley Kauffmann, *The World on Film: Criticism and Comment* (New York: Harper & Row, 1966). General LeMay's preemptive policy is revealed in Fred Kaplan's important study, *The Wizards of Armageddon* (New York: Simon & Schuster, 1983). Hook sought to invalidate the premises of Sidney Lumet's thriller in a pamphlet, *The Fail-Safe Fallacy* (New York: Stein & Day, 1963). Riesman criticized the fanaticism of a single cause in "National Purpose" (1963), which is reprinted in *Abundance for What?*.

President Johnson's imputation of Communist inclinations to opponents of military escalation in Vietnam was first transcribed in Eric F. Goldman's *The Tragedy of Lyndon Johnson* (New York: Knopf, 1969) and is amplified in Goodwin's *Remembering America.*

On the donnybrook over Professor Genovese at Rutgers, see Hook's *Academic Freedom and Academic Anarchy* (New York: Delta Books, 1971). On the academic career of Sir Moses Finley, see Ellen W. Schrecker's *No Ivory Tower: McCarthyism and the Universities* (New York: Oxford University Press, 1986), itself a major contribution to the study of civil liberties and political freedom in the 1950s. One eloquent protest against the California loyalty oath is quoted in Robert Coles, *Erik H. Erikson: The Growth of His Work* (Boston: Little, Brown, 1970). The attack on Senator Humphrey is noted in Robert Marsh's *Agnew: The Unexamined Man* (New York: M. Evans, 1971), in Wills's *Nixon Agonistes,* and in Lewis Chester, Godfrey Hodgson, and Bruce Page, *An American Melodrama: The Presidential Campaign of 1968* (New York: Viking Press, 1969).

The 1950s should not be permitted to recede without drawing attention to the following anthologies: Allen Guttmann and Benjamin Munn Ziegler, eds., *Communism, the Courts, and the Constitution* (Lexington, Mass.: D. C. Heath, 1964), Paul Holbo and Robert W. Sellen, eds., *The Eisenhower Era* (Hinsdale, Ill.: Dryden Press, 1974), and Joseph Satin, ed., *The 1950s: America's "Placid" Decade* (Boston: Houghton Mifflin, 1960). The best political cartoonist of the era (*né* Herbert Block) could write and think as trenchantly as he could draw and can be (re)discovered in *Herblock's Here and Now* (New York: Simon & Schuster, 1955), *Herblock's Special for Today* (New York: Simon & Schuster, 1958), and *Straight Herblock* (New York: Simon & Schuster, 1964).

See also Ellen W. Schrecker's "Archival Sources for the Study of

McCarthyism," which appeared in the *Journal of American History* 75 (June 1988): 197–208. Finally, aficionados of historical irony will cherish Strobe Talbott's "Rethinking the Red Menace," *Time* magazine, January 1, 1990, 66–72, which acknowledges that, "for more than four decades, Western policy has been based on a grotesque exaggeration of what the U.S.S.R. could do if it wanted."

INDEX